The Implicit Relation of Psychology and Law

The Implicit Relation of Psychology and Law brings an innovative, feminist analysis to these affiliated fields. Fiona E. Raitt and M. Suzanne Zeedyk explore the role of psychological syndromes (i.e. Battered Woman's Syndrome, Rape Trauma Syndrome, Premenstrual Syndrome and False Memory Syndrome) within the courtrooms of the UK and the US. In addition to the explicit relationship between the two fields, they argue that there is an unrecognised implicit relation existing within the intersection of psychology and law, which they find works to the disadvantage of women.

Both novel and controversial, and written in a highly accessible style, *The Implicit Relation of Psychology and Law* will engage readers from a wide range of disciplines including: psychology, law, critical theory, criminology and women's studies.

Fiona E. Raitt is a solicitor and a senior lecturer in law. **M. Suzanne Zeedyk** is a lecturer in psychology and co-editor of the *Journal of Reproductive and Infant Psychology*. Both are at the University of Dundee.

The Implicit Relation of Psychology and Law

Women and syndrome evidence

Fiona E. Raitt and M. Suzanne Zeedyk

London and Philadelphia

First published 2000 by Routledge
11 New Fetter Lane, London EC4P 4EE

http://www.psypress.co.uk

Simultaneously published in the USA and Canada
by Taylor & Francis Inc
325 Chestnut Street, Suite 800, Philadelphia, PA 19106

Routledge is an imprint of the Taylor & Francis Group

© 2000 Fiona E. Raitt and M. Suzanne Zeedyk

Typeset in Galliard by Keystroke, Jacaranda Lodge, Wolverhampton
Printed and bound in Great Britain by Biddles Ltd, Guildford and King's Lynn

British Library Cataloguing in Publication Data
A catalogue record for this book is available from the British Library

Library of Congress Cataloging in Publication Data
Raitt, Fiona E.
    The implicit relation of psychology and law : women and syndrome evidence /
Fiona E. Raitt and M. Suzanne Zeedyk.
        p. cm.
    Includes bibliographical references and index.
    1. Law–Psychological aspects. 2. Women–Psychology. 3. Women–Legal status,
laws, etc. I. Zeedyk, M. Suzanne (Mary Suzanne), 1963– II. Title.

K346. R35 2000
340'.19–dc21   00–028088

ISBN 0–415–14782–4 (hbk)
ISBN 0–415–14783–2 (pbk)

To

Elizabeth Craig Morrin
who shared with me her extraordinary sense of
justice and lived her life by example

Winifred Gene Zeedyk
who, by believing in her boundaries, allowed me to
break free of my own

Jan Stephens
who has nourished in me and so many others the
courage to speak our truths

Contents

Table of cases

Preface

Only if we understand what is at stake can we care about scientific questions.
Margaret Wertheim[1]

We wrote this book because we are concerned about what is at stake for women when the science of psychology enters the legal realm. The relationship between law and psychology has, in the past two decades, become a strong and vibrant one. This is particularly true in the domain of the courtroom, where psychological explanations are used to account for a wide variety of behaviours. Our particular interest is in the way that psychological syndromes have increasingly been used to account for women's behaviour. While many commentators have welcomed this trend, we wish to draw attention to its more detrimental consequences. We argue that there is an unacknowledged, implicit relation between the two disciplines, and it is one which operates to the disadvantage of women. As a lawyer and a psychologist, we set out to examine this inter-relation between our two disciplines and to consider ways in which it might be countered.

As an applied epistemological project, our intention was always to produce a book that offered a critical account of the topic. That is not to say we deliberately set out to be captious, rather that we wished to theorise and to challenge some of the accepted tenets of our fields. Like others, we no longer find many of the mainstream theories operating within our disciplines convincing. Traditional textbook explanations and established 'givens' fail to provide adequate answers to our questions and to satisfy our intellectual concerns. Our particular perspective is a feminist one, not simply because our primary concern is women's differential treatment, but because we think that it is only by viewing the psychology–law partnership through a feminist lens that some important problems can be discerned.

We hope that readers of this book will come from a broad spectrum of backgrounds and occupations – individuals involved in psychology, law, and other disciplines, either as academics or practitioners. We anticipate that this will include those interested in feminist critiques, whether new to them or extending their knowledge of them, as well as those who may disagree with a feminist perspective but who are willing to engage in critical debate about the assumptions of science and law.

The inter-disciplinary nature of our enquiry provides an opportunity to encourage cross-disciplinary debate, but it also makes our endeavour difficult. When one's intended audience is drawn from a single cohort, the assumptions that can be made about the reader's level of knowledge and understanding make the project relatively straightforward. When the intended audience is drawn from more than one group, it necessarily makes the undertaking more difficult. Inter-disciplinary writing may be, simultaneously, too simplistic and tedious for some readers and too advanced and inaccessible for others. Although there is much talk about the need for inter-disciplinary work, there seem to be strikingly few examples of its actual execution, possibly because of this precise difficulty. Perhaps it is better to try to reach a smaller audience and succeed, than to aim for a larger one and fail to reach anyone?

Yet, the re-examination of basic concepts and assumptions can produce exciting outcomes. Advances and insights often emerge only because a theorist is willing to look again at the accepted assumptions of her or his field. As Thomas Kuhn (1970: 90) observed, it is those who are 'little committed by prior practice to the traditional rules of normal science [or any other discipline] who are particularly likely to see that those rules no longer define a playable game and to conceive another set that can replace them'. Subjecting concepts to continued critique sustains the impetus for re-evaluation and change. For readers who are familiar with psychology or with law, whether from a critical or a mainstream perspective, we hope our arguments will be sufficiently thought-provoking to encourage fresh consideration of accepted ideologies. Perhaps if no risks are taken, the larger audience is never reached?

Structure of the book

We have structured the book so that it supports these aims. The first three chapters are intended to lay the groundwork for our thesis. Chapter 1 introduces our claim that an implicit relationship exists between psychology and law. In Chapter 2, we discuss what we perceive as the explicit relation between psychology and law, including a discussion about the evolution of syndrome diagnoses and their place within the legal process. In Chapter 3, our theoretical arguments concerning the implicit relationship are more fully developed. This incorporates a historical perspective, which we believe to be fundamental, for it is in understanding the development of the fields that it becomes possible to grasp the degree to which key qualities are embedded within both of them individually and, thus, within their intersection.

Establishing a theoretical argument is only a first step, however. The next step is to test our arguments by applying them to the practice of law. In Chapters 4 to 7, that will be done by examining areas of the law in which psychological syndromes have been, or shortly may be, accepted by the courts as explanations of women's behaviour. We will look in depth at four different syndromes: Battered Woman's Syndrome, Rape Trauma Syndrome, Premenstrual Syndrome, and False Memory Syndrome. We argue that in their treatment of syndrome evidence, psychology and law create adverse consequences for women, and we wish to make these consequences transparent.

In the final chapter we offer suggestions for countering the implicit relationship. In a critical enterprise such as this, we feel we have a responsibility to propose alternatives to those aspects of our fields that we find problematic. It is generally easier to deconstruct and destroy than to reconstruct and rebuild. But since one of our aims in writing this text is to improve the position of women, we face the task of articulating a vision of something better. We will therefore make suggestions at both the epistemological and pragmatic levels, for we think change has to happen at each level in order to be effective and enduring.

Scope of legal jurisdictions and litigation

The legal concepts and cases that we will discuss throughout the book are drawn primarily from jurisdictions within the United States of America and the United Kingdom (specifically, England and Scotland). These jurisdictions were chosen because they have provided the arenas within which most of the debate and litigation concerning psychological syndromes has occurred, and published litera-ture has therefore tended to focus on them. We will supplement this scope, where helpful, with examples of legal reasoning found in other countries such as Canada and Australia. All of these jurisdictions depend upon a common law tradition.[2] That is, they favour an adversarial approach to litigation, where the issues in dispute are argued by the parties to the litigation before a presiding judge, whose role is intended to be adjudicative rather than interventionist. In addition, common law systems rely on precedent and *stare decisis*, where the judicial decisions of higher courts are binding on lower courts and where earlier decisions play a significant role in the development of legal reasoning.

It is often difficult to write about a range of judicial systems in an integrated fashion. However, jurisdictions operating within a common law tradition face similar issues in deciding what kinds of evidence they will admit into court, what standards for admission they should adopt, and how much weight they should give to the evidence. Thus, it is reasonable to encompass breadth in a single theoretical analysis. We have tried to avoid the discussion becoming entangled in non-essential details and to focus on illuminating similarities and differences in the ways that jurisdictions have chosen to address these issues. We hope that employing such a comparative strategy will be helpful not only in elucidating the operation of the implicit relation, but also in devising strategies to counter it.

Litigation within the courts can pertain to criminal and civil matters. Our main focus here will be upon the former, because it is in the criminal domain that much of the debate surrounding syndrome evidence has arisen, especially when attempts are made to have such evidence function as part of a defence. Domestic abuse, rape, homicide, theft, assault, road traffic violations, and child sexual abuse, all of which are criminal offences and will feature in this text, are only some of the crimes that have now become associated with the use of syndrome evidence. Even where civil actions are raised, they may have been preceded by related criminal charges;

the increasing tendency of men who file civil claims (for example, against a therapist or health authority) after having had criminal charges brought against them for committing child sexual abuse is a good example. The critiques we raise in this book in regard to syndrome evidence, and in regard to the implicit relation of law and psychology more generally, apply equally well to civil and to criminal matters, but by keeping our primary focus on the criminal domain, we can bring a new dimension to those issues already receiving most attention in the literature.

A feminist consciousness

Since the second wave of feminism in the 1970s, there have been many advances in the position of women in society. A glance at the recent media lends a few arbitrary examples: a report by Unicef recognises that violence against women is one of the factors that undermines the health and stability of a nation (*The Guardian*, 24 July 1997); Elizabeth Dole, a woman, announces her bid for the US Presidency (*The Guardian*, 3 March 1999); a group of male clergy are quoted as welcoming use of the phrase 'God Our Mother' (*The Independent*, 13 March 1999). Such changes are to be celebrated, but they should not lead to the conclusion that feminism's aims have been achieved. There is a need to remain vigilant, for the evidence of disparity between the sexes has become more subtle, as have the factors responsible for it. This has practical consequences for women's (and for men's) everyday lives, and it is not in anyone's interest that these consequences be allowed to remain invisible.

Bonnie Spanier (1995: 14) has written, 'I have learned that the privilege of access to and love of science becomes a responsibility when we also achieve a feminist consciousness'. We feel similarly about our chosen fields of psychology and law. As powerful societal institutions, they each have the potential to do much good – and much harm. In offering the present analysis of their current performance in relation to women, we take up Spanier's banner in the hope that we can encourage our disciplines to reflect on what they wish their future performance to be.

Acknowledgements

It is a pleasure to begin this book by expressing our appreciation to those who have supported us throughout its long gestation. We were inspired by the circumstances faced by our women clients, students, friends, colleagues, and those whose stories we knew only through the media. We wished to write a text that placed their personal struggles in a wider, theoretical context, such that it would become clear how and why theory matters in everyday life. We hope that they and others find our account useful.

Many people contributed directly to the progress of this work. The opportunity to discuss our ideas at professional conferences helped in developing our thesis. These included the British Psychological Society Annual Conference (Heriot Watt University, 1997), the Law and Science Seminar (University College London, 1997), and the Gender, Sexuality and Law Conference (University of Keele, 1998). Conversations with colleagues, often enriched by good food and excellent wine, were as valuable as they were fun, with particularly memorable occasions having been shared with Jan Bebbington, Dorothy Degenhardt, Nick Hopkins, Elizabeth Kirk, Ellie Lee, Deirdre McCloskey, Susan Marshall, Angela Roger, Joan Schulz, Fiona Smith, Bonnie Spanier, and Stephen Whittle. Audrey Harrow and Jill O'Hara were enthusiastic research assistants, ably locating literature and checking references, while Mhairi Gray and David Hart provided valuable library assistance in tracking down esoteric sources. Thanks, too, to the staff at Routledge for their patience and good humour. Most importantly, we appreciate the enormous benefits we gained from observations offered by those who read early drafts of the manuscript and associated journal articles, including Anne Walker, Patrick Ford, Julie Casey, Irina Anderson, Ruth Woods, Noelle McAra, several anonymous referees, and especially Pamela Ferguson, who gave us endless hours of her time.

We wish also to express our thanks to those who contributed to this text in less direct ways. It has been both frustration and delight to spend so much time in the textual company of the women and men on whose ideas we have drawn in writing this book. Our students, particularly those enrolled in the courses 'Gender and the Law' and 'Developmental Theories and Epistemology', kept us mindful of just how challenging and uncomfortable these topics are, as well as of the unexpected rewards that tackling them brings. We have received unceasing support from the Psychology of Women Section of the British Psychological Society and from the

Focus on Women Network of the University of Dundee. Suzanne Zeedyk owes a debt to Bill Kessen, whose teaching transformed her into an incessant epistemopathectomist (to borrow Koch's phrase) and who sadly passed away before this book, which he had encouraged, could be completed; Larry Fenson has, over the years, pushed her to think and write more sharply, even though he may not have expected that his influence would result in these particular arguments. Her wider research programme benefits immensely from the dynamic organisational skills of Joanne Gray, and the work would be so much less fulfilling without the other members of the team: Mandy Baranowski, Julie Rattray, and Morag Smith. Fiona Raitt's debt is to all those who over the years collaborated in the firm of Wilson and Raitt, during which time the hugely political nature of law became ever more apparent. In particular she is indebted to Marion Foy, who acted as Edinburgh court correspondent and who, on a daily basis, continues to champion the cause of abused women and children; to Fiona Reed, who offered regular insight and support; and to Liz Wilson, partner and co-founder of the firm, for her immeasurable contribution to that and other enterprises. Finally, we would like to note our appreciation for the efforts of the gardeners employed by Dundee City Council, who provided the colour of the local parks in which we so often walked while talking over our ideas.

Most importantly, we wish to thank our families and friends, from whom authors derive the essential energy to complete the task they have set themselves. Liz Wilson and Florence Germain ensured that spaces were created for tranquillity and restoration. Patricia McGrane and Judith Adkins made sure that the flow of support never slowed, even with an ocean between us. Numerous other friends lobbied assiduously to guarantee we spent some time in the sunshine, away from the computer. And it is a relief to satisfy the curiosity of our family members, varying in age and geographical locations, as to whether this book would ever be finished. The diversion of attention to our parents, siblings, nieces, and nephews (and to Folly and Callum) was often enjoyable and sometimes painful, but always cherished. It is to our mothers, for their influence in our lives as women, that this book is dedicated.

Permissions

The authors would like to thank the following for permission to quote extracts from their work:

The Good Terrorist by Doris Lessing. Published by Grafton Books. Reprinted by kind permission of Jonathan Clowes Ltd on behalf of Doris Lessing.

The extract reprinted on p. 11 is from *The Charlotte Perkins Gilman Reader* edited by Ann J. Lane, published by The Women's Press Ltd, 1981, 34 Great Sutton Street, London EC1V 0LQ.

The Handmaid's Tale by Margaret Atwood. Published by Jonathan Cape; used by permission, McClelland & Steward Inc. The Canadian Publishers. For the same excerpt from *The Handmaid's Tale* by Margaret Atwood. Copyright © 1985 by

1 Introduction

We are not here to make ourselves comfortable.

Doris Lessing[1]

The relationship between law and psychology is thriving, and it now encompasses a variety of domains: eyewitness identification, the process of jury deliberations, the accuracy of children's testimony, the reliability of confession evidence, and theories of criminal behaviour, amongst many others. This book focuses on one domain – the use of syndrome evidence in the courtroom – and argues that, underlying the apparent pragmatic relation of these two disciplines, in which psychological evidence is used explicitly to assist law in interpreting human behaviour, is another type of relation. This one is implicit, based on epistemological assumptions that the disciplines share. When the two work together, the biases inherent in such assumptions are strengthened. We are particularly concerned about the ways in which these hidden assumptions work to the disadvantage of women. The intention of this book is to theorise this implicit relation, exploring the ways in which it shapes the use of scientific facts and the pursuit of legal truths.

The last two decades have witnessed increased willingness to bring evidence about psychological syndromes into the courtroom. Donald Downs (1996) has provided a glimpse of what he terms the 'syndrome society', territory now occupied by a vast range of syndromes including Post-Abortion Syndrome, Abortion Survivor Syndrome, Battered Child Syndrome, Parental Alienation Syndrome, Child Sexual Abuse Accommodation Syndrome, Attention Affective Disorder, Multiple Personality Disorder, Postnatal Depression, Failure Syndrome, Gambler's Syndrome, Racial Hatred Syndrome, Internet Addiction Syndrome, Hope Deficiency Syndrome, and Divorce-Related Malicious Mother Syndrome (this last being one of our favourites). Within the courtroom setting, attempts are often made to use syndrome evidence as an explanation for the behaviour of one of the parties in a case. In particular, syndrome explanations are becoming a common way of accounting for the actions of women in cases where they are accused of, or accuse others of, criminal offences.

Diagnoses such as Battered Woman's Syndrome and Premenstrual Syndrome have become familiar to the public in this way. Lawyers seek to have evidence about a relevant syndrome admitted in a case in the hope that this will act as a mitigatory factor on their client's behalf or that it will reinforce the credibility of a key witness. While the appearance of syndromes has been most frequent in the US courts, there have also been a number of high-profile cases occurring in other countries. As the impetus builds to permit more of this type of evidence into the courts, it is reasonable to consider whether it has a wholly beneficial effect. What purpose does such evidence serve? How valid is the explanation it provides? In what ways are syndrome explanations gendered? Are there ramifications beyond the outcome of any specific case? To what hazards should the legal system, psychology, and society itself be alert?

In this book we examine the evolution of syndromes as a psychological condition and their incorporation into law. In contrast to the large number of commentators who welcome the potential for syndrome evidence, we have reservations about its value. We argue that the origins of psychological syndromes, rooted as they are in the medical diagnostic process and classified as pathological disorder, ultimately render them incapable of protecting the interests of women as a whole. This is the case even where they appear to benefit individual women. Our argument is based on the premise that the problems caused by syndrome evidence derive from connections between the disciplines of psychology and law. The connections exist at two levels: first, within the mechanisms that overtly govern the admission of psychology into the courtroom – what we describe as the *explicit relation* between the disciplines – and secondly, within the covert epistemological relationship that underlies such mechanisms – what we describe as the *implicit relation*. We believe the implicit relation works to the disadvantage of women and that this effect will be reinforced as the legal process makes greater use of psychology to assist in its decision-making. The implicit relation has gone too long unacknowledged, perhaps unrecognised, and certainly unarticulated.

The perspective from which this text pursues its theoretical critique is feminism. As a form of critical thinking, feminism encompasses many variants (for discussion see Beasley, 1999; MacKinnon, 1989; Naffine, 1990; Olsen, 1990; Rich, 1980; Ussher, 1991), but it is palpable that virtually every discipline in the academic spectrum has now been subjected to feminist analysis and found to be wanting. For example, English literature has traditionally ignored the contributions of women authors (e.g. Gonda, 1992a). Economics endorses models that obscure the ways in which 'women's work', including housework, childcare, and emotional labour, contribute to the economy (e.g. Waring, 1989). Chemistry, physics and mathematics have failed to give attention to the way in which their epistemic values marginalise women's interests (e.g. Wertheim, 1997). Architecture prioritises public and commercial structures over those of more private, household spaces (e.g. Berkeley and McQuaid, 1989). Anthropology does not yet treat sufficiently seriously the contributions of women to the cultural, linguistic, economic, and agricultural environments (e.g. di Leonardo, 1991). Geography has constructed its theories based on a masculinist gaze, which conceives of landscape in terms of ownership and control, rather than in terms of a reciprocal relationship with the physical environment (e.g. Rose, 1993). Psychology has characterised Woman as inferior to Man, invoking biological, sociological, and cognitive models to sustain that comparison (e.g. Bohan, 1992). The standards against which law evaluates behaviour reflect male experience and expectations (e.g. MacKinnon, 1989). (See volume edited by Kramarae and Spender (1993) for a comprehensive survey of feminist critiques of these and other disciplines.)

It is not only feminism that has challenged orthodox thinking. Major critiques have been undertaken by movements such as postmodernism, social constructionism, post-structuralism, Marxism, dialogics, symbolic interactionism, and critical legal studies, all in the quest for transformation, insight and 'truth', even where that truth is necessarily subjective, variable and fluid (for review in law, see Minda, 1995; and in psychology, see Smith, Harré, and van Langenhove, 1995). All owe a debt to Michel Foucault's intellectual vision as he charted new territory in his dissection of truth, power, and knowledge.

> Truth is a thing of this world: it is produced only by virtue of multiple forms of constraint. And it induces regular effects of power. Each society has its regime of truth, its general politics of truth: that is, the types of discourse which it accepts and makes function as true; the mechanisms and instances which enable one to distinguish true and false statements, the means by which each is sanctioned; the techniques and procedures accorded value in the acquisition of truth; the status of those who are charged with saying what counts as true.
>
> (Foucault, 1980: 131)

For Foucault, science (including psychology) and law are two of the foremost social institutions implicated in this 'regime of truth' and in the exercise of power.

The premise basic to feminist analysis is that human relations are arranged on a power dynamic that favours the male, and that if structural change is to be effected, account must be taken of gender. Most feminist analysis has been confined within the limits of individual disciplines. This is perhaps odd, given that a broader multidisciplinary perspective reveals more effectively the extent to which women have been excluded from full societal participation. An inter-disciplinary perspective, such as the one we adopt here, brings particular strengths, too. It is well suited to uncovering the obscure mechanisms that facilitate that exclusion. The implicit relation between psychology and law is one of those mechanisms.

The explicit relation between psychology and law

Contemporary interest in the intersection of law and psychology could be described as explosive. A glance at a library catalogue reveals a sharp rise in the number of books published on 'psychology and law' over the last 20 years. Numerous journals have been launched to highlight and encourage psycholegal research: *Issues in Criminological and Legal Psychology* (1973), *Law and Psychology Review* (1975), *Law and Human Behavior* (1977), *Behavioral Sciences and the Law* (1982), *Criminal Behavior and Mental Health* (1991), *Psychology, Crime, and Law* (1994),

Psychology, Public Policy, and Law (1996), and *Legal and Criminological Psychology* (1996). Associations and societies have also been founded, such as the British Psychological Society's Division of Criminological and Legal Psychology (1977), the Psychology and Law Division of the American Psychological Association (1981), the European Association of Psychology and Law (1991), and the UK-based Behavioural Science and the Law Network (1994). Recent international conferences that have been hosted include the European Conference on Psychology and the Law, in Siena (1996); Controversial Expert Evidence, in London (1997); and the joint European Association of Psychology and Law and the Psychology and Law Division of the American Psychology–Law Society, in Dublin (1999). New terminology and specialist areas, such as 'psycholegal studies' and 'forensic psychology', have even emerged. It is now possible to complete whole degree courses in these areas, with undergraduate and postgraduate textbooks (e.g. Kapardis, 1997; Memon, Vrij, and Bull, 1998) having been published to facilitate such programmes and professorial chairs being founded to head them. This brief survey makes it obvious just how much interest in the links between psychology and law has been 'mushrooming' (Farrington, 1997: viii) within recent years.

The specific ways in which psychology intersects with law vary. Police make use of criminal profiling, deception detection, interviewing strategies, and other techniques developed within psychology. Psychological theory is used extensively in prison systems, in developing approaches to working with offenders, designing clinical treatment programmes, and enacting parole supervision. Lawyers under-taking family casework seek opinions of clinical psychologists on the suitability of applicants as parents in cases involving the care, adoption and custody of children. Lawyers acting for defendants in criminal cases seek the opinion of clinical and forensic psychologists on the mental status of clients, including their IQ or neuropsychological functioning, to assist in the preparation and conduct of the case.

It is, however, in the realm of expert evidence that psychology has perhaps gained most recent attention within the legal setting. This occurs through psychologists serving as expert witnesses in the courtroom. The function of an expert witness is to provide to the trier of fact (i.e. the jury or the judge) knowledge that is considered to be so specialist, abstract, or complex that it requires an expert to explain it. Expert testimony constitutes an exception to the general rule that witnesses must confine their testimony to matters that they have directly observed. Experts are the only witnesses permitted to give an *opinion* (based on the facts), as opposed to recounting information that may *make up* the facts. The particular benefit of an expert is that s/he is able to offer specialist insight and to exercise professional judgement.

> [I]t is clear that expert opinion is not the mere conjecture, surmise or speculation of the expert: it is his [sic] judgment on a matter of fact; it differs from ordinary evidence on matters of fact in that it is not based on the untutored senses or on the observations of the average man [sic], but on

specialised training, experience out of the common, and/or theoretical information of a recondite kind.

(Kenny, 1983: 199)

There is no limit to the categories of knowledge that are potentially eligible for expert assistance. However, there are limits as to what kind of information can be offered within those categories. The rules of evidence restrict expert testimony to certain types of knowledge, such as that which has gained enough recognition within its field to permit it to be described as 'generally accepted' (*Daubert* v *Merrell Dow*, 1993). As will become apparent, the consequences of these constraints are very significant.

The range of topics on which psychologists have been asked to give expert evidence includes eyewitness testimony, child witness testimony, criminal profiling, reliability of confession evidence, sexual discrimination, crowd behaviour, and psychological syndromes. The number of psychologists offering information about such topics, in the capacity of expert witnesses, has risen dramatically in recent years (Gudjonsson, 1996). Entire careers can now be built around the expert role, supported by training materials developed to enhance psychologists' ability to fulfil that role, such as the instructional video marketed by the British Psychological Society, entitled *Expert Testimony: Developing Witness Skills* (1994), and *The Handbook of Psychology in Legal Contexts*, edited by the lawyer/psychologist team of Carson and Bull (1995). This expansive growth has contributed to calls for an extension of the boundaries of admissible expert psychological evidence (e.g. Blau, 1984; Mackay and Colman, 1991). Indeed, numerous commentators have expressed confidence about the future, including Andreas Kapardis (1997: 179), who believes there is 'greater readiness to admit psychological evidence' amongst even traditionally conservative jurisdictions, and Stephan Landsman (1995: 157), who predicts that '[o]ver the course of the next decade a great deal [in regard to the use of expert witnesses] is likely to happen'.

Expert evidence is one area which has been the subject of extensive debate within the psycholegal literature, with attention focusing particularly on admissibility rules. These are the processes by which evidence, including that relevant to psychological syndromes, is allowed into the courtroom. It is these processes that frame what we perceive to be the explicit relation between law and psychology. They include, for example, the *Daubert* guidelines, the *Turner* rule, and the concepts of reliability and helpfulness, all of which are discussed in more detail in Chapter 2. This debate about admissibility has highlighted differences in the philosophical approaches that psychology and law have each adopted in their attempts to make sense of human behaviour. Much attention has been directed to devising ways in which tensions and conflicts between them can be overcome. We wish, conversely, to draw attention to the ways in which the philosophies of law and psychology are similar. It is this harmony, inherent within the explicit relation, that gives rise to the implicit relation, the effect of which is to restrict the kinds of explanations about human behaviour that can be offered for law's consideration in the first place. We wish to illuminate the way in which such restrictions are particularly deleterious to women.

We argue that the implicit relation comprises three key characteristics: the tenet of objectivity, a male normative standard against which human behaviour is evaluated, and an individualistic model of human behaviour. These characteristics are central both to psychology and to law; when the two join forces, the characteristics are reinforced and further empowered. Crucially for our interests here, they shape the development and the operation of syndrome evidence. Although each of these three characteristics has been criticised within the separate disciplines, there has been little consideration of the three characteristics from an inter-disciplinary perspective.

The implicit relation between psychology and law

The intersection of law and psychology holds advantages for each field. Law already has the benefit of the power derived from the political significance of 'the rule of law' fundamental to Western democracies, but it welcomes assistance from psychology in interpreting aspects of human behaviour about which it may be less informed. Psychology seeks to supply knowledge that upholds the rigour and reliability of scientific methods, thus offering trustworthy insights and expertise to law. Overall, it is believed that by bringing together two apparently independent and autonomous fields, the search for justice and knowledge is furthered.

The key to the success of the relationship rests on the promise of the scientific method. Whilst it owes its origins to philosophy, psychology now regards itself as a science (as discussed in Chapter 3). It conducts empirical research using scientific methods, such as experimental designs and statistical techniques, which test hypotheses designed to be supported or falsified. In Western culture, considerable kudos attaches to knowledge that is considered 'scientific'. Massive amounts of money from government and private enterprise fund scientific research; media attention is given daily to scientific developments and discoveries; scientists continue to be regarded with esteem. Small wonder then that many psychologists strive to secure for psychology a reputation as a science, by emphasising its biological, neurological, and empirical basis (e.g. Eysenck, 1998; Gleitman, Fridlund, and Reisberg, 1999; Rosenzweig, 1991; Santrock, 1996; Staats, 1991).

The ideology of law is one that presumes to reflect political society: its socio-economic basis, cultural norms, and moral consensus. Law derives its authority from these foundational elements and in a modern democracy is assumed to mirror social attitudes. Only occasionally does law lead in the formation of societal values and norms. Rather, governments claim legitimacy for legislative reform by reference to manifesto commitments endorsed by an electorate. Once that legislation reaches the courtroom and is clothed in recognisable legal form, ready to be interpreted and applied by an independent judiciary, its political origins are deemed irrelevant to the decision-making process, underpinning law's apparently value-free universality.

Feminist analyses in psychology and law reveal that neither discipline achieves its objectives. Psychology's knowledge is problematic because (like all science) it assumes a neutrality and generalisability in its enquiry that ignores the agency of those designing and conducting the research (Bohan, 1992). Legal theory is prejudiced in a similar manner (Smart, 1989). Among the biases that disciplines exhibit is support for androcentric values and assumptions. The conjunction of the two disciplines can only serve to reinforce kindred dispositions and to aid the resistance directed against any challenge for reform. It is the scrutiny of that conjunction that concerns us in this book.

If we now take a brief look at each of the three key characteristics that underpin the implicit relation, the framework for our theoretical argument will be complete. The first characteristic, objectivity, is fundamental to both fields. Psychology, like other sciences, takes as its primary aim the discovery of generalisable, objective truths. The use of decontextualised, empirical methods is believed to achieve that. Law, too, places a high value on objectivity, in that objectivity appears to offer an impartial, stable criterion by which behaviour can be measured and evaluated. Qualities such as rationality, reason, and logic are regarded as close siblings of objectivity, and all of these are highly valued by both psychology and law, because they are viewed as the path to 'truth'.

The notion of objectivity has been criticised by many commentators, but these observations tend not to be regarded as seriously problematic by mainstream scholars in either science or law (e.g. Hart, 1961, 1968; Morgan, 1996, 1998; Sokal and Bricmont, 1998; Wolpert, 1998). Many critics within psychology (e.g. Alcoff and Potter, 1993; Bohan, 1992; Bradley, 1989; Burman, 1994; Gilligan, 1993; Kessen, 1990; Kitzinger, 1991; P. Nicolson, 1995; Prilleltensky, 1989; Sampson, 1981; Ussher, 1991; Wilkinson, 1997) have deconstructed the presumed neutrality of the scientific actor, contesting that no person or system can separate their interpretations of data from the methods used to collect those data, nor can they stand outside the society which endorses those methods. They highlight the ways in which the discourse of 'objective science' is used to support various political and societal aims. Within law, critiques of the notion of objectivity have come largely from the movement known as Critical Legal Studies (e.g. Boyle, 1991; Cornell, 1991; Fitzpatrick, 1992; Minow, 1986; Sandland, 1995; Tushnet, 1991; Williams, 1991), a body of scholarship that encompasses diverse groupings including critical race theorists, postmodernists, political economists, and feminists. Critical legal theorists assert that 'law is "rational" or "objective" only because it appears to conform to a particular liberal political ideology' (Minda, 1995: 110), and they point out that that ideology denies the pluralism and multiculturalism of industrialised society. Research drawn from hermeneutics and linguistics underlines the fragility of claims for the objectivity of law by pointing to the 'relativity of values' and 'subjectivity of interpreting language' (Greenawalt, 1992: 7).

The second characteristic is the insistence of both disciplines that human behaviour be measured against a male norm. This attribute is closely related to the first because it is the male point of view that occupies the objective ground. The two are conflated; the objective stance does not reflect a gender-neutral perspective, but an androcentric (i.e. male-centred) one. Psychology has adopted an androcentric perspective from its very origins. Theories accounting for virtually all aspects of human functioning, from brain structure to moral capacity, have been fashioned on a male normative model (Bohan, 1992; Kitzinger, 1991; Ussher, 1991). Where women do not fit that norm, they are characterised as inferior, deviant, inadequate, abnormal. Despite continuing criticism of this model, psychology has largely refused to examine or alter its premise. Law, too, adopts an androcentric model. From the gendered language that continues to be used in drafting legislation and writing legal texts, where 'he' is explicitly presumed to include 'she', to the types of behaviour on which criminal defences are based, the dominant and often exclusive, but unacknowledged, perspective is male (Allen, 1987; MacKinnon, 1987, 1989; O'Donovan, 1985; Rhode, 1989; Smart, 1989, 1995). Like psychology, law has been criticised for its use of this model; like psychology, law resists self-examination and change.

Finally, both disciplines choose an individualistic model to explain human behaviour. The problem with this focus is that it ignores contextual influences on behaviour and implies there is no need to look further than internal features for explanations of behaviour (Bohan, 1992). The importance of an individualistic analysis can be seen for psychology in that this is the very way in which it defines itself (Prilleltensky, 1989; Sampson, 1981). Law prioritises this account of behaviour by assigning rights and duties to the individual person; it assumes and requires that s/he accept responsibility for and control of behaviour, artificially divorcing actions from their external sociological influences (Hart, 1961). Human behaviour simply cannot be explained meaningfully by focusing only on the individual person; actions must be embedded within a socio–historical–personal context in order to understand their meaning. Law and psychology have, in the main, been reluctant to respond to calls that they accept and act on this precept.

Our intention in this book is to explore the domain of syndrome evidence, illuminating the presence of these three characteristics and their central role in the implicit relation that we claim underpins the explicit relation between psychology and law. We have chosen to focus on syndrome evidence, as opposed to other domains within the psycholegal field, because it exemplifies so well the contemporary societal dependence on science as the access route to 'knowledge'. Although science is under siege from some quarters, as information emerges of its limitations in medical, social, and environmental arenas, there remains a deep faith in the capacity of science to provide answers about the world and human experience of it. Law's preference for scientific explanations can only reinforce that faith, as well as force other disciplines that work with it towards closer approximations of accepted scientific models.

The syndromes

We have already observed that it is in the courtroom that the partnership of psychology and law has particularly flourished. The growth of their relationship has been made possible through a burgeoning tendency in modern society to classify behaviour in psycho-medical terms. 'Advances' in scientific and medical knowledge that have been disseminated to an eager public have been greeted with a willingness to label and to be labelled. This is nowhere more apparent than in regard to the diagnosis of psychological syndromes. The four syndromes which we have chosen to examine were selected because, as a group, they span the spectrum of acceptance within the psychological and legal communities. They range from those that have become firmly established within both disciplines to those that have not yet gained official acceptance within either. Those emerging more recently already exhibit patterns discernible in the more established syndromes. While these four are not the only syndromes we could have selected for critique, they represent well the typical patterns of application of psychological evidence in law.

Specifically, Battered Woman's Syndrome (BWS) was chosen for inclusion because it was one of the earliest psychological syndromes to gain acceptance by both communities. It has become established practice within many legal jurisdictions to admit evidence of BWS in cases where a woman kills her abusive partner. Because of the extent to which this syndrome has gained professional acceptance, it is relatively easy to distinguish the operation of the implicit relation. Rape Trauma Syndrome (RTS) was chosen for inclusion because of the frequency with which RTS has begun to be used to explain women's actions following an alleged rape. Like BWS, the syndromatic nature of the 'diagnosis' characterises a woman's reaction to rape as pathology, providing clear evidence of the implicit relation. Premenstrual Syndrome (PMS), in which women's mood fluctuations are attributed to biological factors, occupies a position mid-way on the acceptance spectrum. This diagnosis has acquired legal status, featuring in crimes ranging from homicide to road traffic offences, despite the fact that professional opinion remains divided about the very existence of PMS. False Memory Syndrome (FMS) represents a recently emerging syndrome. FMS has, very recently, become a subject of intense debate within the psychological literature. It is alleged by its proponents that when adults recover memories of childhood sexual abuse, the memories may well be false, arising from misdirected therapeutic techniques. The lack of resolution about FMS (or recovered/repressed memories) within the psychological community has not restrained the law from beginning to admit evidence on the syndrome into the courtroom, and we think that it is useful to make predictions about its future development.

We claim that within each of these syndromes, it is possible to observe the implicit relation in operation. Each of them explains women's behaviour as the result of a pathological disorder, classifying it as deviant and abnormal. This is the case regardless of whether or not such a classification was intended by the original advocates of the diagnoses. The consequence is that, despite the many contemporary advances in women's societal position, women's behaviour continues, as it has for centuries, to be regulated in key ways. The processes by which the regulation is achieved are so subtle as to be invisible without critical analysis. We have organised the chapters so that the syndromes are examined in the order in which they have been described above, for in adopting a chronological framework that discusses the most established syndromes first, it becomes easier to recognise the operation of the implicit relation in those emerging more recently. However, the chapters were written so that they could stand independently, and they need not necessarily be read in the order in which we present them. Readers may prefer to start with those domains about which they are already informed or impassioned.

Amidst the celebratory rhetoric of the 'unfulfilled promise' (Tremper, 1987: 267) and the 'goldmine' of research opportunities (Kapardis, 1997: 290) offered by the alliance of law and psychology, few critical voices are heard. Of the critiques that have been offered, the majority address methodological issues such as limitations on the generalisability of findings, the employment of too narrow a range of research methods, and the risk of overselling psychology (e.g. Bruck and Ceci, 1995; Lloyd-Bostock, 1981; McCloskey and Egeth, 1983). Only a very few commentators have been willing to contemplate issues of a deeper epistemological nature. Among those are King (1986) and Haney (1993), who have drawn attention to the issues of power, values, models of human functioning, and beliefs about the nature of science that underlie the entire psycholegal enterprise. They have argued that social inequalities and injustices are perpetuated by an unwillingness in either field to face these issues. Such observations are usually ignored or resisted, because they are troublesome and gloomy and discomfiting. However, we contend that, because it is currently so enthusiastically maintained that psychology can offer to law 'valid and reliable data about behaviour and experience on which may be developed adequate accounts which have both predictive and explanatory power' (Blackman, Muller, and Chapman, 1984: 3), those working in the two disciplines must begin to engage in the uncomfortable process of self-reflection. Failure to do so will result in the repetition of patterns of the past with all the inequities they embody. A fresh approach is needed.

2 The explicit relation

Until we can see what we are, we cannot take steps to become what we should be.
Charlotte Perkins Gilman[1]

The contemporary inventory of psychological syndromes is, as we observed in Chapter 1, striking in its breadth and variety. Whatever the (perceived) origin of individual syndromes – mental trauma, physical injury, substance ingestion, stress, hormonal fluctuations, genetic predisposition, psychological or physical addiction – it is hard to ignore the expansion in diagnoses that is under way. What should have brought about such escalation? Have advances in medical and psychological science enabled a more accurate understanding of human behaviour to develop, as the language of most published papers and diagnostic manuals implies (e.g. DSM-IV, 1994)? Might it be that such maladies have been recognised in the past, but the official labels have changed, as Showalter (1997) argues? Perhaps the increase is due to the invention (Lee, forthcoming) or construction (Scott, 1990; Young, 1995) of entirely new illnesses? Has, as Downs (1996) proposes, Western society begun to use psychological logic as the means for determining moral and social responsibility?

The use of psychological syndromes to explain women's behaviour and experience is particularly prevalent. Mental health statistics, documented by a number of authors (e.g. Busfield, 1996; Chesler, 1972; Gove, 1979; Showalter, 1987; Ussher, 1991), show there is a gendered dimension to mental health. General-practice statistics for England and Wales for the period 1981–1982 reveal that women were between two and three times as likely as men to be diagnosed with an anxiety disorder or neurotic depression (Busfield, 1996: 21). In 1986 more than twice as many women as men were admitted to psychiatric units for treatment for neurotic disorders and unclassified depressive disorders (Ussher, 1991: 165). These patterns are replicated in the US where, in the 1990s, studies produced for the National Institute of Mental Health by the World Health Organization, the World Bank and Harvard University confirmed that nearly twice as many women as men are affected by a depressive illness each year and that women are twice as likely as men to develop a panic disorder (National Institute of Mental Health, 1999).

Various explanations have been proposed for women's greater representation in the statistics, including a willingness to self-report, their fulfilment of the dependent social roles constructed for them, and the likelihood of women's behaviour being pathologised if they challenge societal expectations (e.g. Allen, 1987; Bordo, 1990; Chesler, 1972; Ehrenreich and English, 1979; Roberts, 1985). Many theorists have also suggested that there is a tendency to ascribe a mental health explanation to women's behaviour, where men's behaviour is typically explained through another mechanism, such as wilful misbehaviour (e.g. Showalter, 1987; Ussher, 1991). It may be that women dominate only in some diagnostic categories, and more theoretical attention needs to be given to the way in which both men's and women's lives are regulated by mental health discourses (Busfield, 1996).

Regardless of the reason for contemporary statistics, professional and societal acceptance of mental health explanations has assisted in admitting psychological syndrome evidence into the courtroom. Indeed, many women's advocates have struggled monumentally to achieve that goal. The campaign to gain legal recognition of Battered Woman's Syndrome as an 'explanation' of why some women kill their violent partners provides a prime example of that struggle (see Chapter 4). Thus, a text that ventures against the tide of opinion needs to lay firm foundations for its argument. The reader might reasonably ask, 'But don't these syndromes help women? Don't they explain why a woman might act in a particular way and allow treatments to be developed that could help her? Don't they demonstrate why serving a prison sentence may be unjust?'

The answer is complex. The label of 'victim' improves the treatment that a woman receives at the hands of society and the criminal justice system; it evokes sympathy rather than condemnation. It decreases the level of responsibility assigned to that person for their behaviour and may reduce their sentence as a result. Practical benefits such as access to therapeutic treatment and the right to claim medical insurance may follow diagnosis. Thus, the logic of syndromes undoubtedly carries advantages. However, their 'discovery' and application are embedded within an ominous context. Explaining a woman's experience by using a diagnostic label characterises that experience as disordered, abnormal, and pathological. It places the victim in a passive role, with power retained in the hands of legal and psycho-medical professionals. To use Foucault's (1979) terminology, 'disciplinary power' is exerted over inert 'docile bodies', who are accorded little say in how their experience is interpreted or explained. As legal devices, syndrome-based explanations do not work efficiently or consistently, and they may just as easily be used against women as in their favour. In short, we fear that the negative consequences of syndromatic labels have not been fully recognised, even by those who work most actively to promote the interests of women. We would argue that the collaborative efforts of psychology and law in regard to syndrome diagnoses render societal and legal change for the benefit of women less, rather than more, likely.

We will begin our analysis by reviewing the means through which diagnostic categories are established and come to be accepted within the psychological and medical communities. We will then go on to explain the mechanisms by which syndromes and other types of evidence are admitted into the courtroom. It is these processes that make up the formal relationship between psychology and law and to which we wish to bring a critical perspective.

Syndrome diagnoses

The term 'syndrome' has been defined as 'a group of concurrent symptoms of a disease' (*Concise Oxford Dictionary*, 1995). This definition makes clear that a syndrome is not simply a group of symptoms, but denotes a classification of those symptoms as illness. The sufferer's experience is interpreted as disordered, abnormal, pathological.

Confirmation that a psychological syndrome 'exists' is generally accomplished through one of the authoritative diagnostic manuals used by health professionals. The primary sources are the *Diagnostic and Statistical Manual of Psychiatric Disorders*, which is published by the American Psychiatric Association and is currently in its fourth edition (DSM-IV, 1994), and the *International Statistical Classification of Diseases and Related Health Problems*, published by the World Health Organization and now in its tenth edition (ICD-10, 1992), which tends to be regarded as the European manual. Although the ICD was designed primarily to facilitate the collection of basic health statistics, in contrast to the DSM which was specifically developed as a diagnostic manual, the degree of difference between the two sources has decreased substantially over the years. Both have attained international standing, and extensive efforts have been made with a view towards 'increasing the congruence and reducing meaningless differences in wording between the two systems' (DSM-IV, 1994: xxi). Compatibility of the codes and terminology has explicitly been sought, resulting in a 'mutual influence' that is seen as desirable by the editorial boards of both the ICD and the DSM (DSM-IV, 1994: xxi).[2]

It is useful to understand how decisions concerning diagnostic classifications are reached. Each edition of the DSM and ICD emerges after a lengthy process of two to four years of discussion amongst relevant professionals about the current state of research and opinion. Working parties of six to twelve 'experts' are formed to review the available literature, and recommendations about whether or not to include a diagnostic category in the manual are made by them. They also attempt to gain agreement about what the precise description of symptoms should be. Disagreements within the working parties must be arbitrated by the committee chair, and a vote as to the final decisions may need to be taken. The chair is also in charge of dealing with input from any organisations raising objections to inclusion of the diagnosis. The Board of Trustees associated with the manual have to approve drafts of the new editions, and they have the power to delete entries or recommend changes to terminology. Thus, the process of identifying and endorsing – indeed, creating – diagnostic categories is a matter of conflict, consensus, and compromise.

The process is not, as Anne Figert (1996: 146) points out, a simple matter where the 'players merely feed the best scientific studies through the machinery of the DSM revision process – and out comes the new diagnosis (no struggle at all)'. Political, economic, and scientific factors all make significant contributions to the final outcome. Having conducted extensive sociological analyses of the construction of diagnostic categories, Figert argues that, after the decisions are taken and the controversies surrounding them forgotten, it is the 'rational account' of diagnostic construction which survives. This account explains the diagnostic labels, symptoms, and code numbers as 'an inevitable outcome of bureaucratic procedure and scientific truth or method' (Figert, 1996: 143). The contribution of other factors is neutralised, obscured. The introductory comments to the DSM-IV, with their emphasis on the systematic, empirical nature of the endeavour, illustrate this point very nicely:

> In arriving at final DSM-IV decisions, the Work Groups and the Task Force reviewed all of the extensive empirical evidence and correspondence that had been gathered. It is our belief that the major innovation of DSM-IV lies not in any of its specific content changes but rather in the systematic and explicit process by which it was constructed and documented. More than any other nomenclature of mental disorders, DSM-IV is grounded in empirical evidence.
>
> (DSM-IV, 1994: xvi)

On the basis of this account, it would be reasonable to assume that the contemporary increase in diagnostic categories is the result of scientific discovery. As medical science progresses, technical equipment becomes more sophisticated, and knowledge 'advances', it is expected that new discoveries should be made. However, the point that those conducting critical analyses of the diagnostic process seek to make is that the process does not occur within a vacuum (e.g. Lunbeck, 1994; McGovern, 1985; Tavris, 1992). Knowledge of any type is contextual. 'All of our knowledge is conditional knowledge, constructed within our conceptual systems, and thus knowledge is a communal achievement and is relevant to time and place' (Polkinghorne, 1983: 13). From this perspective, the contemporary increase in diagnoses has as much to with modern societal and political concerns as it does with scientific discovery.

The social construction of illness, particularly mental illness, has of course been widely discussed in previous decades by a succession of anti-psychiatry critics, such as R. D. Laing (1960) and Thomas Szasz (1972, 1973). Numerous contemporary theorists have added their voices to this perspective. Judith Herman (1992), for example, focusing on the effects of psychological trauma and Post-Traumatic Stress Disorder, argues that all conceptions of psychological trauma are affiliated with a political movement: '[w]ithout the context of a political movement, it has never been possible to advance the study of psychological trauma' (Herman, 1992: 32). She supports her claims through identifying those periods in the twentieth century when the study of psychological trauma prospered. Herman suggests there were three such periods, the first of which occurred during the early years of the century. Attention at that point was focused on the study of hysteria, which she describes as 'the archetypal psychological disorder of women' (Herman, 1992: 9). She argues that this focus grew out of the republican, anticlerical political movement of the late nineteenth century in France. The focus of the second period was shell shock, the study of which began in the UK and the US after the First World War and reached its peak after the Vietnam War. Its political context was 'the collapse of a cult of war and the growth of an anti war movement' (Herman, 1992: 9). The most recent trauma to come into public awareness is sexual and domestic violence, its affiliated political context being the feminist movement in Western Europe and North America. Pointing out that the trauma suffered by female victims of violence has a similar configuration to that of male war veterans, she draws the stark conclusion that there is indeed a war between the sexes. This analysis leads Herman to argue forcefully that the pathology of trauma is a social construction. 'Our contemporary understanding of psychological trauma is built upon a synthesis of these three lines of investigation' (Herman, 1992: 9).

This theme is also explored in the work of a number of other writers. The work of Phyllis Chesler (1972) and Elaine Showalter (1987) applies a specifically feminist and constructionist approach to female madness, siding with anti-psychiatry theorists in contending that diagnoses of mental illness are used to control and regulate women's behaviour. Donald Downs (1996: 4) has examined the ways in which psychological syndromes serve contemporary notions of justice, reflecting a societal wish to acknowledge fully the position of the victim, in the belief that '[a]ny adequate and just accounting of criminal responsibility must take the mental states engendered by such abuse into consideration'. The role of economic factors in shaping the contemporary mental health profession has been emphasised by Tavris (1992), particularly in regard to the US, where insurance companies stipulate that financial compensation can be secured only through reference to an 'official' medical diagnosis. Bayer's (1987) review of the debates that took place over the classification of homosexuality as a mental illness is now well known, and a critical approach has also been applied to the diagnoses of Self-Defeating Personality Disorder, Masochistic Personality Disorder, and Premenstrual Syndrome (Caplan, 1995; Figert, 1996; Walker, 1984). Very recently emerging syndromes, such as False Memory Syndrome and Post-Abortion Syndrome, have already begun to be subjected to similar critiques (e.g. Lee and Gilchrist, 1997; Webster, 1996).

In highlighting the political factors that contribute to the construction of syndromes, all of these writers expose the expedient qualities of using psychological syndromes to explain human behaviour. Diseases of the mind need not necessarily have an organic or psychological foundation; rather, a society's conception of what constitutes mental illness can originate from the need to regulate social dysfunction. Rather than simply offering a method with which to treat mental malfunction, diagnostic categories can assist society in achieving a desired structural outcome. While 'being diagnosed' offers advantages, the cost of this regulatory system is that the sufferer must accede to classification as disordered, abnormal, and submissive. The significance of this account for our purposes is that it highlights the role that medical and other sciences can – and do – play in controlling society. The contrast with the established rhetoric of objectivity and neutrality is important. The mainstream scientific rhetoric, with its guise of apolitical impartiality, fits very nicely with the values and aims of law. It is this fit that, in part, explains the reception of (scientific) psychology into the legal process.

Before we examine the application of syndrome diagnoses within the courtroom, it is important to pause and ask: what relevance do *psychiatric* manuals hold for a book on *psychology* and law? The answer lies in the degree of overlap that exists between the two professions, demonstrated by the increasing reference within the literature to the composite unit of the 'psy disciplines'. Foucault (1979) originated this conception, critiquing the power exerted by the disciplinary discourses of psychiatry, psychology, and psychoanalysis. Other theorists have built upon this notion (e.g. Boyle, 1997; Sheldon, 1997; Smart, 1989; Thomson, 1998), arguing that the 'psy discourses' serve as contemporary mechanisms of surveillance, normalisation, and regulation. Given the power and influence exerted by these discourses, there can appear little reason to discriminate between psychology and psychiatry. Certainly the disciplines both address issues of human mental functioning, and they have close associations in terms of their clinical applications. Both owe theoretical debts to the neurological discoveries of Charcot and to the psychoanalytical concepts of Freud, among other theorists. The DSM and ICD are highly influential within the teaching of psychology, featuring prominently in abnormal psychology textbooks (e.g. Comer, 1998)[3] and forming a key component of the curriculum in clinical psychology courses. Surveys indicate that a majority of psychologists and other mental health professionals use the DSM, 'even . . . therapists who doubt the value of formal diagnosis' (Kutchins and Kirk, 1988: 6). The DSM was specifically designed to fit such a broad range of applications, as the editors stress in their preface to the current volume.

> An official nomenclature must be applicable in a wide diversity of contexts. DSM-IV is used by clinicians and researchers of many different orientations (e.g., biological, psychodynamic, cognitive, behavioral, interpersonal, family/systems). It is used by psychiatrists, other physicians, psychologists, social workers, nurses, occupational and rehabilitation therapists, counselors and other health and mental health professionals. . . . Fortunately, all these many uses are compatible with one another.
>
> (DSM, 1994, xv)

It is this breadth that helps to give the DSM its power, and which ensures that it will influence psychologists' thinking, practice, and research, even where they may disagree with some of its diagnostic categories. Such similarities between psychiatry and psychology can lead lawyers to treat the two fields as relatively interchangeable, and for many purposes, law can now be equally content with the expert testimony of a psychologist or a psychiatrist (Thornton, 1995). It is therefore reasonable to argue that distinctions between the two disciplines are often unimportant.

There remain, however, meaningful contrasts between the two disciplines. Critically for our purposes, the functions of psychologists and psychiatrists differ with regard to how widely they conceive the boundaries of their interest and expertise. Psychiatrists focus entirely on pathology; as medical doctors, they are interested in treating mental states and behaviours that are abnormal. Psychologists, on the other hand, regard pathology as only one component of their field; they are interested in human behaviour more generally, studying 'normal' behaviour more often than abnormal behaviour. As a recent report on the role of expert witnesses, produced by the British Psychological Society (1998: 1), stated:

> The evidence of psychologists and psychiatrists departs when the former begin to comment on the development and mental functioning of ordinary individuals. Psychologists do devote more of their training to the understanding of normal human behaviour than their psychiatrist colleagues, who focus principally on the presence or absence of mental disorder.

This differential focus is important because, we would contend, one of the key problems in the 'symbiotic relationship' (Smart, 1989: 20) between the psy professions and law is the classification of behaviour as 'abnormal'.

If the implicit relation is to be challenged (a possibility we explore in Chapter 8), then the tendency to conceive of women's behaviour as the result of a psychological syndrome must be altered. Alternative explanations of behaviour are possible, derived by placing behaviour in its context(s) before assigning it a meaning. Psychology has the potential to offer such alternative characterisations, given its philosophical origins and the insights that critics have offered the field. Indeed, a model for admitting expert psychological testimony on 'normal human behaviour' already exists in the form of social framework data (Monahan and Walker, 1994), which provides general, contextual information about human behaviour to the courts. The use of this model in explaining phenomena such as eyewitness memory, sex stereotyping, and crowd behaviour has been very effective when allowed into court, precisely because it acts in an 'educational' capacity. Testimony on psychological syndromes has already sometimes been used in this way (as we discuss in Chapters 4 and 5). Thus, this model is one that provides a good basis for conceiving of new ways in which knowledge about women's (and men's) behaviour could be admitted into the courtroom without necessarily characterising it as disordered. We believe that it is possible for psychological evidence to make a valuable contribution to the processes of the courtroom, but only if – and this is the imposing 'if' – psychology is willing to adopt a more reflexive approach to the production of its own knowledge. It is because we believe that psychological models have such capacities that we have directed our analysis toward the intersection of law with psychology, rather than the psy disciplines more generally.

Psychology in the courtroom

Men of authority have, for centuries, been called to testify in legal cases. In the Middle Ages, authority was lodged in (male) religious figures; as the Enlightenment proceeded, this shifted toward practitioners of science (and so the gender composition did not change) (Szasz, 1972, 1973). As psychology began to make use of scientific methods (a transition which will be described in more detail in

Chapter 3), this placed it in the same category as other sciences and made the findings, techniques, and knowledge it produced of likely interest to the law. Hugo Muensterberg, a German psychologist, was one of the earliest advocates of this position. In 1908, he published a book entitled *On the Witness Stand*, in which he took issue with judges and lawyers for failing to take notice of the emerging findings of experimental psychology. Muensterberg urged lawyers to utilise psychological methods, particularly in testing the reliability of witness memory and suspects' consciousness of guilt.[4]

J. H. Wigmore, one of the great American jurists, disagreed vehemently with this view, however. Wigmore belonged to the intellectual tradition of 'optimistic rationalism', which maintained that the proof process in court can be reduced to a set of logical principles, allowing law to function with the formulaic precision of a science. Indeed, those who aligned themselves with this movement saw law itself as a science (for discussion, see Minda, 1995; Redmayne, 1997; Twining, 1985). When Wigmore was writing in the early twentieth century, psychology was in its infancy and had not yet gained widespread acceptance as a science. Wigmore challenged the need for psychology in the courtroom, arguing that the reliability of experimental psychology and the methods proposed by Muensterberg and others for testing memory and consciousness of guilt were 'highly controversial and that there was a considerable body of opinion . . . to the effect that the specific methods [Muensterberg] had recommended were not yet sufficiently developed to be relied on by courts' (Wigmore, 1908, cited in Twining, 1985: 136). He did not believe that experimental psychological findings could add anything to a court's deliberations.

Today, the relationship between psychology and law in the courtroom is very different. Although there remains in many quarters substantial discomfort with admitting expert evidence about people's 'state of mind' (e.g. Hagen, 1997; Jonakait, 1994; Richardson and Ginsburg, 1998), the early antipathy has given way to a 'growing détente between law and medicine' (Sprince, 1998: 59), in the belief that there is perhaps something for law to learn from psycholegal research in general and from 'objective psychological tests' in particular (per Henry LJ, *Frost* v *Chief Constable of the South Yorkshire Police*, 1997: 565). Indeed, psychology has gained a clear foothold in the courtrooms of many jurisdictions, and the trend is unarguably towards greater admissibility of expert testimony. In the last two decades, psychologists have been asked to serve as expert witnesses in cases dealing with a wide range of topics, among them eyewitness identification (e.g. Kassin, Ellsworth, and Smith, 1989; Loftus, 1991; Penrod, Fulero, and Cutler, 1995), persuasion (e.g. *Processed Plastic* v *Warner Communications*, 1982), sexual stereo-typing (Fiske *et al.*, 1991), reliability of confessions (e.g. Sheldon and MacLeod, 1991), crowd behaviour (e.g. Colman, 1991), and the effect of psychological trauma (e.g. Frazier and Borgida, 1985). This breadth of topics has encouraged some writers to predict 'the dawn of a new era of legal psychology' and to look forward to its 'promising future' (Kapardis, 1997: 18).

Having established the principle that psychology might have a contribution to make to the proof process, rules of evidence began to be adapted so that they could provide mechanisms by which psychological evidence (along with other forms of scientific evidence) could be admitted to court. Although the legal jurisdictions considered in this text each have their own distinctive procedural rules, the ethos governing the admissibility of evidence is similar across all of them. This is an important point for our purposes, for it is such rules and processes that formalise the relationship between psychology and law. The judicial interpretations made in the application of these rules in legal cases form official and authoritative decisions. Thus, they comprise what we term the 'explicit relation' between psychology and law.

Evidence of a scientific nature is introduced into court cases by asking witnesses who are considered to be expert in their field to provide informed views about their specialist knowledge. They are classified as 'expert witnesses', and their evidence constitutes a special kind of testimony known as 'opinion evidence'. Generally, only expert witnesses are allowed to offer opinions in court. The testimony of most other witnesses is restricted to factual evidence: observations of what they have directly seen, heard, or experienced. Opinion evidence is only admissible when the information being sought is deemed likely to be outside the experience or knowledge of the judge and/or jury. Experts are given scope to interpret complex findings for the benefit of those judging the facts in a case, who are unlikely to be knowledgeable about evidence of a scientific or technical nature. This places expert witnesses in a privileged position, for they have much potential to influence the case. That is why rules of evidence governing the admission of expert testimony were developed: to counteract the potential imbalance of their privilege.

The rules of evidence state the criteria that should be used to evaluate and regulate the admissibility of expert evidence. There are two primary principles governing admissibility that operate across jurisdictions: reliability and helpfulness.[5] In the US reliability is considered the primary criterion, while in the UK helpfulness is considered to be the more important (for discussion see Raitt, 1998). These principles echo the arguments of Muensterberg, providing a reminder that, a century later, both science and law continue their search for certainty and generalisability.

Reliability

Reliability is an attribute central to the considerations of both scientists and lawyers.[6] Unless the expert evidence to be presented in court can be shown to be reliable, it will carry little weight with a judge and/or jury. A traditional way in which the reliability of scientific evidence has been evaluated by law is through the concept of 'general acceptance'. The general acceptance rule originated in the 1923 case of *Frye* v *United States*, where the court refused to admit the results of an early polygraph test. In its judgement the court declared:

> Just when a scientific principle or discovery crosses the line between the experimental and demonstrable stages is difficult to define. Somewhere in this

twilight zone the evidential force of the principle must be recognized, and while courts will go a long way in admitting expert testimony deduced from a well-recognized scientific principle or discovery, the thing from which the deduction is made must be sufficiently established to have gained general acceptance in the particular field in which it belongs.

(*Frye* v *United States*, 1923: 1014)

The court did not feel that the evidence presented in the *Frye* case met this standard, and evidence about the polygraph test was disallowed. The decision set a precedent, and it was the 'general acceptance standard' or '*Frye* rule' that became the basis against which admissibility of scientific evidence was generally evaluated within US courtrooms.

This standard received support because it took account of the views of the wider scientific community. The findings presented in the evidence were presumed to be reliable and valid because they had been subjected to the procedures of science: replication, theoretical and methodological scrutiny, and especially peer review. Any knowledge that had withstood these processes was considered to be reliable, trustworthy, and ultimately truthful. The principles of the *Frye* test were often invoked even where the term 'general acceptance' was not used explicitly or the *Frye* case was not cited (Bernstein, 1996: 127). In effect, general acceptance came to be regarded as a barrier against the inclusion of unorthodox, unreliable, untrustworthy theories and techniques. This reasoning has been applied in the courts to a variety of topics, including the detection of narcotics, voiceprint identification, electron microscopic analysis in testing for gunshot residue, neutron activation analysis in blood testing, and syndrome evidence. (For a review of these and other decisions see Giannelli, 1980.)

The concept of general acceptance plays a role in the evidential processes of countries other than the US, although this may occur in a less explicit fashion or make use of marginally distinctive terminology. For example, the South Australia Supreme Court made the following statement in a 1984 case.

Before admitting the opinion of a witness into evidence as expert testimony, the judge must consider . . . whether the subject matter of the opinion forms part of a body of knowledge or experience which is *sufficiently organized* or *recognized to be accepted* as a reliable body of knowledge or experience.

(*R* v *Bonython*, 1984: 46, emphasis added)

In reference to English law, Cross and Tapper (1995: 558, emphasis added) state that evidence should be admitted into court 'so long as a field is *sufficiently well-established* to pass the ordinary tests of relevance and reliability'. Recent legislation extending to the whole of the UK states that the definition of mental impairment includes 'an impairment resulting from or consisting of a mental illness only if the illness is a clinically *well-recognised illness*' (Disability Discrimination Act 1995, schedule 1, para 1(1), emphasis added). Although slightly different terms are being employed across these examples, the general intention behind them is to establish the reliability of the evidence by referring to its acceptance within its scientific field. Despite the attempts of some legal commentators to differentiate between such terms (e.g. Gless, 1995), there is little difference between the meanings of 'general acceptance', 'general recognition', 'sufficiently well-established', 'well-founded', and 'sufficiently organized'.

Problems with the general acceptance standard have for a long time been debated. As the margins of scientific knowledge expanded, confusion grew over the boundaries that demarcated expert knowledge from everyday experience. Did normal human behaviour require specialist explanation; why was common sense not sufficient? There was disagreement in the courts regarding which levels of scientific study required to be generally accepted – a theory? a technique? scientists' conclusions? all of these? What if there was disagreement at some of these levels but not others? And how was general acceptance of any of them to be demonstrated?

Problems such as these resulted in increasing confusion and disagreement regarding the use of the general acceptance test. There was an attempt to address this confusion when codification of the US *Federal Rules of Evidence* occurred in 1975. The *Rules* attempted to take a more liberal stance toward the admission of expert testimony, but unfortunately they did not explicitly address the general acceptance standard and so the confusion continued. In 1993 the matter was resolved to some extent in the US Supreme Court decision in the case of *Daubert* v *Merrell Dow Pharmaceuticals*, a case brought by the families of two children, Jason Daubert and Eric Schuller, who had been born with birth defects. They believed the defects had been caused by the mothers' ingestion of the anti-nausea drug Bendectin, which had been prescribed to them during pregnancy. Merrell Dow Pharmaceuticals was the manufacturer of the drug. Both parties relied heavily on expert testimony, although it was based on very different kinds of evidence. The pharmaceutical company relied on epidemiological evidence (i.e. human statistical evidence) which showed that no studies had demonstrated a statistically significant association between Bendectin and birth defects. Against this, the plaintiffs offered expert testimony based on test-tube and live animal studies exposing a link between Bendectin and birth defects. They also arranged for re-analysis of previously published epidemiological studies. At the District Court level, judgement had been granted in favour of the company on several grounds, including the findings that epidemiological studies were the most reliable evidence of causation of birth defects, that test-tube and live animal studies were not based on epidemiological studies, and that the re-analyses carried out had not been published or subjected to peer review.

On appeal to the Supreme Court, the specific question for determination was the appropriate standard for admitting expert scientific testimony in a federal trial. In responding to this question the court issued a set of four guidelines:

1   Is the theory or technique at issue testable, or has it been tested?
2   Has the theory or technique been subjected to peer review and publication?
3   In the case of a particular technique, what is the known or potential rate of error?

4   What is the degree of general acceptance in the scientific community of the theory or technique?

The court stated clearly that general acceptance should no longer be seen as the sole standard for admissibility. These new guidelines were envisioned as being more appropriate for making contemporary determinations about whether or not to admit scientific evidence. They were intended to provide a clearer and better framework within which judges could perform a gate-keeping role. It was recognised that on occasion the exercise of their discretion might 'prevent the jury from learning of authentic insights and innovations' but that was regarded as inevitable in the execution of a trial applying rules of evidence 'designed not for the exhaustive search for cosmic understanding but for the particularized resolution of legal disputes' (*Daubert*, 1993: 485). The *Daubert* guidelines have thus come to be regarded as a new standard for evaluating expert testimony.

The momentous nature of this decision can be seen in that it has already begun influencing the legal community beyond the US. Reference to the decision has been made in literature and textbooks published for consumption in England (Cross and Tapper, 1995; Imwinkelried, 1995; Pizzi, 1995; Uglow, 1997), Australia (Freckleton, 1994), and Canada (Roberts, 1998). Appeal courts in several of these countries are reported to have invited presentations on the implications of *Daubert* from informed academics (Richardson and Ginsburg, 1998: 266).

However, there was from the beginning also heated debate about the extent to which the guidelines could accomplish their aim. Imwinkelried (1995), Gless (1995) and Goodman-Delahunty and Foote (1995) were among those who held the view that the guidelines would result not in flexibility but in greater restriction, while other scholars (e.g. Zonana, 1994; Feldman, 1995; Pizzi, 1995) feared that the guidelines were not yet strong enough. Even two of the Supreme Court Justices, in their dissent from a portion of the judgement, regretted that the generality of the guidelines detracted from their value as 'they are not applied to deciding whether or not particular testimony was or was not admissible, and therefore they tend to be not only general, but vague and abstract' (*Daubert*, 1993: 486). In practice, since 1993, the *Daubert* standards have been rejected by many state courts (which are not obliged to follow federal precedents), in favour of the old *Frye* standard, due to its stricter demands upon scientific evidence (for review, see Penrod, Fulero, and Cutler, 1995). In 1997, the Supreme Court was again required to rule upon the gate-keeping role of the trial court judge, in the case of *General Electric Co. et al.* v *Joiner*, where the justices' discussion focused on the distinction (or lack thereof) between scientific methods and conclusions. Thus, it is clear that *Daubert* has not settled the debate over admissibility of scientific evidence. What the decision has re-confirmed is the importance that courts place on scientific methods and reliability, and the key role that general acceptance continues to play in evaluating those qualities.

The pressure placed on psychology by this state of affairs is obvious. If it wishes to maintain its status as a science (a desire about which there can be little question), then the evidence it produces in the courtroom will need, at the minimum, to meet the standard of general acceptance. The *Daubert* criteria impose additional expectations upon it: that its theories and conclusions will be testable (i.e. falsifiable), that they will have been subjected to peer review, and that the error rates of psychological assessments be determinable. These are not necessarily problems, however. Psychology has always endorsed the need for peer review, and findings are not really regarded as reliable or valid until they have been replicated and drawn support from a fair proportion of the professional community. The testing and falsification of hypotheses are integral to the empirical methods of psychology. Thus, psychology is arguably well placed to meet the *Daubert* standards.

We would contend, however, that problems do exist – ones of a deeper, more philosophical nature. A primary one is that the conservative model of science contained within the concept of general acceptance and within the *Daubert* guidelines discourages reflection: reflection about the epistemological assumptions of psychology's theories and methods, about the political and social consequences of those assumptions, and about the nature of psychology's interaction with the law. Rather than promoting debate about these important issues, decisions about admissibility criteria in cases such as *Daubert* encourage psychologists to endorse the prescribed model of science even more enthusiastically than they might do otherwise, precisely because fulfilling it accords them greater status.

Indeed, those psychologists most invested in promoting psychology within the courtroom have been particularly active in discussing how the discipline can meet established admissibility criteria. For example, Penrod and colleagues advise that to maximise the acceptability of eyewitness evidence

> [e]xperimental psychologists should be able, and increasingly will be called upon, to talk authoritatively about the role of basic scientific concepts and practices [including] empiricism, the operationalization of independent and dependent variables, objectivity, theory development and testing, the use of null hypotheses and tests of statistical significance, notions of reliability and variability, the importance of experimental control, internal validity and rival hypotheses, and external validity.
>
> (Penrod, Fulero, and Cutler, 1995: 245)

Psychologists preparing to give expert testimony on psychological injuries in cases of employment discrimination were recently apprised that

> the *Daubert* standards . . . will require the psychologist to articulate a strong scientific basis for the conclusions reached about the client. . . . It may be helpful . . . to assess whether [a theory] is 'time tested'; however, the absence of consensus in the scientific community alone will not serve as a bar to the admission of the proffered testimony if other indicia of reliability and trustworthiness are present to establish the element of falsifiability.
>
> (Goodman-Delahunty and Foote, 1995: 198)

In his examination of the probative value of psychometric evidence (i.e. tests that measure mental abilities and psychological states), Marlowe counsels that

> [t]he *Daubert* case has elevated 'good' science to a threshold evidentiary standard, mandating judges and forensic experts to understand, evaluate and apply scientific reasoning to proffered evidence. This explicit coupling of evidence law to the Scientific Method and Empiricism necessitates the further development and refinement of a hybrid evidentiary vocabulary. The constructs contained in this vocabulary must . . . educate the courts on the principles and techniques of science.
>
> (Marlowe, 1995: 226)

Thus, the result of decisions such as *Daubert* is to make it even less likely that psychology will reflect critically upon its basis as a science. It cannot afford to query the criteria that have been suggested by law for evaluating the reliability of evidence, for if it fails to achieve any of the established criteria, then psychology sacrifices that which it holds most dear: its status as a science. The consequences of this reluctance are an issue to which we will return shortly.

Helpfulness

The other primary principle used in making decisions about admissibility is helpfulness. This principle states that evidence presented in court must be more than 'common-sense' knowledge. It must assist the deliberations of a judge or jury by adding to the knowledge that they already possess. The English *Turner* rule is an excellent example of this standard. This rule emerged in the case of *R v Turner* (1975), in which Turner was charged with the murder of his girlfriend, whom he admitted killing with a hammer. She had informed him that she was pregnant by another man, and he argued that this admission had provoked him into violent action. He wished to submit psychiatric evidence that supported this claim. Relying on the precedent of *Folkes* v *Chadd*, a 1782 case, the Court of Appeal famously confirmed that

> [a]n expert's opinion is admissible to furnish the court with scientific infor- mation which is likely to be outside the experience and knowledge of a judge or jury. If on the proven facts a judge or jury can form their own conclusions without help, then the opinion of an expert is unnecessary. In such a case if it is given dressed up in scientific jargon it may make judgment more difficult. The fact that an expert witness has impressive qualifications does not by that fact alone make his opinion on matters of human nature . . . more helpful than the jurors themselves; but there is a danger that they may think it does.
>
> (*R v Turner*, 1975: 841)

In short, the *Turner* rule, as it has come to be known, contends that judges and jurors will be able to appreciate the nuances of human behaviour without the help of expert opinion, due to their own life experiences and common sense.

This rule has been extensively criticised but remains relatively intact today in all three jurisdictions in the UK (England and Wales, Scotland, and Northern Ireland). Although the judgement was expressly concerned with psychiatric evidence, the rule applies to all psychological evidence. Critics have attacked the assumptions about common sense on which the rule was founded. For example, Colman and Mackay (1993) describe a range of behavioural phenomena, such as obedience to authority, group polarisation, cognitive dissonance, and bystander apathy, for which studies have demonstrated the fallacy of treating human behaviour as 'transparent'. Empirical research has revealed the extent to which people behave in ways counter-intuitive to common sense predictions. Colman and Mackay (1993: 48–49) claim that '"ordinary, reasonable men and women" have a systematically biased under-standing of normal human behaviour', leading them to conclude that 'this leaves the *Turner* rule without any discernible justification or force'.

The UK emphasis on helpfulness is mirrored in the US in the *Federal Rules of Evidence* (1975). Rule 702 states that expert testimony should be permitted in any case where it will 'assist the trier of fact to understand the evidence or to determine a fact in issue'. Rule 402 provides that 'all relevant evidence is admissible' except where prohibited elsewhere in the *Rules*. The emphasis is therefore on helpfulness; unless there is good reason to exclude it, there is a presumption in favour of admitting evidence. This has contributed to the evolution of a permissive regime in the US, where the inclination has been to admit, rather than exclude, evidence. It was just such indulgence that gave rise to the concerns about junk science that culminated in the *Daubert* decision.

Like the *Turner* rule, the *Federal Rules* on helpfulness have been subjected to criticism. In particular, critics charge that law's resistance to expert psychological testimony is based less on concerns about the nature of helpfulness than on beliefs about its status as the gate-keeper of knowledge. According to Jones (1994: 122), the struggle is 'less to do with an ideological preference for the ordinary layperson and more to do with professional power struggles between the judiciary and persons who have special knowledge'. Alldridge (1994: 138) adds that it is law's reluctance to confer authority on certain types of science that has contributed to the 'pecking order of respectability' among the sciences, with the 'hard sciences' residing at the top. From these viewpoints, conflicts between law and psychology are not pragmatic ones, as the notion of helpfulness implies, but epistemologically based. Which areas of knowledge command expert status? Who should have control of that knowledge? The 'pecking order' amongst the sciences is thus a reflection of wider academic and political disputes, swathed in notions about objectivity, reliability, falsifiability, and all the other indicators of scientific merit.

The helpfulness of expert testimony is not always evaluated by giving attention to its content. The credentials of the expert also frequently play a key role. By emphasising the title, professional training, years of service, and professional reputation of an expert, it can be demonstrated that the expert indeed possesses specialist knowledge. Technically, according to Rule 702 of the US *Federal Rules*, anyone with the relevant 'knowledge, skill, experience, training, or education' is qualified to serve as an expert witness. Testimony from real-estate agents, narcotics officers, foreign-language specialists, and counsellors has occasionally been accepted on this basis in US courtrooms (Giannelli, 1980). A leading UK text states, similarly, that the two qualities most important in establishing expert status in the UK are (a) possession of specialist knowledge and (b) ability to 'use that knowledge by virtue of training and/or experience in that field' (Hodgkinson, 1990: 11). Thus, in theory, anyone with specialist training or experience could serve as an expert witness.

In practice, however, the reality is somewhat different. This is particularly true for psychological evidence, where evidence of the sciences' pecking order emerges once again. When hearing expert evidence, courts prefer that it be presented by those who can demonstrate an established research background, complete with peer-reviewed publications. Traditionally it has been established experimentalists, researchers, and academics who have been most successful in having such testimony admitted into court. During the last two decades, clinical psychologists working as practitioners have begun to perform more often in an expert capacity, in concert with the increased willingness to admit expert testimony. This trend has highlighted tensions within psychology, with experimentalists criticising their clinical colleagues for encouraging the admission of non-empirically-grounded 'junk science' into the courtroom. Margaret Hagen (1997), professor of psychology at Boston University, recently published a book entitled *Whores of the Court: The Fraud of Psychiatric Testimony and the Rape of American Justice*, in which she attacked the 'forensic mental health professionals and self-styled pyschoexperts' who produce 'psychobabble' about trauma and abuse and rely on 'anti-scientific intuition' in making diagnoses (Kassin, 1998: 321–322). Randolph Jonakait contributed a key paper to the first volume of the influential journal *Shepard's Expert and Scientific Evidence* (1994), in which he argued that psychotherapists' techniques are subjective and their testimony no more than personal opinion, so he recommended that practising psychotherapists not be permitted to provide expert testimony unless it is based on scientific methodology. Richardson and Ginsburg worry about the scientific validity of much psychological syndrome evidence, going 'so far' as to '*even* suggest that political and popular opinion about certain issues can influence decisions to admit allegedly scientific evidence' (Richardson and Ginsburg, 1998: 268, emphasis added). Such criticisms resonate well with the expectations of *Frye* and *Daubert*, making it seem that decisions about admissibility and exclusion are largely a matter of procedure and definitions. However, critical reflection reveals the extent to which beliefs about what constitutes expert knowledge, 'real science', and 'junk science' underlie such decisions, and as greater use is made of expert testimony, such beliefs take on a more powerful role. One consequence is that, within psychology, old rifts between experimentalists and non-experimentalists re-emerge with renewed vigour.

Thus, it is clear that the notion of helpfulness is not based simply on pragmatic matters. Like reliability, assumptions are harboured about what counts as knowledge and who counts as an expert. Discussion of these two key principles, in the academic literature or in the courtroom, rarely highlights the epistemological nature of these concerns. Instead, the focus is placed on how reliability and helpfulness can be assessed and demonstrated. Disregard of more fundamental philosophical issues helps to maintain the image of law and psychology as objective, neutral institutions. Once epistemological suppositions are revealed, it becomes intellectually (and even morally) necessary to explore their consequences. What results flow from their collaboration? In the final section of this chapter, we will consider briefly some of the problematic consequences, which have tended to be overlooked in the psycholegal literature despite their far-reaching implications.

Critique of the explicit relation

These principles which govern the admissibility of scientific evidence – general acceptance, *Daubert* guidelines, *Turner* rule, Rules 702 and 402, expert credentials, reliability, helpfulness – are examples of the formal ways in which the law–science relationship is regulated. They constitute the official, overt, explicit relation between psychology and law in the courtroom. Although they are applicable to all scientific evidence, such rules are particularly important when it comes to information about human behaviour, because this is an area which law has traditionally regarded as its own area of expertise. The historical distrust between psychology and law still casts its shadow. Their 'marriage' has been described as an 'uneasy' one; their state as 'bedfellows' has 'not always been happy' (Farrington, 1997: viii). While considerable progress has been made towards harmony, there remains scepticism about the degree to which close collaboration can or should occur. The persistence of the *Turner* rule exemplifies law's suspicion of other disciplines 'muscling in' on its patch. For their part, psychologists are 'appalled when lawyers continue to ignore what the psychologists consider good empirical research results and, consequently fail to resolve issues in law' (Kapardis, 1997: 14).

However, the two disciplines derive mutual benefit from their interaction. As Jasanoff (1995: 42) observes, '[t]he legal system has long looked to science as an indispensable ally in the shared project of truth-finding', and what better than a scientific psychology to augment law's understanding of human behaviour? Psychology, on the other hand, has a new domain in which to test its theories and develop new ones. Psychologists can feel proud that their findings are being used to contribute to societal goals and enforce justice. Best of all, psychology achieves status, for in accepting psychology into the courtroom, law tacitly affirms that the discipline has matured sufficiently to be acknowledged as a science. Thus, the partnership has become secure and productive; there is a general aura of excitement and confidence. 'The era of [psychologists' and lawyers'] most productive relationships built on mutual respect and realistic idealism may be only just beginning' (Judge Wald, 1982, cited in Blau, 1984: 6).

Ultimately though, despite the appearance of mutuality, science comes to law *on law's terms*. While science can propose who might be considered an expert, it is law that has the final say. It is law that decides whether an expert's testimony will be heard in the domain of the courtroom, and it is law that decides whether that testimony will eventually be accepted or discarded. Psychology can recommend, but law is the final arbiter. It is perhaps therefore timely to reflect on some of the problematic aspects of the psychology–law partnership, before being engulfed in the wave of enthusiasm. There are at least three reservations that can be identified: (1) the particular model of science endorsed by admissibility rules; (2) the infallibility of the peer review system; and (3) the discouragement of disciplinary self-reflection. It is useful to consider briefly each of these broad critiques, for they provide a framework within which our more specific critique concerning the implicit relation can be made in the next chapter.

1 Admissibility rules tend to endorse a particular model of science

Whenever jurisdictions use the notion of general acceptance to help them judge reliability of evidence, they are endorsing one of several possible epistemological models of science. General acceptance implies that knowledge which has been endorsed by the wider scientific community is better than knowledge which has not. However, this reasoning makes the crucial mistake of equating validity with popularity. If an idea is generally accept*ed*, that is because it is accept*able*. It is popular. This does not provide guarantees about the accuracy or validity of the claim.

General acceptance does provide a type of safety valve. It increases the likelihood that the techniques and findings which survive the process of professional scrutiny meet some methodological standards (but it must be kept in mind that these standards may in themselves be problematic). Elements (but only some elements) of the methodology and approach will have been considered by reviewers and by the wider field. Alternative interpretations of findings may (or may not) have been generated by the work. Unknown, risky, and extreme (as well as unusual, insightful, and unpopular) ideas are likely to have been 'weeded out'. Overall, general acceptance offers the safeguard of 'organized skepticism' (Merton, 1973).

Scepticism is not always a useful tool, however, and science applies this doubt to only some aspects of its practice. General acceptance provides no *guarantees* of truth or certainty or 'good science'. The tacit assumption on which it is based – that accepted science is 'better' – is a false one. In Dan Tarlock's (1996: 13) words, it 'revives the false dichotomy between "good" and "bad" science'. The law is nervous about 'new' science because it is seen as risky. 'Old' accepted knowledge is seen as safer. However, as Tarlock tries to make clear, this is an inaccurate model of knowledge production. 'For better or for worse, knowledge is contingent and experimental. Thus, new science is not good or bad: it is just science' (Tarlock, 1996: 16).

Just as scientists' 'organised scepticism' can be used to guard against 'junk' claims, it can keep scientists wedded too long to ideas, as illustrated by those theories and techniques that have achieved general acceptance for some time but which have later lost support or been proven inaccurate. Bloodletting, leeching, and the use of purgatives for psychological disturbances represented the height of generally accepted medical science during the Victorian period (Showalter, 1997). The Greiss test, developed to detect nitroglycerine on the hands of persons suspected of handling bombs, was crucial in the 1975 convictions in England of the

'Birmingham Six', who maintained their innocence until 1991, when they were finally released from prison because the reliability of the test had been called into question (*Maguire and others*, 1992). DNA tests, regarded for the last 15 years as producing indisputable proof of a person's identity, are now regarded as potentially so unreliable that some defence lawyers have quipped that the acronym should stand for 'Do Not Accept' (Farrington, 1993). These randomly chosen examples could be used to argue that since science eventually moved beyond these views, it proves that science does progress toward more accurate, 'better' knowledge. However, this can only be claimed with the benefit of hindsight. The point is that the 'objective accuracy' of *contemporary knowledge* is impossible to judge. Unfortunately, but crucially, it is on the basis of contemporary knowledge that legal and medical decisions must be made, and these hold very real consequences for the lives of the men and women affected by them.

The term 'general acceptance' originated within law, but it is an accurate way to characterise the approach to knowledge which scientists themselves employ. The general acceptance model is analogous to what Rorty (1980) has labelled the 'up the mountain' account of scientific progress. Although scientists may accept that they do not currently know what is true, they believe that scientific testing allows them to progress steadily towards that truth. That which is generally accepted at present may later (i.e. with hindsight) turn out to be inaccurate, but it is the closest that a field comes to truth at the moment. Therefore, it is regarded as 'good enough' because it lies on the path to truth. Loftus and Monahan (1980: 281) capture this account of scientific progress perfectly when they describe it in the following terms in a paper entitled *Trial by data: psychological research as legal evidence*.

> The truth is like a mountain, there for all to see. Research is the guide to help us avoid the slippery slopes and the passages that lead nowhere. Benefiting from the work of previous climbers, we reach the summit and all rejoice. Nobody loses when the truth is scaled.

Although Loftus and Monahan (1980: 281) consider this an 'idealized perspective', it is this image that, surreptitiously but powerfully, guides the empirical research programmes of psychologists.[7]

The problem with the 'up-the-mountain', general acceptance model of truth is that it assumes all knowledge has an equal chance of being discovered. It fails to take into account the factors that influence research in pragmatic and theoretical ways: research funding, publication practices, political preferences, social values, and economic forces. These factors are not *external* to science's knowledge; they are the factors which *constitute* that knowledge. The scientists' site on the mountain cannot be separated from the route they took to get there. Had they taken an alternative route – endorsed a different set of funding practices, methodological expectations, research questions, societal values – they might have been led to a very different, but perhaps equally 'accurate', site. In choosing their current path, they may also have unknowingly by-passed more useful or important sites. Most scientists who offer their disciplinary knowledge to law are doing so with a sense of faith in its reliability and accuracy. It is a genuine offer, not a ruse of some sort. The trouble is that it is a misplaced faith, for in real-life practice science does not operate in the way its mythology says it does. Kuhn (1970), Koch (1981), and Kessen (1990) have each chided those who continue to adopt a positivistic stance with science and psychology, urging them to see that the accumulation of ideas does not render the field closer to truth, but rather represents shifting ideas that are formulated, refined, and revised.

Thus, scientists' current position on the mountain is not inherently 'better' than other sites simply because it is the position they presently occupy. The value of their position can only be assessed in a wider context and against other markers. The use of general acceptance as an admissibility criterion, either on its own or as one of several criteria, discourages – and relieves – scientists from developing any alternative epistemological compass with which to navigate the wilderness of knowledge they wish to explore. Indeed, general acceptance allows those who do try to encourage the field in undertaking that development to be more easily marginalised – in the figurative sense, pushed off the side of the mountain.

2 The peer review system cannot provide what is expected of it

The peer review process is regarded as the cornerstone of the general acceptance model. Subjecting findings to the system of peer review is presumed to strengthen their reliability and validity, for unorthodox or unreliable theories and techniques will be discarded. It is by this process that scientists police their boundaries, judging which research findings will be published and in which journals, determining which research applications will be funded, and exerting considerable influence over knowledge production and dissemination in general. As Jasanoff (1995: 95) observes, 'the scientific community often presents peer review to courts and other social institutions as a fail-safe process for evaluating the merits of science'. It is not.

One of the problems with reliance on the peer review system is the belief that it operates fairly and neutrally. Unfortunately, the practice often does not live up to the theory. Empirical studies confirm that reviewers tend to reject manuscripts not because the methodology is flawed but because the findings or the authors' interpretation disagree with the reviewer's own theoretical perspective (Mahoney, 1977). Publication is biased toward studies that produce a particular kind of finding: differences, rather than similarities, between groups under study (see Sommer, 1987, for review). Research conducted at high-ranking institutions is more likely to be accepted than is work from low-ranking institutions, regardless of the actual quality of the research (Peters and Ceci, 1982). Journal editors acknowledge that the work of established researchers may be published at the expense of less well-known, but equally competent, people (Alexander, Coleman, and Schauer, 1995). Men's contributions to the scientific literature are still rated more positively by reviewers (of research grants) than women's, with women having to produce as much as 250% more work to be regarded as equally meritorious (Wenneras and Wold, 1997).

A particularly good illustration of the problems caused by relying on the peer review system to produce accurate, balanced sets of findings can be found in Ruth Bleier's (1988) attempt to publish work on brain structure. (See also Spanier, 1995: 74–76, for an account of Bleier's story.) In 1982, the respected journal *Science* had published an article by DeLacoste-Utamsing and Holloway showing that the corpus callosum (a set of nerve fibres linking the two halves of the brain) was larger in females than in males. Bleier identified a number of significant flaws with the study, including a sample size too small to provide reliable results (14 people), unclear methodology in obtaining the sample, and fallacious assumptions as a basis for interpreting the data. Indeed, one of the authors later reported that he had 'felt horrible' about the small sample, but that his team had felt that the data were 'so intriguing we decided to publish. I didn't think it was premature at all' (San Francisco *Examiner*, 22 February 1987, quoted in Bleier, 1988: 193). Bleier and others replicated this work, using more valid procedures, but all of their studies failed to reveal any sex-related differences. *Science*, however, refused to publish Bleier's findings. The journal also refused to publish a review article by Bleier, in which she identified errors in methodology and interpretation in several areas of sex-differences research. As she recounted subsequently, one of the reviewers had recommended against publication, arguing that

> [w]hile many of Bleier's points are valid, she tends to err in the opposite direction from the researchers whose results and conclusions she criticizes. While Bleier states . . . that she does not 'deny the possibility of biologically based structural or functional differences in the brain between women and men', she argues very strongly for the predominant role of environmental influences.
>
> (Bleier, 1988: 191)

Thus, the reviewer accepted that many of Bleier's criticisms were valid and that the authors of the original paper might perhaps have erred. However, because the reviewer believed that Bleier had also erred in her theoretical arguments (that is, the reviewer *disagreed* with Bleier's interpretations), publication of her work was not supported. Her 'mistake' was deemed less valid or justifiable than the mistakes of the scientists whose work had already been published in *Science*.

These kinds of failings are a problem because the notions of peer review, admissibility, objectivity, validity, and reliability become rather interchangeable in scientific and legal discourse. If something has been published in a scientific journal or included in a diagnostic manual, it seems it must be true – or at least true 'enough'. At least one District Court judge has been willing to observe that 'peer review [has become] something of a catch-phrase for admissibility' (Feldman, 1995: 795). This view exists despite judicial comment in *Daubert* (1993: 483) that publication should not be regarded as a 'sine qua non of admissibility' and acknowledgements that the practice of peer review may 'sometimes function imperfectly' (Gellatly, 1997). That the system has been shown to be routinely subject to problems that some consider 'pernicious and counterproductive' (Mahoney, 1977: 173) has not decreased the faith that scientists place in it and the power that law accords it.

We are not advocating the dissolution of the peer review system. If performed thoughtfully, it unquestionably serves an important and useful function, ensuring that at least some degree of quality control operates within the scientific disciplines. The general quality of published material is significantly enhanced as a result of referees' and editors' observations. The point is that that quality control is not absolute. Like all regulatory systems, peer review is constrained. It is dependent on the views of those who designed it and those who maintain it; published literature reflects the beliefs of those individuals concerning what should be allowed in and what kept out. It is not simply a matter of tightening up or modifying the system to get it to work 'properly', as some have suggested (Richardson and Ginsburg, 1998). The peer review system, in any form, will be subject to limitations, for this is an inherent aspect of all forms of knowledge production. The extent of one's dissatisfaction with those limitations will, of course, depend on one's concerns about the consequences that derive from them.

3 Disciplinary self-reflection is discouraged

We have already seen how decisions about the admission of expert knowledge into the courtroom are inherently epistemological choices. Beliefs about what 'counts' as scientific knowledge and who 'counts' as an expert constitute the basis on which such decisions are made. Disciplines resist examination of these epistemological assumptions, and that resistance is fortified through regulatory mechanisms such as peer review and research funding. One of the problematic aspects of the explicit relation is that it reinforces this resistance even further, for if another discipline endorses the mainstream position, it is easier to ignore or discredit challenges to it. Law and psychology do exactly this for one another: reinforce the other's mainstream position, thereby decreasing the likelihood that either will engage in disciplinary self-reflection. Theorists who seek to represent human experience in non-traditional ways, including feminists wishing to reformulate understanding of women's experience, will be among those marginalised by such exclusionary practices.

If law trusts psychology's peer review system, why should psychology be concerned about it? If psychology is willing to try to meet the admissibility standards set by law, what call is there for law to re-examine them? If the legitimacy of either discipline's perspective is accepted by the other, why is there a need to listen to the disgruntled few who disagree? Evidence of such resistance can be seen in the comments of psychologists and lawyers to their colleagues. For example, Kassin, Ellsworth, and Smith (1989: 1095), well-known researchers in eyewitness phenomena, suggest that 'only those psychologists with a record of publications should be counted as part of the relevant scientific community' called upon to explain eyewitness phenomena. Jonakait (1994: 449), a legal commentator whose work on evidence and forensic science has been very persuasive for practising judges in the US (e.g. Gless, 1995), argues vigorously that syndrome evidence does not constitute the kind of psychology that should be admitted into courtrooms because it tends not to be 'based on testable propositions that have been rigorously tested through investigations containing appropriate controls'. More generally, Harry Edwards (1992: 47), a US Circuit Court judge, maintains that legal scholarship is useless unless it has 'direct utility for practitioners, judges, administrators, or legislators', and he praises the 'heroic battle' that is being waged by some against the 'legal nihilism' of critical legal studies.

In arguing that expert or scholarly knowledge should fit a particular mould, these authors disclose their preference. The fact that they *have* a preference is not problematic; of course choices will be made about which professionals and which knowledge should represent a field. The issue here is the *content* of that preference. Kassin, Jonakait, and Edwards advocate a very conservative position; their preference fits mainstream models of scientific and legal knowledge. While they may have considered what it is they *gain* by excluding evidence that does not meet 'established standards', they do not seem to have considered what it is they also *lose*. Our concern is that the recommendations of these authors increase the likelihood that others will also fail to engage in that reflection.

It is not just in regard to psychological and syndrome evidence that such limited vision exists. Tarlock (1996) highlights a similar situation in the field of environmental regulation in the US. Legal decisions concerning the release of toxic substances into the environment, public health, and biodiversity protection are now, like those concerning other sciences, subject to the *Daubert* guidelines (at least at the Federal level). Tarlock argues that these are inappropriate and irresponsible standards for environmental regulation. Decisions about the environment must often be made under extreme conditions of uncertainty. Waiting until conclusive evidence of harm (i.e. generally accepted evidence) has been collected carries serious and possibly irreparable risks. Moreover, many of the problems in environmental regulation cannot be addressed through testing falsifiable hypotheses; rather, conclusions must be drawn from site-specific work conducted to support particular regulatory programmes. Tarlock argues that responsibility for harm should be conceived as a continuum, with standards of proof adjusted to take account of public-health risks.

> A case can be made that the standard of proof should be even less for public health-based regulation. In contrast to criminal and civil liability, regulatory liability is a form of tax imposed on those who directly profit from harmful activities which is then partially spread to larger segments of the population in the form of higher product prices.
>
> (Tarlock, 1996: 14)

The narrowly constructed *Daubert* guidelines are entirely ineffective in producing the flexible scientific framework that is needed for reasoning about the issues involved in environmental regulation. Indeed, Tarlock fears the judgement 'may make it more difficult to protect legitimate public health and biodiversity objectives' (Tarlock, 1996: 11).

The result of formalised links between law and science is that there is both less *impetus* and less *scope* to question the basis of knowledge. Attention has already been drawn to the way in which the need for 'alternative' forms of knowledge seems to decrease when that knowledge which is already available is widely endorsed. Tarlock's discussion makes clear that, as the admission of evidence comes to be more rigidly regulated, non-mainstream forms of knowledge face even greater impediments in gaining admissibility. These are points also made by Sheila Jasanoff in her examination of the interaction of law, science, and technology.

> [C]ourts are prepared to honor science's claims of autonomy, but only so long as they do not conflict with the legal system's major substantive and procedural interests, including the law's own claim to autonomy in finding facts relevant to litigation.
>
> (Jasanoff, 1995: 96)

As long as scientists' boundaries do not infringe on the territory law sees as its own, there is no problem. Likewise, as long as a scientist's methods (and other claims) do not conflict with the view of science that law has developed, there is no problem. It is when the two elements are discordant that there is difficulty. As law develops rigid mechanisms with which to represent and regulate its view of science (developed in concert with some bodies of scientists but not with others), there is less scope for scientists who do not share that view to make an argument about why their evidence is nonetheless useful to law. The possibility of such a dialogue is precluded by the procedures that have been drawn up to police the boundaries, such as those contained in *Daubert*. Even if a judge wished to engage with the problem, her/his decisions would be tied by the existing standards.

The resistance of science and law to pragmatic and epistemological critique has been discussed at length in the psycholegal literature. However, many critics have tended to focus on the way in which the disciplines are reluctant, even in their collaboration, to submit to *external* critique (e.g. Jasanoff, 1995; Jones, 1994). Neither science nor law wishes to have its power or its expertise questioned. By erecting boundaries between what they consider to be 'their own' knowledge and that which can be said to 'belong' to the other, they protect themselves from scrutiny. We wish to extend the analyses of the authors by emphasising the ways in which the science–law collaboration increases resistance to submit to *internal* critique. When a discipline's ownership over a knowledge domain is endorsed 'from the outside', there is less need for the owners themselves to reflect on it. The consequences of such neglect, as we will see, are substantial, particularly for those groups whose interests have been marginalised from the outset.

Conclusion

This chapter has provided an overview of the explicit relation between psychology and law, explaining the ways in which it operates via diagnostic categories and admissibility standards and highlighting the epistemological assumptions on which these processes are based. The critique we have begun here is abstract, deliberately oriented toward general issues. That is because the formal rules on which the law–science relationship is based are themselves intended to be generalist and broad in scope. Such a diffuse analysis does not, however, give much sense of the real-life consequences that admissibility decisions hold for people's lives, especially women's lives. A primary aim of this project is to illuminate the consequences of those decisions by bringing a critical perspective to specific areas of the law. Our contention that there exists an implicit relation between psychology and law could be seen as a particular kind of critique of the interaction between the two disciplines. In Chapter 3, we wish to frame that critique theoretically and then go on in subsequent chapters to examine specific domains for evidence of the more tacit aspects of the disciplines' coalition.

3   The implicit relation

It is high time this whole legend was exploded, because it is not just a myth pure and simple: it is a political myth.

Elaine Morgan[1]

Whereas the previous chapter examined the overt connections between psychology and law, the aim of this chapter is to expose their underlying links. In particular, we will consider the key characteristics of the implicit relation: the tenet of objectivity, the evaluation of human behaviour against a male standard, and the tendency to account for behaviour at an individualistic level. In the course of this exploration, we will touch on the history of psychology and of law, for without a historical perspective, it is not clear why these particular characteristics should have come to be so important to each of the disciplines. The theoretical overview provided by this chapter will establish a framework within which specific syndromes can be examined in subsequent chapters.

Objectivity

Objectivity in psychology

Psychology is a diverse field, encompassing a variety of specialised areas, including clinical, personality, developmental, cross-cultural, social, cognitive, neurological, physiological, organisational, and educational psychology. Because psychology is perceived as relevant to so many aspects of life, there is a substantial popular market in psychological theories and information. Bookshops have racks of self-help psychology books, categorised under headings such as Personal Development, Self-esteem, Mental Health, Well-being, Women's Studies, Communication, Assertiveness, Therapy, Counselling, and Sexuality. Psychology has thus come to be regarded by laypeople as primarily a clinical field, and if asked what psychologists do, non-psychologists might well answer that 'they help you get to know yourself or others better'.

This personalised, therapeutic account of psychology is a perception that many of those who hold the title 'psychologist' would not share, however. This is particularly the case for academic, research psychologists. They are much more likely to view psychology as a science, in which scientific reasoning and methodology are employed in order to better understand human behaviour and to discover the universal laws that explain it. Undergraduate textbooks, for example, typically define psychology in their first few pages as 'the science of the mind' or 'the science of behavior' (Gleitman, Fridlund, and Reisberg, 1999: 1). For Gross (1996: 19), psychology is 'the scientific study of behaviour and cognitive processes (or mind or experience)'. More elaborate definitions have also been devised, such as that offered by Eysenck (1998: 2): 'Psychology is the science which uses introspective and behavioural evidence to understand the internal processes which lead people to think and to behave in the ways they do'. Virtually all textbooks stress the scientific nature of contemporary psychology.

The kinds of questions that psychology asks are, of course, the ones that have been asked for centuries: what motivates human behaviour? what explanations can be given for behaviour? how do we come to understand the world around us? what distinguishes humans from animals? Such questions were originally the domain of religion, and later philosophy. Indeed, it is from philosophy that psychology emerged towards the end of the nineteenth century, when psychologists were seeking more systematic, measurable ways to address these questions. Wilhelm Wundt's establishment in 1879 of a scientific laboratory to study consciousness and perception is celebrated today as the 'birth' of psychology. Once questions about human experience began to be formulated in a way that permitted empirical investigation, psychology's rise as a discipline was assured.

It is precisely this uncomplicated, positivistic account of psychology's history that is usually taught to psychology undergraduates. The central message imparted by most textbooks and instructors is that the scientific, empirical methods adopted by psychologists were naturally better than the introspective approaches adopted by philosophers. Their techniques 'lacked objectivity and investigated mental processes that were too vague' which resulted in those methods going 'the way of the dinosaur' (Santrock, 1996: 5). One gains the impression that it was inevitable that non-empirical approaches to the study of human behaviour should become 'extinct' as more advanced (i.e. scientific) approaches were developed. The confident assertions provided by Gleitman and his colleagues capture this sense particularly well.

> Fifty years ago, psychologists tended to be rather defensive about the status of the field and were perhaps a bit too loud in proclaiming that 'Psychology is a science!' But by now there is no need for such defensive proclamations, for that assertion has become a simple statement of fact. In the last half a century, psychology has assuredly become a real and vigorously progressive science.
>
> (Gleitman, Fridlund, and Reisberg, 1999: xxiii)

The actual history of psychology is considerably more complex, as many historians have tried to stress in their discussions of the epistemological debates that took place during the early decades of psychology's growth (e.g. Bohan, 1992;

Kessen, 1990; Polkinghorne, 1983). There has been an anti-positivistic movement operating within psychology since its establishment, and it was certainly vigorous during the late nineteenth century. Brentano, Dilthey, Weber, James, and Wundt[2] were among those who aligned themselves with this dissenting position, and although there were considerable differences between their particular viewpoints, the common link between them was their conviction that the study of human behaviour and experience required methods additional to those employed in the natural sciences. While quantitative laboratory methods might be useful for studying physical objects in the world and even the physiological sphere of human functioning, such methods could not yield insight into the *meaning* of human experience. These theorists felt that the newly emerging psychology should be seeking to address questions about the cognitive, social, emotional, and expressive aspects of life, and they maintained that this would require the use of alternative hermeneutic, historical, and linguistic methods. In the end, the 'anti-positivist position did not carry the day, and the sciences of the human realm ended up with a methodology grounded in the procedures and logic of the physical sciences' (Polkinghorne, 1983: 20). While it can be interesting to consider the reasons for this outcome (e.g. lack of unification within the anti-positivistic movement, the higher status accorded to scientific subjects), the important point for our discussion here is the consequences of that outcome. Psychology's adoption of a positivistic scientific model has generated the kinds of conceptual and material problems we are addressing in this text. The length of time that these epistemological debates have been raging within the field, and the extent to which that controversy has been excised from psychology's history, is evidence of the significance of the concerns.

One consequence of the positivistic model's victory was that objectivity became both premise and pursuit for psychology. As psychologists began to classify themselves as scientists, their esteem of objective methods and findings increased. This is not surprising, given that objectivity is one of the features that discriminates science from less rigorous disciplines; it is objectivity that transposes knowledge from opinion to fact. Ibanez (1991: 190) describes the transition this way: 'Scientific Reason has progressively constituted itself into the ultimate foundation of truth, and . . . scientific practices have been imposed as the only social practices legitimately capable of producing truth.' The effect of presumptions about truth and objectivity can be observed at every level of the scientific enterprise: in the preference for quantifiable data, in the dependence on decontextualised laboratories, in the language of passive verbs and third-person pronouns, in the mandatory expulsion of experimenter subjectivity. In short, standard scientific theories and methods are founded on the conviction that it is possible to divorce human experience, both the experimenter's and the 'subject's', from context. Through that process of decontextualisation and generalisation lies objectivity, which enables one to discover the 'truth' about phenomena in the world, including human experience.

In short, most (academic) psychologists believe that, because their discipline is scientific, objectivity exists and operates at some level of their theory and/or practice. There is general agreement about this point; the disagreement pertains to the level at which such objectivity can be found. For some, it lies within the minds of individual scientists. This is the view taken by John Flavell and his colleagues.

> Unlike scientists, children and lay adults often either ignore discrepant evidence or attend to it in a selective, distorting way. They sometimes adjust evidence to fit their theories; the processing of evidence is biased toward a favored theory. . . . [In contrast], scientific thinkers understand, monitor, and direct their own higher-order reasoning.
>
> (Flavell, Miller, and Miller, 1993: 161 and 163)

Annette Karmiloff-Smith and her co-author share the same perspective.

> [U]nlike professional scientists, the intuitive scientist [i.e. the layperson] manifests a major shortcoming known as the self-serving bias. . . . [A]dults and children will distort information to bring it into line with their own predictions. Lay people fail to show the objectivity in hypothesis testing that scientific inquiry is purported to adhere to.
>
> (Spencer and Karmiloff-Smith, 1997: 52)

Objectivity is characterised by these authors as residing within scientists themselves. Adults and children show a 'bias' in their reasoning processes that scientists ostensibly do not. This view endorses the myth of science which maintains that scientists, via some mystical process (e.g. their training, their individual personality characteristics, or the white coat they don upon entering the laboratory), are endowed with the ability to step outside the influence of culture and personal history to obtain an objective view of the phenomena they study.

For others, objectivity lies in the systems of science. Gellatly, for example, challenges Spencer and Karmiloff-Smith, above, by arguing that

> [s]cience achieves objective knowledge not because scientists are privileged with a special faculty of objective thought but as a result of the institution-alised practices of information-sharing, peer review, replication, and so on, imperfectly though these may sometimes function.
>
> (Gellatly, 1997: 58)

Objectivity does exist for Gellatly, although it lies not in the minds of individual scientists but in the processes of science. He maintains that where 'mistakes' occur, the system of science will ensure that they do not remain. This exemplifies the 'up the mountain' model of science described in Chapter 2. Science is seen as progressing slowly towards an ultimate Truth, and it is vaguely expected that one day science (and society) will reach a point where the phenomenon in question will be so well understood that no more questions need be asked about it. The systems of science are believed to be capable of guiding that progress. Gellatly acknowledges that sometimes these systems may not operate perfectly, but in theory it is possible for them to guide the search for Truth.

For many, objectivity also lies in the language that scientists employ. For example, one of the authors of this book (Zeedyk) recently received the following comments from a referee on a paper she had submitted for publication in a professional journal.

> The style of writing needs some attention. . . . Writing in the [singular] first person diminishes the authority of the argument because it makes it seem more like personal opinion than a scientific argument.

Just as dressing up people in formal clothing increases their authority and importance, dressing up language in an impressive vocabulary alters its power and influence. Of course, clothing does not make the person, nor does vocabulary create the content. The fact that they may appear to do so is a useful tool, for it is that appearance from which the authority stems. That is why, even in their earliest essays, students of science are taught to use particular forms of language and why scientists continue to demand such language from their colleagues. Plural pronouns replace singular pronouns: 'I' becomes a more sizeable 'we'. Passive verbs replace active ones: 'it was revealed that. . . . ' suggests that the findings were waiting to be discovered, independent of any actions of the experimenter (Kitzinger, 1990).

And certainly, for almost all scientists, objectivity lies in the pre-eminent tool of science: the scientific method. As Gleitman and colleagues (1999: A1) explain in their student text, the essential difference between the way that psychologists and 'philosophers, novelists, theologians, and sages of all sorts' approach the understanding of human behaviour 'lies in psychology's commitment to the scientific method'. Testable hypotheses, systematically gathered data, and replication are key principles of that method, and while psychology does utilise a range of designs within which these principles are applied (e.g. correlational, observational, self-report, and case studies), its most esteemed design is that of the experiment. The control that that particular design offers over confounding variables, through random assignment, control conditions, and independent and dependent variables, is valued highly within the field. This clarifies Santrock's observation that '[s]cience is not defined by *what* it investigates but by *how* it investigates' (Santrock, 1996: 13, emphasis in original). He later elaborates: 'The scientific method is an approach used to discover *accurate* information about mind and behavior' (p. 14, emphasis added). The scientific method is very simply seen as better and more objective than other methods.

Objectivity is thus simultaneously 'an act, a goal, and a personal attribute . . . a primary aspiration for our investigations' (Morawski, 1994: 73). This bountiful concept has increasingly come under fire during the second half of the twentieth century with the rise of postmodernism and critical theory. Within psychology, the movement has been led by feminist psychologists (e.g. Bohan, 1992; Burman, 1994; Kitzinger, 1991; Morawski, 1994; P. Nicolson, 1995; Sherif, 1979; Ussher, 1991; Wilson, 1998) and by critical social psychologists (e.g. Billig, 1987; Gergen, 1985; Prilleltensky, 1989; Shotter and Gergen, 1989; Smith, Harré, and van Langenhove, 1995). They charge that many of the traditional aims and assumptions of science, including 'objectivity', 'value-neutral facts', and 'truth' are an impossibility. As a human activity, psychology is infused with the social, cultural and moral assumptions of the time period in which it was undertaken. This is true for all forms of knowledge; content cannot be divorced from context. Each stage of the knowledge acquisition process is 'vulnerable' to this influence: the questions science chooses to ask, the experiments society is willing to fund, the conclusions scientists draw from their data. These are what Prilleltensky (1989) refers to as 'nonepistemic values': the sociocultural and political beliefs that enable a discipline to remain congruent with the dominant social ideology. Knowledge, including scientific knowledge, can never be de-politicised.

Fundamental to the postmodern project is the challenge it poses to the notion of objectivity. While this insight has transformed a range of academic disciplines, from English to history to architecture, science has proven particularly resistant to re-examining the nature of its knowledge (Harding, 1991; Spanier, 1995; Tuana, 1993). Such reluctance is perhaps understandable, for once contemplation of the dilemma of objectivity begins in earnest, it is no longer possible to feel sure about anything, including the way the world is constructed and the place of one's self or one's discipline within it. Such epistemological pandemonium is particularly jarring for those who believed themselves to be discovering facts and amassing truth.

Such a reaction is demonstrated, for example, in the comments of Michael Morgan (1996, 1998). He rejects the observations made by critical theorists, arguing that

> [t]he real problem [with critiques of positivistic science] is that they reject the notion of something 'out there' which can be studied objectively. . . . I argue that it is potentially misleading, to both students and the public at large, to invest these methods with the authority of objective science.
>
> (Morgan, 1998: 488)

Morgan remains resolutely wedded to the view that objectivity exists and that it is superior to other forms of knowledge. He makes clear that those who dare to question the notion of objectivity and to challenge accepted methods are unwelcome in the discipline, for they risk disturbing psychology's authority and power.

> My opinion is that we have to reject postmodernism from scientific psychology, if only to have a coherent teaching programme. We cannot have one set of lecturers explaining to students how to study psychology scientifically, and another set of lecturers telling the same students that when studying people, the methods of science are no use. It won't work, and psychology departments won't work.
>
> (Morgan, 1998: 483)

Morgan is more concerned about the harmony of the curriculum than the effectiveness and accountability of psychological methods, and he is willing to engage in intellectual autocracy in order to prevent students and others from reflecting on those issues as well.[3]

Such hostility is regrettable, for psychology is particularly well-placed to help science undertake a critical analysis of objectivity (Koch, 1981). Some commentators have inferred that the point has been accepted: 'the controversy is no longer about *whether* values influence scientific practice, but rather about *how* values are embedded in and shape scientific practice' (Howard, 1985: 255, emphasis in original). Yet Morgan's comments, taken in conjunction with those made by other authors (e.g. Baars, 1984; Kimble, 1989; Rosenzweig, 1991; Schneider, 1992; Staats, 1991), make clear that that is an overly optimistic view. '[T]he majority of academic psychologists seem not at all bothered by [these] harsh criticisms, maybe they are not even aware of the existence of the critical currents that attack their most basic assumptions and methods' (van Langenhove, 1995: 10). The objective characterisation of psychology will not change in the near future. The debate is occurring at the fringes of the discipline; it has affected neither theoretical nor methodological approaches in a substantial fashion.[4] Moreover, its status as an (objective) science brings desired rewards, its relationship with law being an important one. Were psychologists willing to use their knowledge and their power in a more reflexive manner, that association might be the cause of celebration rather than unease.

Objectivity in law

Law too has close associations with philosophy, where (Western) debates about the nature of law, statehood, citizenship, freedom, and justice emanated from early political theory espoused by Plato and Aristotle. Over the ensuing centuries, a range of theories have been produced within the field of jurisprudence, the most dominant of which has been the positivist tradition. Within this school of thought, law is seen as capable of producing truth, accomplished through the application of logic and objective methods to facts and legal rules. Law is not regarded as having any essential moral content; rather, laws are viewed as the product of political authority. The rules and doctrines that are derived within such a system are intended to provide 'abstract, universal, objective solutions to social ills' (Scales, 1986: 1373). The emphasis on generalisability and objectivity illuminate the similarities between the positivist models of both law and science.

Over the course of the twentieth century, law's claims to objectivity and truth have come under substantial criticism. Contemporary jurisprudence is now heavily influenced by the school of critical legal studies, a broad set of scholarship embracing Marxism, communitarianism, critical race theory, queer theory, and feminist theory (see Minda, 1995, for review). While these theoretical approaches differ in important ways, the key characteristic that unites them is the challenge that they bring to the notion of the autonomous individual that inhabits liberal ideology. This individual has full citizenship, is capable of making rational choices, is able to participate fully in economic life, and is believed to behave in a reasonable, impartial manner. Law ascribes these qualities to its legal subjects and in so doing creates consistent standards against which behaviour can be measured.

Of the various schools that fall under the critical legal studies banner, it is feminist theory that has provided one of the most sustained and searching critique of these assumptions (e.g. Lacey, 1998; MacKinnon, 1987, 1989; Smart, 1989, 1995; Williams, 1991). Feminist theorists have deconstructed law's claims to rationality, neutrality, and objectivity through identifying the gender biases inherent in those concepts. Behind each of these descriptors lies a set of dualities: objective/ subjective, rational/irrational, active/passive, reason/emotion. The 'desirable' qualities with which the apparently gender-neutral legal subject is endowed have been revealed as those that are typically regarded as masculine. 'Feminine' qualities such as subjectivity, irrationality, passivity, and emotionality are shunned in the construction of the legal subject.

Of these dualities, it is the claim to objectivity that has been most influential in achieving and maintaining the elite status of law. There are a variety of methods through which law claims it achieves objectivity. First, there is the process of rule-making and rule-application. The creation and operation of a body of rules is a primary means by which the law asserts its objectivity. A legal system that is to have any efficacy and integrity must, it seems, have a body of easily discernible and applicable rules. They are usually written down, accessible to any person who wishes to understand the codes of behaviour acceptable to a society, and easily internalised by citizens, who can behave according to the publicised rules. Rules provide a framework within which consistency and apparent equity can be pursued, thereby creating further public support for and confidence in the rule of law.

Another means by which objectivity is fostered is in the premium that law places on tangible, physical evidence. Evidence which can be measured quantitatively and recorded using replicable techniques is regarded as 'best' evidence. Narrative accounts and subjective impressions are much less favourable, because they are vague and more difficult to assess. Indeed, physical evidence is commonly referred to as 'real' or 'objective' evidence, signifying that other types of evidence are less real and certainly less reliable. The rules of evidence entrench this view, classifying expert testimony on physical injury as 'factual evidence' and expert testimony on psychological injury as 'opinion evidence'. By confining information about psychological harm to the realm of 'opinion', the inherent and unfavourable subjectivity of the evidence is highlighted. This reconfirms the superiority of tangible, objective evidence.

Perhaps the most fundamental mechanism through which law maintains its search for objectivity is in the standards against which it measures behaviour. Very often law evaluates the behaviour of a person by reference to what it believes a 'reasonable man' would have done under similar circumstances. This fictional person features in both legislation and in caselaw, covering topics ranging from murder to employment conditions. A single, objective standard of behaviour is thus devised, against which the conduct of all other parties can be judged. On the rare occasions when the standard of an ordinary reasonable man has been deemed inappropriate (e.g. *R* v *Lavallee*, 1990; *R* v *Morhall*, 1995), an alternative standard has been identified against which the behaviour of the person in question can still be evaluated.

Law's attachment to objectivity is thought by many lawyers (and laypeople) to be entirely appropriate, given that this quality is perceived to be necessary in the pursuit of certainty and fairness (Minda, 1995). There are legal theories that break with this view, however. One of the earliest to emerge was that of American legal realism, the origins of which are generally attributed to Oliver Wendell Holmes, a leading judge in the US Supreme Court. Holmes (1881) believed that law was fundamentally about prediction. Rather than being the rather sterile study of authority, rules, and logical deduction, he said it was about predicting what judges and the courts would actually do in any given case. Holmes asserted that the study of law would be better served by examining the socio-political make-up of legislators, lawyers, and the judiciary, as these people were the real actors in the drama of the law in action. Jerome Frank, who served as a judge during the 1930s and 1940s, argued similarly that if law were only about rules, no one need bother going to court. A lawyer would need only to discover the appropriate rule, apply it to her/his case, and the outcome of a dispute would be obvious.

Litigation is not, of course, just about rules. Other considerations such as witness reliability and credibility in establishing the facts are also important. Frank was the first to insist that the inevitable personal biases of the personnel involved in the legal system be confronted. He demanded that the prejudices of judges and juries be taken into account, because, he pointed out, a legal decision would not in practice be reached merely by reference to rules but would be affected by:

> hidden, unconscious biases of trial judges or jurors – such as, for example, plus or minus reactions to women, or unmarried women, or red-haired women, or brunettes, or men with deep voices or high-pitched voices, or fidgety men, or men who wear thick eyeglasses, or those who have pronounced gestures or nervous tics – biases of which no one can be aware.
>
> (Frank, 1949; cited in Lloyd, 1994: 681)

Frank's outspoken views were one of the first indicators that the positivist presumption of the objectivity of law was under siege. Those who followed in his footsteps (e.g. Dewey, 1963; Llewellyn, 1960) ensured that his insights were not forgotten. Research conducted since that time has illustrated the extent to which he was correct. The effect of personal beliefs on the decision-making processes of juries (Schuller and Hastings, 1996),[5] as well as those of lawyers and judges (Soothill, Walby, and Bagguley, 1990; Soothill and Soothill, 1993), is now well documented.

The attack on objectivity brought more recently by postmodernists is of a much more sophisticated and theoretical nature than was probably ever envisioned by Frank. Rather than seeking ways to guard against subjective elements of the law, postmodern theorists seek to accentuate and augment them (e.g. Boyle, 1992; Fitzpatrick, 1992; Kennedy, 1983; Tushnet, 1991). They emphasise the value of pluralism, subjectivity, and multiple narratives to legal theory and legal process, pointing out that the traditional objective structure excludes perspectives which do not accord with its own one. That is, postmodern theorists wish to expose the biases of the law, not to eliminate them, but to understand and accept them as an integral component of any regulatory system. Having demonstrated that an objective stance is impossible, they have begun to explore the ways in which a legal system could be constructed with the explicit aim of accommodating diversity. What would such a system look like? How could it be regulated? Would it be fair? How would behaviour be evaluated? These are the apprehensive questions that tend to arise most immediately in response to the suggestion that law discard its attachment to objectivity and embrace diversity.

Critical theorists address such concerns by arguing that the incorporation of subjectivity would result not in a *collapse* of the legal system, but in *greater* transparency and fairness. They point out that law has already demonstrated its capacity to accommodate plurality, in that it frequently does so under the guise of 'exceptions to general rules'. There cannot therefore be a sustainable argument that law *must* have singular standards to be efficacious (Smart, 1989). This is neatly demonstrated by the campaign led in the 1970s in which Sikhs sought to be excepted from the effects of the UK road traffic legislation which require a person riding a motorcycle to wear a helmet. Sikhs argued that this violated their devout religious custom of wearing turbans in public places. As a result of their lobbying efforts, the legislation was amended to exempt Sikhs from the general rule. Similarly, when considering the criminal defences of provocation and self-defence, juries are now sometimes advised to consider the personal circumstances of the defendant (see Chapter 4). As Smith and Hogan (1999: 361) put it: '[t]he reasonable man must now be endowed with the age, sex and other relevant characteristics of the accused'. Thus law can, and already does, accommodate subjectivity by taking account of the needs of different social groups. It has not foundered as a consequence.

Despite this, the search for objectivity continues to govern the approach to law taken in lecture rooms, in lawyers' offices, and in courtrooms. Part of its success in remaining relatively impervious to critique lies in the relationships it has forged with other disciplines – associations that endorse law's existing theoretical foundations. Thus, inter-disciplinary analysis presents a valuable way of addressing the question first posed by Frank's pragmatist movement: 'what difference can it make in practice to adopt a sociological (or realist or contextual) approach to law?' (Twining, 1973: 383). By examining the intersection of psychological and legal theory, the material consequences of the traditional objective approach are illuminated. This provides a powerful demonstration of the difference that could be made by adopting an alternative approach.

Male norm

Male norm in psychology

The characteristic of the male norm is closely linked to that of objectivity because the two are conflated. That is, the male point of view is frequently taken to be objective. Where there is a difference in masculine and feminine perspectives, an objective stance will inevitably reflect the former. Social sciences typically depict themselves as seeking generalisable truths that apply equally to all people. Gleitman, Fridlund, and Reisberg (1999: 11) state, for example, that the 'main goal' of psychology is 'to get at what is true for all of humankind'. The issue of gender can appear to be relatively unimportant when contrasted with the fundamental category of 'human'. Yet, the model for human functioning that psychology has adopted is an androcentric one. The standards by which psychology has defined, described, measured, and affirmed human processes are ones based largely on male experience and expectations.

It is not surprising that it is feminist work which has highlighted the nature of this standard. For example, Bernice Lott (1985) documented the way in which women's abilities and competencies are devalued. Erica Burman (1994) identified assumptions about maternal instinct that fuel political policies. Carol Gilligan (1993) revealed the way in which women were excluded from and discounted in work on moral reasoning. Naomi Weisstein (1971) went as far as entitling her paper on psychology's constructions of women the 'Fantasy Life of the Male Psychologist'.

The historical debate over the relation between brain size and intellectual functioning provides a particularly vivid example of the operation of a male norm. Stephanie Shields's classic 1975 article reviewed the psychological literature published in the mid-nineteenth and early twentieth centuries, the period during which psychology became established as a formal discipline. In particular, she examined the degree to which evolutionary theory, also emerging during this period, shaped psychological explanations of human behaviour – including the hierarchical relations between men and women. One of the key issues being addressed by the 'men of science' (Shields, 1975: 81) during this period was the biological foundation of intellectual functioning. The science of phrenology, in which the size and indentations of the skull are examined to provide information about the person's mental functioning and personality, had demonstrated that women's brains were smaller than men's, and it was deduced that this size differential accounted for women's lower intelligence. 'More brain necessarily meant better brain' (Shields, 1975: 82). However, when it was discovered that the ratio of women's brain weight to body weight was higher than the ratio for men, questions arose about whether absolute brain size was indeed the most appropriate measure of 'mental powers'. Attention began to shift to specific areas of the brain. Some researchers had found that the frontal lobes in men's brains were more developed in size and complexity than in women's. For them, this was taken as the reliable evidence for men's greater intellectual capacities. For other physiologists, the parietal lobe was regarded as the repository of intellectual function, and its predominant size in men could also be demonstrated. Some researchers were (generously) willing to grant that women were compensated for their intellectual inferiority by an increased capacity for instinct or perceptual ability. However, these qualities still contained 'the germ of female failure' because they rendered women more subject to emotionality (Shields, 1975: 83).

Since these early studies, physiological research on the brain has continued to be interpreted as evidence for neuroanatomical 'deficiencies' of the female (Shields, 1975: 84). The gyri and sulci, the cortex, neuronal attributes, brain lateralisation, and hormonal influences have each had a heyday in the headlines of professional publications and the media, drawing popular attention and scientific debate. Predictably, when critiques of such work become available, they tend to receive much less acclaim. Ruth Bleier's (1988) account of her work on gender differences and the corpus callosum, discussed in Chapter 2, illustrates this point vividly. As Spanier (1995: 75) commented in her summary of Bleier's story, 'clearly the prevailing paradigm of sex differences, not balanced presentation of different perspectives, influences publication decisions'.

The findings of research on sex differences often matches contemporary social expectations about men and women, leading to their acceptance with little questioning. They do not appear as blatantly biased as, for example, Paul Mobius, who proclaimed in 1901 that

> [a]ll progress is due to man. Therefore the woman is like a dead weight on him, she prevents much restlessness and meddlesome inquisitiveness, but she also restrains him from noble actions, for she is unable to distinguish good from evil.
>
> (cited in Shields, 1975: 84)

It is only by embedding contemporary findings and conclusions within a broad history that it becomes possible to discern the long pattern of characterising women as inferior. Rosser (1994: 32) queries whether the search for sex/gender differences represents an attempt to 'find biological bases for the social inequality between the sexes? . . . [H]ow much money and emphasis are placed upon research on differences in eye color or hair color?' We search for differences based on sex, rather than eye colour, because that is the variable which has been assigned importance by our society (Bleier, 1984; Keller, 1983, 1985; Spanier, 1995). Science is always as short-sighted as our own human perspective. As a social activity, it can never be value-free.

Another way in which the operation of the male norm is facilitated is through the application of standard statistical and peer-review procedures. Due to the way in which the scientific process of experimentation, statistical analysis, and publication operates, it is impossible to estimate a domain's ratio of 'discoveries of similarities' to 'discoveries of difference'. That is, it is not possible to compare, the number of times that men and women have been found to be similar (i.e. not different) on some capacity to the number of times that they have been found to be different on that capacity. This is because, when a scientist 'fails' to find a difference between two groups, the results tend to be regarded as uninteresting (by both the scientist and the field), making it less likely that they will be published, a disposition that Rosenthal (1979) dubbed the 'file drawer effect'.

A primary paradigm within which science operates is that of Popperian logic (named after its originator, Karl Popper). This paradigm is taught to all psychology and other science undergraduates, and it was cited and praised by the judges in the *Daubert* judgement. One of the key concepts of this paradigm is the 'null hypothesis'. The null hypothesis assumes that there is no difference between two groups, while the experimental hypothesis predicts the opposite, that is, that there will be a difference between the two groups. It is the experimental hypothesis for which the experimenter hopes to find supporting evidence, by comparing the findings against the assumptions of the null hypothesis. To take a simplistic example, a researcher who is interested in investigating sex differences in intelligence might administer an IQ test. Scores on the test would be obtained for a group of men and a group of women, the average score for each group would be calculated, and these two mean scores would be compared.[6] The ultimate hope of the researcher is that s/he will be able to reject the null hypothesis; in order to do that a statistically significant difference will need to be shown between the mean scores for the two groups. It is by finding such a difference that the researcher has something interesting to report. In instances where no difference is found, the null hypothesis must be accepted, and generally that outcome will not be perceived as exciting enough to be reported in the literature (Cohen, 1979; Coursol and Wagner, 1986; Greenwald, 1975; Hubbard, 1995; Neuliep and Crandall, 1993; Parlee, 1973; for review, see Sommer, 1987). In short, a finding that merely supports the original statistical assumption (i.e. confirms the statistical status quo) is not regarded as particularly notable. The researcher has merely failed to reject the null hypothesis, which is usually disappointing and less likely to be published.

The knowledge that science tends to make available to society is knowledge of *difference*, not of *similarity*. It is this knowledge that Popperian science values; it is this knowledge that is perceived as novel and interesting; it is this knowledge that editors and referees wish to accept for publication. Recently, the medical literature has begun to consider the effect of this preference on the field's ability to judge the effectiveness of new drugs (e.g. Berlin, Begg, and Louis, 1989; Easterbrook *et al.*, 1991; Naylor, 1997; Smith and Roberts, 1997; Stern and Simes, 1997). Because 'successful' drug trials (i.e. trials in which statistical differences between two groups have been found) are much more likely to be reported in the literature than are 'unsuccessful' ones (i.e. those which showed no effect), false impressions are raised about the efficacy of the drug, particularly given the growing enthusiasm for meta-analysis. In an attempt to solve this problem, there have been calls to create national or international registers, which would keep track of all clinical trials from the point at which ethical approval for a trial is given (e.g. Chalmers, 1993; Simes, 1986; Smith and Roberts, 1997). Such advocates argue that by keeping a comprehensive record of clinical trials, a more accurate assessment of general outcomes could be produced. If establishing such a register in the medical field is a challenge, it is unimaginable how the monitoring of studies examining sex/gender differences might be achieved. It is simply not possible to compare the number of studies finding 'no differences' with the number finding 'differences', for most reports of the former will never leave the scientist's laboratory. We are left with only half the equation – knowledge about differences. But because that 'knowledge' tends to fit with our societal expectations of men and women, the findings are not generally received as contentious or dubious. Of course, Mobius's conclusions about women's 'dead weight' (reported earlier) would have seemed reasonable to the public and scientists of his day, too.

One final brief example of the male norm at work can be seen in the area of syndrome diagnoses. As we noted earlier, there is a tradition of using mental health labels and diagnoses to control and regulate women. Phyllis Chesler's *Women and Madness* (1972) was one of the earliest texts to explain how the construction of mental illness could be gender-based. She argued persuasively that women whose behaviour deviates from the prescribed norms of femininity have been and continue to be classified as pathological, either through the use of the generic notion of hysteria or through specialised forms of neuroses, disorders, and syndromes. This situation contrasts sharply with that of men, where the tendency is to treat their behaviour as wilful; they are viewed as unwilling (rather than unable) to maintain rational control over their behaviour. This is an attitude captured in the criminological cliché 'women are mad and men are bad'. Contemporary theorists who have developed this line of critical gender analysis include Allen (1987), Brown (1990), Caplan (1995), Herman (1992), Showalter (1987, 1997), and Ussher (1991).

Busfield (1996) disputes the claim that mental disorder in general is a female malady, pointing out that women only dominate in the statistics for certain types of diagnoses, especially neuroses, depression, and anxiety disorders. Men dominate in others, such as alcoholism, drug addiction, sexual disorders, and anti-social psychopathy. For diagnoses such as schizophrenia and paranoia, the evidence for gender differences is not at all clearcut. These comparisons lead Busfield to argue that insufficient theoretical attention has been given to the way in which mental health discourses regulate *both* men's and women's behaviour. She maintains that if women's experience is to be theorised adequately, it must be embedded within a wider analysis of men's experience as well. Current feminist accounts, while providing important insights and groundwork, do not yet go far enough in her view in explaining the complex 'gendered landscape' of mental disorder (Busfield, 1996: 13). This question of the role that gender plays in the development and application of syndrome diagnoses is one to which we will return repeatedly throughout this book.

Gender biases are too rarely acknowledged by mainstream theorists. This is particularly the case at the epistemological level, in which consideration is given to the way in which gender influences the *construction of theory*. Gender biases still tend to be treated as a *methodological* problem, corrected simply by including more women in the relevant experiments. Consideration is avoided of the ways in which any understanding of human behaviour shelters an intrinsically normative base. This becomes a greater problem when another discipline, such as law, seeks to utilise scientific psychological theory, because it is presented with male normative accounts of behaviour that do not acknowledge their inherent nature.

Male norm in law

Like psychology, law promotes norms of behaviour. As we have pointed out, the adoption of a single standard against which to evaluate behaviour is one of the primary ways by which law believes it achieves certainty. The question arises as to what the content of that standard should be. Whose perspective should it reflect? It is usually maintained that norms can be derived from human behaviour, rendering them impartial, neutral, and objective. Feminist analyses reveal, however, that norms are not neutral. They typically reflect a male perspective. As Catharine MacKinnon has observed:

> [T]he male occupies both the neutral and the male position. This is another way of saying that the neutrality of objectivity and of maleness are coextensive linguistically, whereas women occupy the marked, the gendered, the different, the forever-female position.
>
> (MacKinnon, 1987: 55)

The single standard that is applied in law is one that endorses and reflects (white, Western) male perspectives. Where the experiences of the two genders differ, the standard will necessarily be biased against women. The male content of the standard is not acknowledged; instead, it is labelled as objective. The conflation of objectivity and male norm renders the two characteristics inextricable.

The most obvious of the ways in which law applies a male normative standard is in the use of language. Legislative codes frequently dictate that law must use the masculine linguistic form to represent both male and female. For example, the American Uniform Commercial Code asserts that 'words of the masculine gender [should be understood] to include the feminine and the neuter' (s. 1–102(5)(b) 1977, cited in Frug, 1985: 1094). The UK Interpretation Act 1978, section 6, states that in any Act, unless the contrary intention appears:

(a)   words importing the masculine gender include the feminine;
(b)   words importing the feminine gender include the masculine.

While this provision suggests a spirit of egalitarianism, in that the masculine and the feminine appear to be treated similarly, the reality is that legislation enacted by the UK Parliament invariably adopts course (a). Codes such as these serve as very powerful benchmarks, for they provide the framework within which primary and secondary legislation is interpreted. Law is neither apologetic nor defensive about its use of specifically gendered terms, for problems have ostensibly been circumvented through neutralising and re-defining terminology. It is an inadequate strategy, though, for law *is* language. The meanings that have been ascribed to the male pronoun over thousands of years of use cannot be eradicated simply by declaring its meaning to be altered. The general use of a male pronoun inevitably establishes a male standard.

Elaine Morgan's observations help to clarify why the gendered nature of language should be so enduring.

> Partly it is due to sheer semantic accident – the fact that 'man' is an ambiguous term. It means the species: it also means the male of the species. If you write a book about man or conceive a theory about man you cannot avoid using this word. You cannot avoid using a pronoun as a substitute for the word, and you will use the pronoun 'he' as a simple matter of linguistic convenience.

Morgan thereby acknowledges the historical, incidental development of a linguistic convention. However, she goes on to stress the consequences of that convention.

> But before you are halfway through the first chapter a mental image of this evolving creature begins to form in your mind. It will be a male image and he will be the hero of the story: everything and everyone else in the story will relate to him. . . . A very high proportion of the thinking on these topics is androcentric (male centred) in the same way as pre-Copernican thinking was geocentric. It's just as hard for man to break the habit of thinking of himself as central to the species as it was to break the habit of thinking of himself as central to the universe.
>
> (Morgan, 1972: 2–3)

It is the *consequences* of the androcentricity of language that have presented one of the primary concerns for feminist theorists. In her ground-breaking text, *Man Made Language*, Dale Spender (1985) detailed the ways in which language has helped to position women societally, in that it serves as a means of ordering and classifying phenomena in the world. She argued that since language was historically constructed by men and written down by men, masculine terminology has had a structural and pervasive effect on communication and knowledge.

The organising force of linguistics is well illustrated in law by a series of cases in the UK in the early twentieth century which became known as the 'person cases'. One of these concerned Sophia Jex-Blake who in 1869 applied to study medicine at the University of Edinburgh. She was one of a number of women who wished to study medicine and practise as doctors. Up until the date of her application all students of medicine had been men and the rules of the University had been framed in the expectation that they would continue to be men. In response to Jex-Blake's application to study, new rules were passed that permitted women to enrol, although they were to attend separate classes from those of the men, and professors were not required to teach those classes. As a result, Jex-Blake matriculated but was unable to graduate, as the refusal of some professors to teach women made it impossible for her to complete the course of study. She sued the University, which responded by declaring its own regulations *ultra vires*; that is, they declared that they should never have altered the regulations in the first place. By a narrow majority the Scottish court agreed with the University, endorsing the view that medicine was not intended as an appropriate pursuit for women since

Universities were not instituted for them, though women would undoubtedly receive indirectly the benefits the Universities were calculated to confer, in making better men of their fathers, their brothers, their husbands, and their sons.

(Jex-Blake and Others v *The Senatus Academicus of the University of Edinburgh*, 1873: 835)

A year earlier, the English courts had rejected the applications of women to have their names included on the electoral register, and thus be allowed to vote, on the similar ground that, in terms of the Reform Act of 1867, only 'a person aggrieved' could take their case to court when complaining about their exclusion from the Roll. Since women were not 'persons' they could not be 'persons aggrieved' (*Chorlton* v *Lings*, 1868). Further examples of women's 'non-existence' as legal persons followed in the next twenty years. Women elected to public political office were declared by the courts to be unqualified to do so, for only a 'person' could be so elected, and women were not persons. The law of course applied this logic to its own sphere when women wished to become barristers, solicitors, and law agents, ruling that reference to 'persons' in the internal regulations of these branches of the profession was presumed not to include the female. (See Sedley, 1997, for wider discussion of the 'person cases'.)

While it is obvious there is more professional and societal inclusivity for women in the latter half of the twentieth century, linguistic reference to a male standard remains commonplace in the jurisprudence of the common law. If a person charged in England with murder wishes to plead that he or she was provoked, the jury must determine whether the provocation was 'enough to make a reasonable man do as [the defendant] did' (section 3, Homicide Act 1957). Scots law has a similar test, established in caselaw, which has been expressed in the following way: 'was it to be expected that a normal average man would lose control as a result of the provocation offered?' (Gordon, 1978: 781). Determination as to what constitutes a 'violent crime' depends, for the purposes of the UK Criminal Injuries Compensation Scheme, on whether or not the 'reasonable and literate man' would label it so (*R* v *CICB ex parte Webb*, 1987: 76). In short, the 'reasonable man' is not just a person. He is a male person.

It is not only in language that gendered prejudices reside. If this were the case, things might be easily remedied. Androcentric biases run much deeper. 'The maleness of the Man of Reason . . . is no superficial linguistic bias' (Lloyd, 1984: ix). Genevieve Lloyd argues that the concepts of masculinity, truth, and reasonableness are linked. They are constructed and defined in opposition to femininity, which is associated with emotion and disorder. Because differences between the sexes are constructed in a binary, hierarchical form (O'Donovan, 1993), when women are characterised as being ruled by their emotions, they are *ipso facto* irrational. Femininity is antithetical to objectivity and rationality.

The male norm is not confined to criminal law, and it is useful to include an example from civil law to illustrate the extent to which male normativity is systemic in law. Employment legislation enacted throughout North America,

Europe, and Australia has attempted to address sex discrimination in the workplace, motivated in part by the increasing economic importance of female employees. One recurring difficulty for law is how to recognise inevitable gender differences between men and women, pregnancy being an excellent example. In *Webb v EMO Air Cargo Ltd* (1994), Mrs Webb was employed on a temporary basis while another member of staff was on maternity leave. Shortly after taking up her appointment Mrs Webb also became pregnant. She was dismissed – an action that she claimed was unfair and amounted to sex discrimination. Her application was rejected by all the UK domestic courts, on the basis that they agreed with the employers that pregnancy should be equated with sickness in a man, and that Mrs Webb had not been dismissed on account of her sex but on account of her unavailability for work. It was argued by the employers that a man who had been unable to work for medical reasons would have been treated in the same manner. Mrs Webb appealed to the European Court of Justice, which upheld her claim, finding that the dismissal was actually on grounds of pregnancy and therefore constituted direct sex discrimination. The Court observed that 'pregnancy is not in any way comparable with a pathological condition' (*Webb*, 1994: 494). These cases highlight the difficulties inherent in the liberal approach to formal equality, which seeks to achieve a level playing field for men and women through legislation. In striving towards such 'equality', it is the existing norms, which reflect male experience, that are applied; new ones are rarely developed. (For further discussion of the failure of law to achieve formal equality in the employment field, see Fredman, 1997.)

Male-normative expectations permeate psychology and law. Yet they are well concealed, having acquired a 'point-of-viewlessness' that is masterly in its simplicity and efficiency, so accustomed are the professions to the notion that there is a specified, objective way to define and to perform psychology or law. It is forgotten that other meaningful alternatives could exist – and that they might even be legitimate.

Individualism

Individualism in psychology

The psychological approach to understanding and explaining human behaviour is exclusively and entirely individualistic. That is, it is expected that the meaning of behaviour can be found within the individual. The introduction to Miller's (1966: 15, emphasis in original) classic text illustrates this point nicely: '*Psychology is the science of mental life*. The key words here are *science* and *mental*.' Zimbardo's definition (1992: 3) updates, but does not alter, this view: 'Psychology is formally defined as the scientific study of the behaviour of individuals and their mental processes.' In essence, psychology is the study of individuals and what happens *inside* them. The problem with this focus is that it ignores the way in which context shapes behaviour, the way in which context gives meaning to behaviour. An individualistic perspective implies that there is no need to look further than the individual her-/himself for an adequate explanation of behaviour.

Psychology's emphasis on the individualistic level is reflected at a variety of levels. In its theory, psychology characterises human beings as asocial, ahistorical beings, explicitly seeking to separate people from their particular social and historical contexts and to discover the general laws that govern their behaviour. The cardinal evidence of this perspective is psychology's endorsement of the cognitivist perspective, in which the structures and processes within the individual's mind are seen as playing the major role in behaviour. This model of human functioning is the dominant one in force today. From babies to adults (Bradley, 1989; Kessen, 1979), contemporary psychology constructs human beings as lone thinkers, making sense of their world through their cognitive reasoning abilities. The social practices and historical influences that play a key role in shaping meaning are ignored. Edward Sampson (1981: 731) argues that the epistemological basis for this choice is that '[t]he knower's psychological states, the ideas in his or her head, are held to be more important, more knowable, and more certain than any underlying . . . interests'. To reflect on the ideological content of the cognitive model is unusual, but Sampson goes even further, examining the consequences of this ideology and arguing that it 'raises serious questions about the nature of psychological science' (p. 730). Not only is cognitivism falsely reductionistic, it reinforces existing inequities in the social order.

The study of identity, a topic of central interest to psychologists, provides another good example of the theoretical bias toward decontextualisation. Identity is concerned with the issue of how people conceive of themselves. How do they decide the social groups to which they belong? Why do they come to value some personal attributes and not others? Which of those attributes do they present in public and which keep hidden? Identity has traditionally been conceived as an internal, stable trait that changes relatively little across time or context (once a person reaches adulthood) (e.g. Cattell and Kline, 1977; Eysenck and Eysenck, 1969). In contrast, critics contend that identity is not stable, that people's views of themselves and others fluctuates across setting and across time (e.g. Turner *et al.*, 1994). For example, what it means to be Scottish will vary depending on whether one is interacting with other Scots or with English people (Hopkins, Regan, and Abell, 1997; Hopkins and Reicher, 1996). The ways in which one's relationships to other people are defined change as a result of life events such as impending parenthood (Oakley, 1979; Smith, 1999). The meaning of any aspect of identity – race, profession, age, height, weight, gender – will always be subject to the influence of context. To conceive of fundamental psychological attributes as dynamic and fluid is a tremendous shift from the way that human experience has been understood by psychology. It challenges, indeed undermines, the reigning ideology of the 'sovereign individual' (Shotter and Gergen, 1989).

The individualistic emphasis of psychology is further reflected in the field's methods, which are specifically designed to decontextualise, to separate people and their behaviour from context. Indeed, if the aim of psychology is to derive generalisable laws of human behaviour, the intention is to discard context from the equation. Thus, questionnaires are typically phrased using general terms, devoid of any context to which the respondent is able to relate their answer. Naturalistic observations often fail to take account of the context within which behaviour is observed, and certainly may be unable to factor in the elements of the context that are important to the individual(s) being observed. Laboratory experiments treat the laboratory as if it were context-free, as if there is no reason to expect that the laboratory environment will have an impact on the people tested within it. Using the model of the natural sciences, the assumption is that if studies are properly controlled, then replicable facts and objective knowledge about human behaviour will accrue as a result of psychological research. There is no need to take account of the meaning assigned by the 'subjects' to their behaviour, for psychologists are satisfied with assigning their own meaning. It is an ironic outcome, for psychology forfeits the very thing it seeks: a better understanding of why people behave as they do.

Thus, psychologists, driven by a theoretical assumption that the individual person constitutes the proper level of investigation, employ empirical procedures that focus on the individual, decontextualised person. The two components work in a circular, self-confirming fashion. Having hypothesised that some factor internal to the individual is responsible for behaviour, the psychologist proceeds to use methods specifically designed for investigation at the individual level. When such methods produce affirmative results, the hypothesis is confirmed and the psychologist is relieved of the need to look further for explanations. Indeed, s/he is discouraged from doing so, because methodological tools with which to do so remain disfavoured and relatively undeveloped. The qualitative tools that have been developed to prioritise participants' perspectives are rarely included in psychology courses or texts, and they tend to be regarded as the dubious equivalent of 'investigative journalism' by experimental psychologists (Morgan, 1998: 483). To employ such tools somehow violates the boundaries of psychology. One is perceived to be doing something akin to sociology or linguistics, subjects which carry the stigma of being non-scientific enterprises. Analysis beyond the individual level, within psychology, has become 'de facto suspect' (Morawski, 1994: 22).

Arguably, this is in part due to the influence of American values and beliefs on psychological theory and practice. American approaches to acquiring psychological knowledge dominate the field. American journals have the highest status and citation rates in the field, and America is able to put considerably more resources into psychological research than most other countries. Baddeley (1998: 312) has expressed concern that the pressure within the UK to publish in North American journals, rather than European journals (as a result of the national Research Assessment Exercise), pushes increasingly larger proportions of the entire psychological discipline toward becoming 'part of the North American scene'. Although Baddeley does not address the issue of individualism, being more concerned about the 'somewhat conservative' nature of American journals, it is relevant here because American referees will bring their cultural preferences to the evaluation of the work they read. The primacy of the individual is, of course, one of America's and capitalism's fundamental values, shaping every aspect of American culture. Such cultural values operate imperceptibly but unrestrained in a field that believes itself to be value-neutral. 'American psychology has been quintessentially a psychology of the individual organism' (Sarason, 1981: 827). Thus, to 'do' psychology is almost necessarily to provide an individualistic account of behaviour. To even contemplate an alternative approach is difficult, for it broaches not only disciplinary nihilism, but also (for Americans) cultural nihilism.

The problem with the individualistic approach is that it fosters 'person-blame explanations', for 'the determinants of human behavior and experience [are located] within the person rather than in the context of behavior' (Bohan, 1992: 13). The implication is that problematic behaviour can be – and should be – corrected at the individual level. It is on that basis that therapeutic models have been developed, with the aim of changing individuals rather than social contexts. There is no need to address poverty, gendered violence, societal myths, and racial prejudices, if individuals can be blamed and perhaps even 'fixed'. '[Psychology's] solutions for human predicaments are to be found, almost exclusively, within the self, leaving the social order conveniently unaffected' (Prilleltensky, 1989: 796). The law's acceptance of syndrome diagnoses exacerbates this languid response. If psychology has determined through objective scientific means that a person's behaviour is the result of internal pathology, law can also be relieved of the need to take account of context. Using psychological syndromes to explain women's (and men's) behaviour ensures that both the law and the existing social order remain secure.

Bohan (1992: 18) has argued that 'context stripping' is particularly marginalising to women because the issues that are of most importance to them are 'by their very nature complex, contextually grounded concerns': interpersonal and familial relationships, institutional issues such as sexism, societal issues such as violence against women. How, she asks, does one address such intrinsically contextualised issues in an explicitly decontextualised laboratory? If you are an experimental psychologist, you do so by arguing that they are not contextualised issues, that they are expressions of the individual person's personality or cognitive style or biological inheritance. And if, like most mainstream psychologists, you have been professionally socialised through the 'reigning ideology . . . of psychological knowledge' to use only individualistic models, you may not even be aware that there are alternatives available for consideration (Prilleltensky, 1989).

The decontextualised, individualistic model forms the bedrock on which the whole of clinical psychology and psychiatry is built. This is made explicit in the introduction to the DSM-IV, which makes the following categoric statement in its introduction.

> [E]ach of the mental disorders [described in the DSM] is conceptualized as a clinically significant behavioral or psychological syndrome or pattern that occurs *in an individual*. . . . In addition, this syndrome or pattern must not be merely an expectable and culturally sanctioned response to a particular event, for example, the death of a loved one. Whatever its original cause, it must currently be considered a manifestation of a behavioral, psychological, or biological dysfunction *in the individual*.
>
> (DSM-IV, 1994: xxi–xxii, emphasis added)

This explicit conceptualisation alleviates any doubt concerning the relevance of the individualistic model to contemporary clinical reasoning. The meaning of abnormal behaviour is taken to reside firmly within the individual, not in relation to the context that frames that behaviour. Indeed, it could be argued that the authors of the DSM have differentiated between two types of behaviour: those *they* consider to be contextual (i.e. culturally sanctioned responses) and those *they* consider to be a manifestation of an individual dysfunction. There is no such thing as Bereavement Syndrome because reaction to the death of a loved one is considered an 'expectable and culturally sanctioned response [to this set of circumstances]'. Behaviours commonly associated with bereavement, such as excessive crying, inability to concentrate, lack of interest in social activities, and lethargy, are not considered by the authors as symptoms of a dysfunctional illness within the individual person. They are the expected responses in the context of the loss of a loved one. The symptoms of psychological syndromes such as Battered Woman's Syndrome and Rape Trauma Syndrome could easily be characterised as 'expectable' in relation to their given circumstances. The authors of the DSM have assigned to themselves the authority to decide when context is and is not relevant to making sense of human behaviour.

The attachment of psychological clinicians to an individualistic model is somewhat ironic, given that authors of many undergraduate texts try, early on, to draw students' attention to the difficulty of defining psychological abnormality and to the important role that context plays in making sense of people's behaviour. Ronald Comer, for example, begins his text entitled *Abnormal Psychology* (1998) with the account of a woman named Miriam, who cries herself to sleep every night and feels certain that the future holds nothing but misery. She talks often of the death that she believes awaits herself and her daughters, is afraid to close her eyes or sleep, and suffers terrible nightmares of blood and destruction. Comer counsels that

> [j]udgments of abnormality depend on *specific circumstances* as well as on psychological norms. The description of Miriam . . . might lead us to conclude that she is functioning abnormally. Certainly her unhappiness is more intense and pervasive than that of most of the people we encounter every day. Before you conclude that this woman's emotions and behaviors are abnormal, however, consider that Miriam lives in Lebanon, a country pulled apart by years of combat. The happiness she once knew with her family vanished when her husband and son were killed. Miriam used to tell herself that the fighting had to end soon, but as year follows year with only temporary respites, she has stopped expecting anything except more of the same. In this light, Miriam's reactions do not seem inappropriate. If anything is abnormal here, it is her situation.
>
> (Comer, 1998: 3, emphasis in original)

Somewhere between entrance into the psychology classroom and graduation as a clinical psychologist, the caution urged by Comer is forgotten by psychologists.

Their training allows them to slip back to more familiar philosophical ground – that the meaning of behaviour lies within the individual, not within its context.

Even feminist psychology is caught in the epistemological struggle between individualistic and contextual accounts of human behaviour. Celia Kitzinger, a leading British theorist, summarises the paradox in the following way.

> The (usually) implicit story . . . goes something like this: Yes, there are social and political features which cause women's unhappiness, but here, in this chapter, this article, this book, we are talking about the personal and individual ways in which women can deal with their misery, and this is not to *deny* structural and political power, but to *choose a different focus* here, because to do otherwise would be to do sociology, or political theory – and we are psychologists, and this individual and personal focus is our particular area of expertise.
>
> (Kitzinger, 1991: 425, emphasis in original)

If one is to remain within the established disciplinary confines of psychology, even as a feminist psychologist, an individual explanation 'has to be the story' (Kitzinger, 1991: 425).

There is little expectation that this perspective will alter in the near future. Despite the admonitions about the neglect of context from a wide range of theoreticians and practitioners, the individualistic level of analysis constitutes the core of the discipline's self-definition. Within the psycholegal field, this characteristic has received particular praise, being identified as the special perspective that psychology can offer to law. Kapardis, for example, emphasises the term 'individual' when acclaiming the insights that psychology has to offer law.

> Psychology has a unique perspective – its concern with the *individual* in a social context – and a unique contribution to make to law. In this regard, psycholegal research differs from such related fields as sociology of law in the way it addresses issues as well as in the methodology it uses. We can now take it for granted that psychology has a contribution to make to law.
>
> (Kapardis, 1997: 14–15, emphasis in original)

An individualistic analysis is *not* seen as problematic by psychologists, including those whose work relates to legal issues. Rather, it is seen as an asset, a quality which differentiates psychological approaches from others. The complex, systemic explanations of human behaviour derived from sociological analysis are difficult for law to make use of, because they differ so fundamentally from law's individualistic models. Psychology's explanations are more convenient for law precisely because they are so similar.

Individualism in law

The most basic presumption of law is that the citizens it governs are separate individuals, each possessing the free will and rationality to control their own behaviour. It regulates the lives of citizens in both the public and the private sphere by according them legally enforceable rights, imposing duties and responsibilities upon them in return. As Norrie (1993a: 26) has observed, '[t]he logic of law is a logic of individual right and self-interest'. It was the Enlightenment period that witnessed the emergence of the 'abstract juridical individual', represented by 'the image of "man" as a metaphysical or calculating, self-interested being, conceived of in an asocial way in a world whose sociality was no more than the coming together of individuals in a social contract' (Norrie, 1993a: 31). Thus, the very foundation of law disregards the influence of context on people's actions.

The decontextualisation of behaviour within law operates in exactly the way in which it does within psychology. Behaviour is stripped of its context, leaving an explanation of actions that is frequently very different from the one which the person her-/himself might have ascribed. The problem is that no useful understanding of crime or of social conflict can be gained with a decontextualised explanation, and widespread societal problems cannot be addressed in an effective way. For example, a full understanding of why abused women stay in abusive relationships can only be achieved by considering the economic and social circumstances within which their relationship is situated. The stereotypical conclusion that 'she must have stayed because she wanted to' is derived by constructing human behaviour as individualistic, rational, and unconstrained. It is assumed she has a 'choice' to make. The economic, social, practical, and interpersonal factors which limit her choices are not taken account of. If the *meaning* of behaviour is to be understood, the context must be taken account of.

Complex social conditions are not the only types of context which law ignores, however. Even in regard to specific acts, the law disregards the context within which behaviour occurs. Thus, when the woman who has been assaulted over a long period of time eventually kills her abuser, the law declares that factors she sees as very relevant to her actions – the previous years of violence, her fear, her sensitivity to danger, her concern for her children – are incidental and collateral. They are irrelevant in law's eyes because *it* has decided that the only factors which need to be taken into account are those involved in the immediate commission of this act. What was he doing immediately prior to her striking the final blow? What other options did she have immediately available to her besides killing him? By pre-determining which elements of the context are relevant for making sense of behaviour and which are not, the law gains no understanding as to how *she* perceived the context and what prompted her to take the action she did.

Technically, then, the law does not *ignore* context. Rather, it *substitutes* an alternative one. By giving attention to some elements of the context but not others, the description of the circumstances facing the woman is selectively altered – so much so that an entirely different context from the one which the woman herself experienced is constructed. The meaning of the behaviour shifts as the description of the context shifts. The act takes on the meaning that the new context permits it to have. With the basis for her fear excised from the story, the woman's action comes to look like revenge or murder, rather than self-defence. The 'story' of an event must make sense, and by limiting the features which can be included in the narrative, an alternative one is created. The meaning of the act becomes that which the law permits it to have, not the meaning that it held for the person committing it.

Law believes it is in the business of impartial moderation of narratives offered by others. It does not recognise that it is also in the business of 'telling tales' (D. Nicolson, 1995). When it pre-determines which elements can feature in a story and which must be ignored, it is dictating the tale that a defendant or witness can offer. Thus, law does not seek to gain an understanding of the event in question, but merely to judge how well the final account 'measures up' against established standards. This comparative exercise does not appear problematic to law, because the standards against which judgement is made are considered to reflect an objective, independent, unbiased perspective. It is only in identifying the biases within them that it begins to be possible to see them as unjust. It is not surprising that men's experience should more frequently and easily measure up against the standards than women's, given that those standards were of a masculine nature from the outset.

There are a variety of ways in which the law is involved in 'telling tales'. The individualistic model on which it is constructed often creates inconsistencies and ambiguities which can only be resolved through the development of legal fictions. For example, offences committed by corporate bodies, such as causing the death of an employee through unsafe working practices or polluting rivers by discharging poisonous effluent, are regarded as crimes. But who is to be charged with the offence – the chief executive? the directors of the company? the employee who pressed the button discharging the effluent? According to the individualistic framework of law, a specific person or persons would need to be identified and held responsible for the crime. However, it is frequently the case that no one person within a corporation carries criminal responsibility, in terms of 'knowingly and intentionally setting out to harm'. The resultant harm is likely to stem from a complexity of factors including neglect, indifference, and/or error. When the law wishes to declare corporate behaviour unlawful, it therefore does so by classifying the corporation as a legal person and on this basis charges it with the offence. The whole corporate body is charged on the grounds that it can have 'a controlling mind' and thus function, in abstract form, as an individual person. This is a pretence, a fiction invented by law in order to accommodate its need for rigid frameworks. Because the model on which it bases its understanding of human action is an individualistic one, all events with which it deals must be forced to fit that model, even if that reshaping leads to an account that is nonsensical. We have seen other examples of such contortionist reasoning processes in the nineteenth-century cases where women were declared not to be persons in the eyes of the law and the attempt to equate the circumstances faced by the theoretical 'reasonable man' and a battered woman.

We have up to this point highlighted the way in which law ignores context, nursing the construction of a story with which it feels familiar and comfortable. There is some evidence, however, that contexts are occasionally being factored into legal deliberations, by taking account of the 'personal characteristics' of individuals who commit crimes. In England, for example, the defence of provocation allows the jury to take account of 'any personal characteristics' that might make the accused person more susceptible to being provoked. Thus, in the case of *R* v *Morhall* (1995), Morhall was convicted of murdering an acquaintance who had nagged him about his addiction to glue-sniffing. On final appeal to the House of Lords, his conviction was reduced to one of manslaughter on the basis that the jury had not been allowed to consider the personal characteristics that would have provoked a person who was addicted to glue-sniffing. That is, they felt that the standard of the general 'reasonable man' should have been replaced by that of a 'reasonable man under Morhall's circumstances' (i.e. a glue-sniffer). Thus, there is evidence that a shift is occurring which accommodates the personal characteristics of a defendant, even where this lends itself to a rather perverse outcome.

Recent developments in rape law in the UK supply additional evidence of such a shift, although the perversity of these decisions makes the reasoning applied in *Morhall* seem mundane. Indeed, it begins to seem that new legal fictions are being erected, rather than old ones simply being dismantled. Rape is explicitly defined from a male perspective. If a man believes that consent to sexual intercourse was given, then the law states that the act cannot be defined as rape. It does not matter what the woman believed to be true of her own (or of his) behaviour. The judgements in the key cases in this area (*DPP* v *Morgan*, 1975; *Jamieson* v *HMA*, 1994) thus apply an even more idiosyncratic standard than is usually found in law.

> The man must have genuinely formed the belief that she was consenting ... [but] this need not be a belief which the jury regards as reasonable, so long as they are satisfied that his belief was genuinely held by him at the time.
>
> (*Jamieson* v *HMA*, 1994: 92)

The man need only demonstrate that he honestly believed that consent had been given; he is not required to meet even the objective standard of a reasonable belief. The personal perspective of the rapist has been accommodated – at the expense of the personal perspective of the woman.

Thus, attention to 'personal characteristics' has not successfully contextualised behaviour. Law is still choosing a route of legal fiction. It has performed an ingenious slight of hand, labelling these new elements 'personal characteristics' instead of identifying them as contextual factors. The purpose that is served – to highlight aspects of the situation as that individual perceived it – is not articulated. To describe it as a contextual approach would create immense tension for a legal system grounded in an individualistic framework.

Contextualised accounts of behaviour are not being encouraged within the legal system. This is because it is *law* that decides when greater contextualisation is appropriate and when it is not needed. It is *law* that decides which additional factors might be informative. It is not the *person* involved in the events who has been awarded this power. As long as law retains the ultimate authority to contextualise, the established individualistic model will prevail.

Conclusion

This chapter has explored in depth some of the key characteristics of psychology and of law. While we have undertaken separate analyses of each discipline, our underlying goal has been to highlight the similarities between them. One of the assumptions guiding their collaboration is that the interaction of two independent fields should help to counteract biases held by the other. This is a misguided assumption. Because psychology and law share the key epistemological character-istics, their knowledge and perspectives actually *reinforce* each other's existing biases. If psychology, with its use of objective, scientific methods, has seen fit to classify certain behaviours as disorders of the individual, how can it be inappropriate for law to share that perspective? There is a need, too often neglected, to examine the bases on which disciplines operate before deciding whether their contribution to society can be considered a beneficial one.

The theoretical framework that has been laid out in this chapter provides a basis from which to address that gap. In the next four chapters, we will examine individual syndromes and situate them within this framework. It is possible to discern the operation of the implicit relation between psychology and law within each of them. We do not believe that that relation is restricted to these four syndromes, however. Wherever the law has the potential to make use of scientific psychological syndrome evidence, particularly in regard to women, we would expect to find the effects of the implicit relation. Rather than adopting a broad approach for our analysis, we have chosen to look at a few diagnoses in detail. It is the details – the proclamations of judges, the affirmations of psychologists, the silence of women's voices – that bring our theoretical arguments to life.

4 Battered Woman's Syndrome

Context is all.
Margaret Atwood[1]

In this chapter, we look at the first domain in which our arguments concerning the implicit relation are applied. Domestic violence is the domain in which syndrome evidence has arguably made most impact in the courtroom. In recent years it has attracted interest from the media, academics, and social commentators, particularly in situations where battered women kill their violent partners. Although such cases represent only a small fraction of the incidence of domestic violence, the circumstances surrounding these fatalities tend to be sufficiently dramatic to ensure media attention. It is also in such cases that Battered Woman's Syndrome has sometimes been used to support a woman's claim that she was acting in self-defence or was provoked, rather than acting in revenge. Amidst the controversies surrounding this issue, evidence of the implicit relation can be identified. We will begin by reviewing the incidence of domestic abuse and the evolution of Battered Woman's Syndrome, followed by a consideration of its application in the courtroom. This provides the framework in which we can situate our analysis.

Incidence of domestic violence

The prevalence of domestic abuse remains very high, despite the variety of measures that have been developed to tackle it in the last twenty years. Statistics for the UK reveal that almost half of all homicides of women are caused by a partner or ex-partner, while one in five of all murder victims (both male and female) is a woman killed by a partner or ex-partner (Home Office, 1985–1993; see also Victim Support, 1992). Official figures for the US report that approximately twice as many women as men are killed each year by a partner or ex-partner (Bachman and Saltzman, 1995). Statistics for Canada and Australia also show that a significantly higher proportion of women are killed by men than is the reverse case (Edwards, 1996). For violence that does not result in death, official surveys have produced figures of 9 in 1000 women in the US reporting physical violence within their relationships (National Crime Victimization Survey, reported in Bachman and

Saltzman, 1995), 19 per 1000 women in Canada (1993 Canadian General Social Survey, reported in Johnson, 1996), and 1 in 10 women in Britain (1992 British Crime Survey, reported in Mayhew, Maung, and Mirrlees-Black, 1993).

Although these official statistics disclose a disturbingly high incidence of domestic violence, they have been criticised for underestimating the real scale of the problem (Gelles, 1997; Stanko, 1988). Academic research reveals a much higher rate of domestic violence, with figures ranging between 20% and 30% of women in heterosexual relationships suffering some form of violence (Gelles, 1997; Johnson, 1998; http://www.brunel.ac.uk/depts/law/dvds). This discrepancy between the official statistics and academic findings is partly attributed to the dependence of official statistics on self-reporting, a notoriously unreliable measure, and to the broad-brush approach used in omnibus crime surveys. Indeed, a recent survey in Canada, conducted using particularly carefully designed materials, obtained figures that exceeded police statistics by a factor of four (Johnson, 1998).

Women's willingness to report domestic abuse is diminished by numerous obstacles. These include fear of retaliation by the abuser, anxiety that involving the police will achieve few outcomes, and doubt that the judiciary will take such crimes seriously (Edwards, 1989). There are also the practical difficulties frequently faced by women fleeing violence, such as an immediate safe refuge, longer-term rehousing, re-schooling for children, and achieving economic independence from her battering partner. Finally, the psychological hurdles are very significant. The sexual, emotional, and mental abuse is considered by many victims to be worse than the physical abuse. There are thus a variety of issues that must be addressed in understanding a woman's decision to report abuse and to leave the abuser (Dobash and Dobash, 1979, 1992, 1998; Edwards, 1989; Kelly, 1988).

Persistent lobbying has achieved some concrete results in addressing these issues over the past 25 years. Much of this has been encouraged by feminist research and activism (e.g. Dobash and Dobash, 1979, 1992, 1998; Edwards, 1989; Hanmer, Radford, and Stanko, 1989; Pahl, 1985; Walker, 1979). In the UK the Women's Aid refuge movement, which was started in 1976 by Erin Pizzey, broadened into a nationwide (indeed worldwide) movement that now provides temporary housing each year for thousands of women fleeing violence. The refuge movement increased awareness of the lack of legal protection available for women, resulting in legislative acts, improvements in police guidelines, and high-profile campaigns (e.g. Domestic Violence and Matrimonial Proceedings Act 1976 in England; Matrimonial Homes (Family Protection) (Scotland) Act, 1981; US Attorney-General Task Force on Violence in the Family, 1984).

Important changes have also been initiated elsewhere within the criminal justice system. During the 1980s many police forces in the UK introduced specialist Women and Child Units to combat complaints about insensitive handling of female victims of physical and sexual violence, although officers assigned to the Units are frequently regarded as doing low-status 'women's work' (Burman and Lloyd, 1993). The 1990s have seen a trend toward multi-agency strategies, with partnerships being set up between relevant agencies, such as the police, the judiciary, social work departments, schools, and health services (e.g. Scottish Partnership on

Domestic Violence Report, by Henderson, 1997; UK Government initiative 'Delivering for Women' (*The Guardian*, 10 November 1998); New Mexico Death Review Team, 1998). These have been established because they are seen as more effective mechanisms for facilitating support to women and tackling the causes of domestic violence than are single-agency efforts (Henderson, 1997).

Yet, despite all this activity, the statistics cited earlier make clear that the prevalence of domestic violence remains intolerably high. Why is it that campaigns should succeed in raising awareness but not in changing behaviour? Proponents of systems theory (e.g. Gelles and Straus, 1988; Straus, 1980, 1990) argue that domestic violence emanates from the dysfunctional family. They argue that by putting greater resources into the support and treatment of such families, rates of violence can be reduced. In particular, they focus on the abuser, proposing therapeutic efforts directed at the level of individual men (within the context of their families). In contrast, a feminist analysis argues that violence results from male power and privilege in society in general (Kelly, 1988; Stanko, 1985). Proponents of this view maintain that the extremely high incidence of violence, across all levels of society, cannot be accounted for satisfactorily by reference to the pathology of individual men and individual families. (For a comparison of feminist and systems theory approaches, see Gelles, 1997; Yllo and Bograd, 1988.) To claim that violence within the family is symptomatic of male power and privilege may seem polemical. There is, however, a substantial body of international research that has convincingly exposed the links between the male as traditional 'head of the household', main breadwinner, property holder and paterfamilias, and the exercising of power and authority that attaches to these positions (Collier, 1995; Stone, 1990). Historically, women were the legal property of their fathers and husbands, and while those historic bonds have been fractured by subsequent legislation, many of their shackles endure within contemporary institutions and societal practices (Leneman, 1998; Stone, 1990). Thus, in England, domestic violence was not acknowledged as a social problem until the mid-1970s, while rape within marriage was criminalised only as recently as 1992.

The very term '*domestic* violence' connotes something that occurs in private, behind closed doors and beyond the public gaze. Reluctance to 'interfere' with the private lives of men and women is deeply embedded within the law. Attacks by partners and ex-partners are still classified distinctively by the criminal justice system as 'domestic' assaults, thus minimising their significance. These cases are unlikely to be prosecuted or, if they do reach court, likely to result in a warning rather than a more serious disposal (Edwards, 1996). When prosecuting authorities are under financial or resourcing pressures, 'domestics' are particularly liable to be dropped (Henderson, 1997; *Scotland on Sunday*, 25 September 1994). Judicial attitudes frequently reflect a similar dismissive tenor. Recent examples include the 1998 Scottish case of William Gallacher, who held his wife down and punched her because, he said, her menopausal mood swings had provoked him. When this argument was offered to the court by his solicitor, the judge dealt with the case by giving Mr Gallacher only a warning, stating that he was taking into account a positive report from the social services department and Gallacher's 'good behaviour' between the offence and the court hearing (*The Scotsman*, 10 December 1998). The judge in the 1997 English appeal case of Michael Creighton was willing to reduce a custodial sentence previously imposed by the trial court. Creighton had harassed his ex-wife, vowing to 'hound her until she died'. Lady Justice Butler Sloss suggested to Mrs Creighton's lawyers that she consider moving elsewhere, on the basis that '[t]here is always the danger of the husband doing something more serious. Your client must protect her situation' (*The Guardian*, 30 October 1997). Whether intentional or not, decisions such as these shift the responsibility for abuse from the perpetrator to the victim. She is assigned responsibility not only for coping with the abuse but also for causing it.

This brief review provides a glimpse of the situation faced by lawyers seeking to protect their clients from violent partners. The difficulties are multiplied when a lawyer is faced with explaining why her/his client has killed her abuser. It is to this end that Battered Woman's Syndrome has been promoted, for, in highlighting the psychological consequences of abuse, it has the potential to contextualise the woman's actions so that they are more comprehensible to the court. This is particularly important where a woman's account of her experience and the law's expectations of her are in conflict. The admission of Battered Woman's Syndrome into the courtroom has been received with celebration in many quarters, but, as we shall see, the implicit relation between psychology and law severely limits the contribution it can make. Indeed, it arguably works against the interests of women as a group.

Battered Woman's Syndrome

In 1979 Lenore Walker published *The Battered Woman*, in which she described the psychological consequences and patterns of behaviour that result from cyclical violence and long-term abuse. The patterns came to be known as Battered Woman's Syndrome (BWS). Walker argued that a battered woman may experience at the hands of her abuser a state of 'psychological paralysis', which can only be ended by an act of violence on her part. In that and subsequent texts, Walker portrays a 'typical' battered woman as one who has been

> subjected repeatedly to coercive behavior (physical, sexual and/or psycho-logical) by a man attempting to force her to do what he wants her to do, regardless of her own desires, rights, or best interests.
>
> (Walker, 1990: 102)

Walker drew on Seligman's theory of 'learned helplessness' to provide a framework for understanding the effects of continued, uncontrollable violence. Working with dogs, Seligman (1975) had shown that administering electrical shocks could induce animals to expect ill-treatment to the extent that, when it became possible for them to leave their cages, they refused to do so. Walker (1984) applied this theory to domestic violence, arguing that women who were subjected to long-term abuse responded in a similar manner. She argued that the cyclical nature of the violence immobilised a woman's ability to act decisively in her own interests, making her feel trapped in the relationship with no means of escape. Walker's emphasis on the dysfunctional mental consequences of abuse was reinforced by the inclusion of BWS in the *Diagnostic and Statistical Manual* (DSM-III), in 1980, as a sub-category of Post-Traumatic Stress Disorder. The current edition of the DSM (DSM-IV) describes the disorder in the following way.

> [The] constellation of symptoms [that] may occur and are commonly seen in association with an interpersonal stressor (e.g. . . . domestic battering . . .) [include]: impaired affect modulation, self-destructive and impulsive behavior; dissociative symptoms; somatic complaints; feelings of ineffectiveness, shame, despair, or hopelessness; feeling permanently damaged; a loss of previously sustained beliefs; social withdrawal; feeling constantly threatened; impaired relationships with others; or a change from the individual's previous personality characteristics.
>
> (DSM, 1994, para. 309.81)

Walker's theory of BWS and her research on domestic violence has had a significant impact on the treatment and prosecution of cases where a battered woman is charged with the killing of her violent partner. As awareness of the high incidence of domestic violence increased, the unfair treatment within the criminal justice system of those few women who were fatally violent towards their abusers was exposed. Some lawyers defending such women were willing to explore the possibilities of the new insights offered by BWS in explaining their clients' behaviour, and to seek to have testimony about BWS admitted as expert evidence in court. The significance of this innovative defence strategy is that it poses a challenge to traditional criminal defences and, in so doing, reveals their inadequacy.

BWS in the courtroom

The admissibility of expert testimony on BWS is inextricably bound up with the construction of the legal defences to a charge of murder or homicide. Across the jurisdictions discussed in this book, there are a variety of charges applicable to the situation in which a battered woman kills her partner. Generally, the charge will be one of either murder or culpable homicide (similar to the term 'manslaughter' used in some jurisdictions). Both of these charges assume that the woman killed the man and that she either intended to do so or that she behaved with such reckless disregard for the outcome of her actions that that intention can be inferred. These charges can be met with a defence that acknowledges that the woman did kill the man but advances an 'excuse' or 'justification' for the killing. The three most probable defences are self-defence, provocation, and diminished responsibility. The precise definition and operation of each of these defences varies from jurisdiction to jurisdiction but common themes are discernible.

To sustain a defence of *self-defence*, the essential element is an attack or fear of imminent attack, which entitles a person to protect her-/himself or a third party, provided that the force used to repel the attack is proportionate to that used in the attack itself. The paradigmatic scenario in which self-defence would apply is that of a man who, being physically threatened by another man with a knife, picks up a broken bottle to defend himself. If he had responded by brandishing a gun instead of a bottle, this would exceed the bounds permitted by a self-defence plea. The retaliatory response must not be angry retaliation or pure aggression (*Palmer* v *R*, 1971), and the court will take into account alternatives open to the defendant, such as leaving, in determining whether the response was appropriate.

To sustain a defence of *provocation*, the essential element is a sudden and temporary loss of control due to a provoking event. If, in the exchange described above, it emerged that a previous threat had been issued, the man who first pulled the knife might reasonably argue that he had been provoked. In some jurisdictions (e.g. Scotland) the provocative event is confined to physical events, but others (e.g. England) accept both physical and verbal events as provocative, as long as verbal provocation is of a very serious nature. In all cases, the time period between the provocative event and the violent act must not be excessive. For example, the threats could not usually have been issued an hour previously, when there would have been time to 'cool off'; the loss of control must occur suddenly and immediately after the event.

Even in those jurisdictions that confine the defence of provocation to physical acts, there is one classic exception to the general expectation that provocation should be physical, and that is words or deeds that amount to a confession of sexual infidelity. A recent illustration of this exception can be seen in the Scottish case of *Rutherford* v *HMA* (1997), in which a plea of provocation was accepted (on appeal). Rutherford had killed his cohabitee by strangling her and throwing her over a bridge after she taunted him with the confession that she had been having an affair with another man for several months. The court accepted that Rutherford had been provoked by her humiliating revelations of sexual infidelity and that he had lost control as a consequence and reacted violently. A conviction of culpable homicide was substituted for that of murder.

To sustain a defence of *diminished responsibility*, it must be demonstrated that the accused suffers an abnormality of mind sufficient to impair normal mental functioning. Diminished responsibility relies on expert psychiatric, medical, or psychological testimony. Although ultimately the question of whether or not a defendant was suffering from a mental abnormality at the time of the offence is a matter for the jury,[2] evidence will invariably be led from experts qualified to comment on the defendant's state of mind. In the English case of *R* v *Byrne* (1960: 3), for example, the Court of Appeal found that Byrne, who had strangled and then mutilated a young woman, suffered from an abnormality of mind. Three doctors who testified on Byrne's behalf considered that he had acted under the influence of 'perverted sexual desires' and that this 'sexual psychopathy could properly be described as partial insanity'.

This discussion illustrates broadly how the defences of self-defence, provocation, and diminished responsibility are framed to operate within the criminal law. Each of them, sometimes singularly and sometimes in tandem, has been used in cases where battered women who have killed their violent partners attempt to defend their actions. However, these defences have rarely been successful. This is because, as many critics have argued, they are intrinsically unsuitable for the circumstances faced by battered women (e.g. Bandalli, 1995; Ewing, 1987; Fox, 1995; Gillespie, 1989; McColgan, 1993; Nicolson and Sanghvi, 1993; O'Donovan, 1991, 1993; Schneider, 1980; Wells, 1994). It is useful to review briefly the arguments of these commentators, for they set the context in which it becomes possible to discern the operation of the implicit relation.

The unsuitability of self-defence

It might be presumed that the defences of self-defence and/or provocation would be appropriate for cases where there is a history of domestic violence, in that (a) the woman is frequently in fear of attack and (b) she has been provoked by cumulative abuse. However, the actions of battered women are typically deemed not to meet the legal standards. Both of these defences emphasise the spontaneity of behaviour. That is, imminence is the key consideration for self-defence, as is sudden loss of control for provocation. An emphasis on spontaneity takes no account of the ways in which women's experience tends to differ from men's, especially when the violence emanates from an intimate partner.

Important differences include the size differential; women are generally smaller and physically weaker than men, thus less able to defend themselves. Women are likely to be economically and even emotionally dependent on their abusers. Abused women who kill are often the recipients of long-term violence, so it is unlikely they are responding to a singular event. Perhaps most critically, the circumstances surrounding women's killing of their abusive partners usually do not fulfil the requirement of spontaneity. Women tend to act when the man is relatively defenceless, such as when he is asleep or incapacitated by alcohol, and they may have earlier hidden a weapon to assist them. These actions stem from their belief that a life-threatening episode of violence is imminent and that if they act when the man is unaware, they will have a better chance of successfully defending themselves. However, because their actions then appear to be planned, the criteria of 'imminent danger' and 'sudden loss of control' appear not to be met. They are therefore typically disqualified from pleading either self-defence or provocation.

The first case to consider fully the question of admissibility of BWS into court was the American case of *Ibn-Tamas* v *US* (1979). Beverly Ibn-Tamas was a neurosurgical nurse who had been systematically abused for a number of years by her husband, who was a neurosurgeon. On the day of his death in 1976, he had beaten her and threatened to kill her with a handgun. In the struggle that ensued Ibn-Tamas, who was pregnant, wrested the gun from her husband and shot him through the chest. He struggled to another room and she followed him, fearful that he was going to the gun cabinet for another gun. She then shot him between the eyes, killing him instantly. She was convicted of second-degree murder and served two years in prison (a sentence that was considered exceptionally light, as Edwards (1996: 239) discusses). An application had been made during the trial to have

Lenore Walker's testimony on BWS admitted as evidence, but this was refused, leading to an appeal. It took several years for the Appeals Court to rule that the trial court had erred in excluding the testimony (on the basis that it would invade the province of the jury). The Appeals Court said such expert testimony would arguably have served two basic functions:

> (1) it would have enhanced Mrs Ibn-Tamas' general credibility in responding to cross-examination designed to show that her testimony about the relationship with her husband was implausible; and (2) it would have supported her testimony that on the day of the shooting her husband's actions had provoked a state of fear which led her to believe she was in imminent danger . . . and thus responded in self-defense.
>
> (*Ibn-Tamas* v *US*, 1979, cited in Monahan and Walker, 1994: 413)

The problem faced by Beverly Ibn-Tamas was that while she may have been able to argue self-defence in relation to the first shooting where she wounded her husband, the parameters of the self-defence plea disallowed her second, fatal shot since, by following her husband to another room, she was no longer deemed to be in 'imminent danger'. Walker's interpretation of events was that Ibn-Tamas's actions were entirely explicable given her steadfast belief and experience of her husband as someone who was 'omnipotent and could heal himself' (Walker, 1990: 75). She was convinced, in her terror, that despite his wounds he still had power over her and would kill her.[3] It is this context, within which the woman's perceptions and actions are based, that a 'BWS defence' seeks to bring to the attention of the court.

The case of Gladys Kelly shows the progression of judicial (and psychological) reasoning about BWS. In 1984, Kelly's conviction of reckless manslaughter, obtained when she stabbed her husband with a pair of scissors while in fear of an attack from him, was overturned by the Supreme Court of New Jersey (*State* v *Kelly*, 1984). Kelly maintained that her husband had assaulted her on the day she killed him and that she had been acting in self-defence. The Supreme Court held that expert testimony on BWS was relevant to a battered woman's defence. In so doing, the court specifically addressed the vexed question of whether BWS had been generally accepted in the scientific field, thus permitting it to be considered reliable evidence.

> [W]e note that judicial opinions thus far have been split concerning the scientific acceptability of the syndrome and the methodology used by the researchers in this area. On the other hand . . . the proffered expert testified that the battered-woman's syndrome is acknowledged and accepted by practitioners and professors in the field of psychology and psychiatry. [The expert] also brought to the court's attention the findings of several researchers who have published reports confirming the presence of the battered-woman's syndrome.
>
> (*State* v *Kelly*, 1984: 380)

The Court went on to note that the topic of BWS had been discussed at several professional symposia, and that numerous books and scientific articles had been written about it. The Court concluded (p. 380) that BWS had by that point obtained 'a sufficient scientific basis to produce uniform and reasonably reliable results'. *Kelly* was thus a significant step forward in the process of gaining admissibility for BWS in US courtrooms as part of a defence of self-defence. Since then, BWS has been admitted on numerous occasions, leading Lenore Walker to assert that by 1989 battered women could expect 'more often than not' to be supported by expert witness testimony (Walker, 1990: 281).

In the UK courts, the self-defence plea in cases of domestic violence has had limited success (Wells, 1994). This is due to the formidable obstacles presented by the elements of the defence that require a perception of imminent danger and proportionality of response. The traditional paradigm envisages a defendant pleading self-defence in circumstances where she/he is confronted by an attacker and has no choice but to injure or be injured. These are rarely, if ever, the circumstances that the battered woman finds herself in. As Kennedy (1993) points out, most women, even if they felt themselves to be acting in self-defence at the time they killed their abuser, are unlikely to offer that as a defence. Instead, they tend to plead diminished responsibility.

> What happens most often in domestic homicide cases is that the woman has available to her a number of different defences, but if one of the avenues affords a manslaughter plea which is acceptable to the Crown, whatever the basis, she is likely to enter that plea rather than fight for a total acquittal [which self-defence would produce] and risk conviction.
>
> (Kennedy, 1993: 209)

In Canada, the case of *R* v *Lavallee* (1990) was considered a landmark victory, because expert testimony on BWS was admitted by the Supreme Court in conjunction with a self-defence plea. Madame Justice Wilson declared in her endorsement of expert evidence in cases of domestic violence that

> [w]here evidence exists that an accused is in a battering relationship, expert testimony can assist the jury in determining whether the accused had a 'reasonable' apprehension of death when she acted by explaining the heightened sensitivity of a battered woman to her partner's acts. Without such testimony I am skeptical that the average fact-finder would be capable of appreciating why her subjective fear may have been reasonable in the context of the relationship.
>
> (*R* v *Lavallee*, 1990: 882)

Despite the successes of *Ibn-Tamas, Kelly, Lavallee,* and other notable cases (e.g. *State* v *Wanrow,* 1977; *Arcoren* v *United States,* 1991), the significance of BWS should not be over-rated. It continues to be a significant struggle, in all jurisdictions, to have BWS testimony admitted in cases where self-defence is pled, and as Edwards

(1996) observes in her extensive review of US cases, even when it is admitted it may function only as mitigation. This implies that the woman has a partial excuse for the killing but no real justification. It rarely results in an acquittal, which is the primary purpose of the self-defence plea.

The unsuitability of provocation

Quite often a plea of provocation is pled in conjunction with a plea of self-defence. Typically, a battered woman will claim that she was subjected to abuse over a long period of time, which elevated her ability to sense imminent danger, and she may also claim that she was provoked by her abuser's behaviour into responding in an ultimate and violent act. However, the crucial element of sudden and temporary loss of control is often absent, for a battered woman who kills rarely acts 'on the spur of the moment'. Her inferior size and strength negate against that, and she will have been generally debilitated by the sustained state of terror under which she has been living (Edwards, 1996). These conditions are not the ones that qualify, in the eyes of the law, as provocation.

In the US provocation has been less favoured as a defence than self-defence, probably because of the scope for a plea of provocation to lead to either acquittal or conviction of manslaughter, while a successful plea of self-defence leads to an acquittal. Better known for provocation are the three prominent UK cases of *R* v *Thornton* (1992), *R* v *Ahluwalia* (1992), and *R* v *Humphreys* (1995), all of which have featured prominently in the media and the legal literature as demonstrations of the law's resistance to taking serious account of women's circumstances. In 1989, Sara Thornton fatally stabbed her husband. There had been a history of domestic violence in the relationship. Prior to the stabbing, an argument had taken place and Thornton had picked up a knife with which to defend herself. Her husband stated that he would kill her when she fell asleep, but he fell asleep first and she then stabbed him in the stomach. Thornton's plea of diminished responsibility was unsuccessful, and she was convicted of murder.

In the first of two appeals, it was argued that the parameters of the defence of provocation should be extended. Thornton's lawyers contended that the concept of a sudden and temporary loss of control was not applicable in the case of 'reaction by a person subjected to a long course of provocative conduct, including domestic violence, which may sap the resilience and resolve to retain self-control when the final confrontation erupts' (*Thornton*, 1992: 313). The Appeal Court dismissed the appeal, declaring that in domestic violence cases there was frequently evidence of prior provocative acts but that the issue for the jury was always whether 'at the moment the fatal blow was struck the accused had been deprived for that moment of the self-control which previously he or she had been able to exercise' (*Thornton*, 1992: 314). A second appeal (*Thornton*, 1996) was made on the grounds that further medical evidence concerning her 'personality disorder' was available by 1995, and that at the time of the trial, the effect of her husband's abuse on her mental state could not have been taken into account. This time, the court was more willing to take account of the special circumstances of the defendant, acknowledging that the effect of prolonged battering was a relevant characteristic in determining whether she met the legal criteria for provocation. Thornton's conviction was quashed, and a retrial was ordered (at which she was convicted of manslaughter and sentenced to five years' imprisonment, which she had already served). This case is a prime example of the difficulties a battered woman faces in convincing a jury that the defences of either self-defence or provocation, as traditionally conceived, are applicable to her, given that a sleeping man does not pose an obvious threat to a woman's safety. Nonetheless, the point is that to a woman who has developed, through years of abuse, a heightened sensitivity to signs of impending danger, her sleeping partner may well pose an immediate threat. It is this point that BWS evidence seeks to illuminate.

In the case of *Ahluwalia*, the court also rejected the argument that the defendant had acted while provoked. In 1989, Kiranjit Ahluwalia killed her husband while he was asleep, dousing him with petrol and setting fire to him. Evidence was led of their ten-year marriage, during which she had been repeatedly beaten and abused, latterly on an almost daily basis, and had incurred injuries including broken bones and teeth, rape, scalding, and being knocked unconscious (Nicolson and Sanghvi, 1993: 729). On the night of the killing, Ahluwalia's husband had taunted her about the affair he was having (which was a particular humiliation within her Muslim culture) and had physically threatened her with a hot iron and a beating. At her trial for murder she pled provocation, based on years of torment and abuse throughout her marriage. Her defence of provocation was rejected by the jury, and she was convicted and given a life sentence. The decision was appealed on the grounds that the jury had been misdirected on the plea of provocation (not having been allowed to consider the effects of long-term abuse) and that evidence was now available that she had been suffering from BWS, affecting her state of mind sufficiently to justify a defence of diminished responsibility. The Court accepted the second ground and agreed to admit fresh medical evidence that Ahluwalia suffered from 'endogenous depression'. A retrial was ordered, and her plea of diminished responsibility was accepted by the prosecution. Ahluwalia was sentenced to forty months' imprisonment, the period she had already served.

Nicolson and Sanghvi (1993) are among those who have argued that the Court's decision in *Ahluwalia* may signal an important step in the liberalisation of the criteria for the provocation defence, for the willingness to consider personal characteristics of a defendant, in particular their power of self-control, could benefit battered women. The rationale is that repeated battering constitutes a form of cumulative provocation which inevitably breaks down a woman's psychological resistance and natural self-control. However, it is important to note that the focus remains on the woman's mental capacity. This emphasis conflicts with the primary purpose of the provocation defence, which should be to lead to acquittal through highlighting the circumstances that provoked the act.

R v Humphreys (1995) reflects the same skewed outcome. Emma Humphreys had been convicted of murder in 1985 when she killed her pimp and cohabitee after years of abuse. She succeeded, after a ten-year campaign, in having her murder conviction quashed and one of manslaughter substituted. It was argued before the Court of Appeal that the trial judge's charge to the jury had been 'fatally flawed' in its direction to ignore evidence of Humphreys' 'abnormal personality', a trait that had developed out of her tragic history of child abuse, prostitution, and drug-taking. The Court of Appeal was willing to accept evidence of her disordered mental characteristics as support for a plea of provocation. While it is notable that the appeal was successful, the acceptance of the plea of provocation is arguably less so. The focus in the case was, once again, placed on the woman's psychological state. The circumstances which gave rise to her actions were not illuminated. The possibility that her actions, although regrettable, could be classified as justifiable by the law remained unrealised, despite this being the aim of the provocation plea. When this decision is added to that of *Thornton* and *Ahluwalia*, the likelihood is eclipsed even further that, in future cases, women's circumstances will be given serious consideration by the courts.

The unsuitability of diminished responsibility

The cases considered so far demonstrate the inflexibility of self-defence and provocation in taking account of the situations of battered women who kill. In contrast, the defence of diminished responsibility has proven more malleable to women's needs. The essence of this defence is that wrongdoing is acknowledged, but with an excuse based on lack of personal responsibility. This defence is utterly dependent on expert testimony, for a defendant cannot plead diminished responsibility without conceding mental abnormality, and expert psychological or psychiatric evidence will be needed to establish that. It is not at all surprising that, of the three defences, the one that has proven most 'successful' in accounting for women's behaviour is the one that characterises it as disordered and irrational.

Diminished responsibility does not provide a complete defence to a charge of murder. It provides only a partial defence. If diminished responsibility is accepted by the jury, the initial charge will be reduced to manslaughter and there is flexibility in whether or not the sentence imposed is a custodial one. A murder conviction in many jurisdictions carries a mandatory life sentence, whereas a lesser conviction of manslaughter can result in a sentence ranging from 'life' to probation, a suspended sentence, or even simply an admonishment.

The extent to which the plea of diminished responsibility has become acceptable as an explanation of women's (irrational) behaviour, but the other two defences have not, is illustrated in *Ahluwalia*. The grounds for her appeal were based on both provocation and diminished responsibility, but it was only the latter that was successful. Because the Court of Appeal had ruled that fresh evidence of her endogenous depression should be admitted, it was the plea of diminished responsibility that was entered at her retrial. This was pivotal in finally gaining the court's acceptance of the manslaughter plea. As Nicolson and Sanghvi (1993: 736) comment in their discussion of the case:

> [t]his willingness to accept evidence of diminished responsibility suggests that battered women are likely to evoke a more favourable judicial response if they

confine themselves to medical-type excuses rather than the partial justification of provocation.

Although Kiranjit Ahluwalia had suffered years of extreme abuse and was acting in fear for her life, the only explanation for her behaviour that the court would accept was that it was due to irrational, uncontrollable impulses brought on by a psychological disorder. It was impossible for them to see it as 'reasonable', in the way that men's behaviour is seen as 'reasonable' when they act in self-defence or are provoked (for example, by their wife's nagging, as we will discuss later).

There is a considerable reluctance on the part of some activists and lawyers (e.g. Gillespie, 1989; Schneider, 1986), particularly in the US, to use BWS testimony in conjunction with a plea of diminished responsibility, because this links BWS to an 'insanity defence'. This was not the purpose for which BWS was introduced. Its aim was to normalise women's actions, that is, to show how they could be characterised as reasonable. The fortification of the link between BWS and the defence of diminished responsibility undermines that aim. Indeed, the receptivity with which that link has been greeted in the UK has created some notable trends. It appears that it has decreased the likelihood that a defence team will advise or even consider a plea of self-defence or provocation. Research by Casey (1999) and by Connelly (1996) has shown that in Scotland, the favoured strategy of defence lawyers in cases of domestic killings committed by women is now to plead to a reduced charge of culpable homicide (manslaughter) on the ground of diminished responsibility. This may also appeal to prosecutors, as the defence will have had to provide them with medical reports that support the claims to a reduced charge, thus providing corroboration of the woman's story through independent, authoritative expert evidence. The prosecution may therefore be willing to accept the plea without the need for a trial. While this may, at first glance, seem an inviting choice for the woman, as it avoids the inevitable uncertainty of a trial, the consequence of the trend is that the options she has available to her are restricted. The woman has less opportunity to have her actions (ever) characterised as self-defence; they are immediately classified as disordered. The decision has already been taken that she killed him as a consequence of her disordered mental state. As it becomes known that an initial plea of diminished responsibility is likely to be 'successful', more and more women will have their experience forced into this mould. Less and less women will have a chance of asserting what it is that they believe and what it is that BWS was intended to help them communicate: that they acted reasonably, in self-defence.

It is in such trends that the implicit relation begins to make itself visible. After twenty years of being admitted into court, it is becoming clear that BWS has not achieved its proponents' aim of drawing attention to the circumstances in which battered women kill. Rather, it has emphasised their disordered psychological state. The traditional construction of criminal defences has remained intact, vindicating Mossman's observation that 'legal method is structured in such a way that it is impervious to a feminist perspective' (Mossman, 1986). Psychology has assisted in that resistance, through proffering the syndromatic explanation of BWS. It is an ironic outcome, given the effort it took to gain its admittance into the courtroom in the first place.

The implicit relation

It was, as we have said, originally anticipated by Lenore Walker that evidence on BWS would be used to strengthen a plea of self-defence. Given that the key requirement of a self-defence plea is that the defendant perceive her-/himself to be in imminent danger, admitting evidence on BWS should make it possible to explain to a jury why a battered woman could perceive herself to be in imminent danger from a sleeping man. In effect, BWS should serve to contextualise and thus normalise the behaviour of a battered woman. To date, however, most jurisdictions have resisted admitting BWS in this way. Instead, it has come to be used in a way that pathologises women, supporting our critical contentions about the intersection of psychology and law. This can be demonstrated by looking at each of the characteristics of the implicit relation in turn.

Objectivity

BWS has come to be of use to law because it was 'discovered' and confirmed through the use of methods regarded as objective and scientific. Providing a diagnostic category such as BWS offers a new way of conceiving the sensibility of women's behaviour, and thus perhaps a new standard against which it can be evaluated. The traditional narrow standard of the reasonable man might be substituted or altered to fit the different set of circumstances faced by women. However, because BWS classifies women's behaviour as disordered – the result of a mental abnormality – no new standard is really created for the criminal law, and certainly not one equal to the traditional standard. Instead it leaves women's behaviour measured against the conventional criterion. The problem is further complicated, as we will show later, by the masculine nature of the standard; it is not a coincidence that the hypothetical reasonable man is indeed a man.

The effect of a singular standard, which denies validity to explanations that are different from those the law expects, is revealed in the case histories of battered women who kill. Women's explanations are only of evidential merit if they conform to the paradigmatic standards of criminal defences, that is, if they are consonant with what the theoretical reasonable man would have done. The law has, in effect, drawn up its own inventory as to what counts as a 'signal of danger', and when women's explanations do not match the entries in that inventory, they are deemed unacceptable. For example, Kiranjit Ahluwalia's explanation that she set fire to her husband while he slept 'to stop him running after me' could not meet the law's definition of provocation, given that she was not acting on an immediate threat. Similarly, Sara Thornton, when asked by the police whether her husband had beaten her on the night of the killing, could only reply 'no'. When asked if he had threatened to beat her, her reply that 'he would have' (R v *Thornton*, 1996:

1027) was insufficient, for she could offer nothing other than her own sense that she was in danger. In each case, the woman's personal knowledge regarding her husband's behaviour, gained over a long period of interactions with him, was subordinated to the law's ideas about what should constitute provocation. Battered women's typical explanations that they act not in rage or revenge but in self-defence, out of fear for themselves or their children, are discounted by the law, a pattern well-documented by researchers (Edwards, 1996: 394–395; Jones, 1980: 281–295; McColgan, 1993: 515). 'His tone of voice' or 'the look in his eyes', signs which women have (rightly) learned to fear after years of practice in reading the man's behaviour, do not appear on law's inventory of authorised danger signals. Women's knowledge is secondary to law's opinion.

Because BWS has been helpful in highlighting the ways in which the traditional standard is insufficient in taking account of women's experience, some courts have tried to create alternative standards against which their behaviour could be judged. In the case of *Lavallee*, Madame Justice Wilson accepted the need for expert testimony on BWS to assist the jury and also attempted to reconfigure the self-defence construct from the perspective of the 'reasonable battered woman', as opposed to that of the 'reasonable man'. Explaining the necessity for this, Justice Wilson stated:

> If it strains credulity to imagine what the 'ordinary man' would do in the position of a battered spouse, it is probably because men do not typically find themselves in that situation. Some women do, however. The definition of what is reasonable must be adapted to circumstances which are, by and large, foreign to the world inhabited by the hypothetical 'reason-able man'.
>
> (*R* v *Lavallee*, 1990: 874)

In *Thornton* the court was also willing to apply a standard of 'the reasonable woman' against which to assess the defendant's actions. The jury was thus instructed: '[E]ven if Mrs Thornton had lost her self-control, you would still have to ask whether a reasonable woman in her position would have done what she did' (*R* v *Thornton*, 1992: 312). Some trends in the caselaw therefore suggest that there has been a relaxation in the extent to which a singular, objective standard is used to judge defendants' behaviour. The definition of provocation appears to have been extended: jurors are now able to take into greater account the personal characteristics of the accused. But do such alterations represent a genuine shift in the parameters of criminal defences? And in any event how much impact do the judgements in these few individual cases have?

Some answers can be found by differentiating between legal transformation and linguistic cosmetics. Reforming the language that is used in court may seem to broaden the definition of reasonableness. It can project an appearance of neutrality and universality. However, little substantive change may be achieved, for the underlying assumptions from which the definition was derived have not been addressed. As O'Donovan (1993) argues, standards that merely substitute the term 'woman' for that of 'man' ultimately leave the understanding of women's experience to founder on the bedrock of a male normative legal method. The same point is made by McColgan.

> [W]here the question concerns a concept such as that of reasonableness . . . the jury has to assess the facts as found against an essentially unquantifiable standard. Where this is the case, the jury will of necessity focus on an idealized model of what is reasonable and assess the defendant's conduct against this standard. The relative scarcity of female killers has resulted in a paradigmatically male ideal model.
>
> (McColgan, 1993: 514–515)

When the gap between women's experience and law's behavioural expectations began to be acknowledged, the implicit relation ensured that this would be filled in a manner that was not advantageous to women. The space law provided for the 'reasonable woman' was inevitably going to be irrational in its contours if psychology's help was sought in redressing this breach. The first attempts to admit BWS to the courts demonstrate this. When it was originally proposed, in the case of Beverly Ibn-Tamas, the *Frye* test had to be satisfied, which stipulated, as explained in Chapter 2, that the diagnosis of BWS could be shown to have acquired 'general acceptance' within its scientific community. Lenore Walker recounts the pivotal point during the trial of *Ibn-Tamas* when she was asked:

> Dr Walker, is the study of battered women a recognized diagnostic category in your profession? By that I mean does it appear in any of the typologies used to recognize mental health disorders?
>
> (Walker, 1990: 269)

Walker correctly identified her dilemma: if she answered in the affirmative then Ibn-Tamas would be labelled 'mentally disturbed'. This would serve not to validate her reasonable perception of danger (thus allowing Ibn-Tamas to meet the established legal conditions for self-defence), but to give law a 'peg' on which to hang the conclusion it had already drawn: that her behaviour was not normal and reasonable, but the result of irrational, disordered perceptions. Walker had to acknowledge to the court that, at that stage in 1977, there were no typologies, only that the group entrusted with the revising of the DSM were considering including battered women's condition as a category in the next edition. Her testimony was therefore ruled inadmissible.

In most of the cases that have come to court since then, the issue of methodology and design in studies of BWS has continued to be raised. That is, the reliability and objectivity of the research has remained crucial to courts' considerations (Monahan and Walker, 1994). Do the studies meet the criteria for scientific knowledge? Are their methods objective and reliable? Are the conclusions they generate generally accepted within the field? With courts stressing such qualities, it is not surprising to find that psychologists conducting work on BWS strive to produce results that conform to these expectations. They rely on research scales and inventories thought to be capable of giving 'objective personality information' (Walker, 1990: 105), such as the Minnesota Multiple Personality Inventory (MMPI) which, as 'one of the most used personality tests, particularly for forensic cases' (Walker, 1990: 105), has the particular strength of demonstrating a specific BWS pattern (Rosewater, 1985, 1988). Other popular scales used to measure and assess symptoms include the Attitudes Towards Women Scale, Levenson's locus of control scale, and the CES-Depression scale (Walker, 1984). Measures such as these produce quantitative outcomes which can be used in evaluating the 'fit' of any particular woman in regard to a diagnostic category in the DSM or ICD. By demonstrating the objective basis on which accounts of women's behaviour can be based, they increase the likelihood that evidence of BWS will be accepted by the courts.

The problem is that these approaches fall into the 'measurement trap' (Smith, Smith, and Earp, 1999). In order to examine women's experience through the use of such techniques, it must be conceptualised in a particular way. That conceptualisation has been criticised as being too narrow, based on data sources that are too poor, expectant of inappropriate outcome indicators, and limited by their quantitative nature. Paige Smith and her colleagues (1999) are among those who have called for the adoption of an alternative framework, in which the 'measurement' methodologies are grounded in women's lived experiences, thus providing a more solid basis for policy or programme development. Dutton (1999) has argued that a quantitative, scaling approach does not necessarily have to conflict with a more experiential approach, as long as women's experiences remain the key focus of the work. The aim of both teams is to increase the accuracy with which research findings represent and explain women's experience. Achieving their admittance to court is not useful if they are misrepresentative.

However, as either framework moves toward lived experience, it necessarily moves closer toward subjectivity, for it is exploring individual experience. This move is one with which law, as well as mainstream psychology, will be uncomfortable. If taken seriously, such a shift would require the examination of epistemological assumptions upon which both disciplines are founded. What counts as knowledge, especially expert knowledge? What counts as evidence? How is human behaviour to be measured and classified? On what basis are definitions of 'normality' and 'abnormality' to be derived? Addressing such questions is central to the reconceptualisation of women's experience, but this is a step to which psychology and law are deeply resistant. It is this opposition that leaves battered women and those who wish to represent them more effectively in the courtroom stranded in the 'measurement trap'. Established, objective measures are the current best hope, but this path does not lead to the resolution of the irrational/rational divide. Demonstrating that a pattern is 'objectively real' does not help in deciding how that pattern should be characterised. It can be real and still treated as abnormality. It is that characterisation of battered women's experience that must ultimately be addressed, and this cannot be done through the acquisition of more data.

The advent of BWS testimony has undoubtedly increased the strategic defence options available to battered women charged with murder. They are better able to counter a charge of murder. This is not, however, because a new way of conceiving of their behaviour has been accomplished. It is still largely judged against traditional, objective standards, and even where a replacement of those specific standards has been attempted, the underlying assumptions in which an objective stance is rooted have not been addressed. Supplying increasing amounts of scientific evidence in an effort to shift law's position will not be effective, for it is too easy simply to choose a new term to represent the same old perspective. A different strategy is required in the long term.

Male norm

It has already been observed that the traditional standards are not, as maintained, objective in character. Rather, their nature is masculine. It is because their perspective is not explicitly marked as masculine that the appearance of objectivity can be sustained. The 'reasonable man' is meant to be an objective, gender-neutral concept that incorporates the perspective of all persons. This linguistic ploy is counterfeit, however, as it intertwines masculinity and objectivity so completely that it is almost impossible to disentangle them.

This is apparent in expectations about women's behaviour, based as they are on male perspectives and standards. For example, a common response to reports of domestic abuse is the question, 'why didn't she leave?' or 'why did she go back?' In the 1979 case of *Greig* (discussed in Connelly, 1996: 215; and in Edwards and Halpern, 1991: 96–97) a woman was convicted of culpable homicide after she had stabbed her husband following years of physical abuse and torture. At the appeal, Lord Dunpark said:

> There are various expedients open to a woman submitted to rough treatment by her husband but a license to kill was not one of them. . . . [H]undreds indeed thousands of wives in this country, unfortunately suffer this fate. . . . The remedy of divorce or judicial separation is available to end this torment.
>
> (Cited in Connelly, 1996: 215)

The judge presiding over Sara Thornton's case in 1992 repeated similar sentiments, explicitly advising the jury to consider the fact that Sara Thornton had had 'other alternatives available, like walking out or going upstairs' (*R v Thornton*, 1992: 312).

No one seems to ask 'why didn't *he* leave?' In the 1992 case of Bisla Singh, who argued that his wife's constant nagging caused him to snap and strangle her, the judge commented that Mr Singh had 'suffered through no fault of [his] own' and awarded only a suspended sentence (*The Times*, 30 January 1992, cited in Bandalli, 1995: 402). Roy Geech, who stabbed his wife 23 times with a kitchen knife following his discovery that she was having an affair, was described by his defence counsel as a 'man of gentleness'. The court agreed that he was a 'good man' and gave him a suspended sentence (*The Guardian*, 22 February 1994, cited in

Lees, 1997: 173). When Joseph McGrail kicked his wife to death, the judge in the case awarded a two-year suspended sentence, on the basis that '[t]his lady would have tried the patience of a saint' (*The Independent*, 1 August 1991, cited in Lees, 1997: 172). Lord Dunpark, whose criticism of June Greig was described earlier, thought a discharge sufficient for a man in another case who had killed his wife and his child, on the basis that he had already 'been punished enough' (*Observer Scotland*, 4 March 1990, cited in Edwards and Halpern, 1991: 96). Nothing in these cases prevented the men from leaving before killing their wives. They are not unusual instances; other contemporary cases where men have successfully used the provocation defence to explain why they killed their nagging, insulting, or demanding partners include Blewis (1983), Bandy (1983), Wilkes (1984), and Corlett (1995) (all cited in Edwards, 1996: 373 and 397). The most recent example of such reasoning is the 1999 case of David Hampson (reported in *The Guardian*, 29 October 1999) who killed his wife with a hammer after suffering years of nagging, buried her body in the back garden, and then pretended for two years to family members and governmental agencies that she was still alive. His defence lawyer claimed that he had buried her in the garden because he 'wanted to have her near him', and the judge accepted that 'your wife behaved in a way which was calculated to impact on your mind'. Giving credit to Hampson for his 'frankness' in making a full confession to the police following his arrest, Judge Francis Allen sentenced him to six years' imprisonment. Judicial attitudes of this sort endorse and reinforce law's ingrained male norm, exposing what Wells (1994: 268) has described as the 'lurking double standard'

The introduction of BWS into the courtroom has not served to counter this double standard. It has not been successful in normalising women's actions, as was Walker's hope. If women's actions could be contextualised through BWS testimony, it should by now have become easier for courts (and others) to see how those actions could be classified as self-defence or provocation. However, reliance on BWS testimony undermines the argument that the woman's response is reasonable, precisely because it is based on an account of her mental health. BWS has gained official recognition as a mental disorder; inclusion in the DSM has ensured that. Thus, the killing of an abusive partner cannot now be considered reasonable, for it is logically impossible that the characterisation of reasonableness co-exist with the characterisation of mental disorder. Women must choose between having their behaviour classified as psychologically abnormal, and thus suited to the defence of diminished responsibility, or as psychologically normal, and thus (ill-) suited to the defences of self-defence or provocation. BWS has done little of substance to change women's position within the law.

It must be stressed how far this is from the original intention of the proponents of BWS. Cynthia Gillespie, a legal commentator, echoes Walker's sentiments that it should serve to normalise women's actions.

> [A] defense based on the battered woman syndrome is in no way an insanity defense. This is sometimes misunderstood because the experts who are brought in to testify about the characteristics of battered woman are often

psychologists or psychiatrists, and the term 'syndrome' is often used to describe mental illness.

(Gillespie, 1989: 160)

Martinson *et al.* (1991) and Dutton (1993) are also vigorous supporters of this view, and an anonymous reviewer for one of our early papers on this topic (Zeedyk and Raitt, 1997) argued that we were 'misrepresent[ing] the essence of the BWS theory of self-defense' in our work, for as a 'feminist forensic psychologist who had testified in many BWS cases', she knew

> full well the difference between a BWS argument, which is a pro-woman contextualising of behavior, and what the authors call a 'madness' defense. . . . If BWS is being used as a madness defense in the UK, then it is being misused, and appropriated by the patriarchy in a manner not intended.

Yet it is patently clear that, in practice, a 'BWS defence' *does* operate as a mental health excuse. The earlier discussion of defences demonstrated that diminished responsibility is the most successful of the three possible defences across all jurisdictions. Ahluwalia's appeal was only successful because evidence of her 'major depressive disorder' (*R* v *Ahluwalia*, 1992) could be demonstrated, not because the law had accepted that she was acting in fear for her life. Thornton's appeal was successful not because the court accepted that she had been provoked by years of abuse, but on the basis of the medical evidence describing her 'personality disorder' (*R* v *Thornton*, 1996). The explanation of mental pathology is being used even where a woman's actions do fit the stereotypical male expectations of law. McColgan (1993) cites the case of Janet Gardner, a battered woman who, while being throttled and having her head beaten against the kitchen wall, reached out for a knife and fatally stabbed her partner. This might be thought a classic case of self-defence, but she was sentenced to five years' imprisonment. On appeal, this was reduced to two years' probation after psychiatric evidence was produced to show that she was suffering from severe depressive illness (*The Independent*, 30 October 1992, cited in McColgan, 1993: 515). By substituting a mental health explanation for Gardner's behaviour, the court is effectively saying a battered woman cannot kill for reasonable reasons – only for disordered ones.

It seems sometimes that proponents of BWS wish to have their cake and eat it too. It is not possible for a BWS defence to operate in the way in which it was originally intended, for its inclusion in the DSM now marks it as a mental disorder. It does not matter how proponents would *wish* a BWS defence to operate; what matters is how law *permits* it to be used. Any defence operates only within the boundaries allowed by law. The rules of evidence and procedure control the manner in which a case can be presented, including the type of evidence that law is willing to consider and the discretion available to a judge in admitting (or excluding) such evidence. Our point is that the implicit relation underlies law's position. It is the implicit relation that has reinforced the untenable position in which battered women who kill now find themselves.

Walker and others welcomed the inclusion of BWS within the DSM because it allowed for recognition of the syndrome (Walker, 1984). It was only through such professional endorsement that an alternative description of women's actions would be accepted into court. It was precisely because there were no generally accepted psychological typologies in 1979 that Walker's testimony was ruled inadmissible in the case of Beverly Ibn-Tamas. The cost of portraying women as pathological was considered by proponents as acceptable, given a judicial process that so thoroughly prevented a contextualised appreciation of women's life conditions. Testimony regarding mental dysfunction was the only way a jury would have been provided with a context for the woman's actions. Proponents of BWS encouraged the use of accepted scientific methodologies in relevant research, because that further increased the law's willingness to admit BWS evidence.

This set of circumstances illustrates vividly the implicit relation in operation. Women's behaviour can only be explained through accounts that characterise it as abnormal. BWS has not been successful in re-characterising them as normal. Its inclusion in the DSM has ensured they remain abnormal. And as long as BWS remains in the DSM, it will not be possible to deviate from that position, for psychology has confirmed, through its use of reliable, objective scientific methods, that long-term abuse results in mental disorder. If a battered woman sought to argue that her abuse had not resulted in psychopathology, the prosecution could now very successfully use the DSM classification to counter her arguments, a pattern which has been observed in regard to rape (see Chapter 5).

Moreover, the implicit relation militates against further change. Law is relieved of the need or responsibility of searching any further for an explanation of women's behaviour. If scientific psychology has determined that abused women are indeed irrational and pathological, why would the law need to seek alternative accounts of their behaviour? It is an account that equates with law's historical view of women, and it is one which has now been independently confirmed by science. In short, it is the implicit relation that has helped to ensure that reliance on BWS testimony, optimistically conceived as a way to 'acquaint jurors with [a woman's] specific predicament', has 'metamorphosed into a mental health excuse' (Edwards, 1996: 227). Two decades after the entry of BWS into the courtroom, women's behaviour continues to be evaluated against traditional male norms. The standard binary constructions of gender – active/passive, autonomous/dependent, rational/irrational – remain resolute, having survived the spectre of reconstruction that once threatened in the form of BWS.

Individualism

In her efforts to gain the admittance of BWS into the courtroom, Walker stressed that experts would be able to bring to the court's attention a blend of 'both general social conditioning and the individual's particular behavior' (Walker, 1990: 11). Her task was monumental, and in many respects she and her colleagues have propelled the topic of domestic violence onto centre stage, not only within the legal arena but before society at large. However, they could not have been expected toanticipate the force of the implicit relation in its insistence on evaluating an individual's actions stripped of background or context.

A diagnosis of BWS does not, as we have shown, call attention to the gendered contexts of violence; instead, it speaks to the impaired mental functioning of the individual.[4] This focus is embedded in the general philosophy of the DSM. As discussed in Chapter 3, the introduction of the DSM states emphatically that the mental disorders listed in the DSM '*must* currently be considered a manifestation of a behavioral, psychological, or biological dysfunction in the individual' (DSM, 1994: xxi–xxii, emphasis added). The introductory comments go on to emphasise that 'conflicts that are primarily between the individual and society are [not considered] mental disorders unless the deviance or conflict is a symptom of a dysfunction in the individual' (DSM, 1994: xxii).

A feminist analysis argues that the conflict of domestic abuse is precisely that – a conflict between the individual and society. From this perspective, BWS is hardly a disorder. It is only the individualistic model adopted by psychology and psychiatry that allows BWS to be classified as a mental disorder in the DSM.

That individualistic model is very convenient for law. It does not currently seek to understand how the context of battered women's lives frame their actions and their perceptions. Detailed evidence of Ahluwalia's ten years of abuse was presented during her trial. However, when the judge summed up for the jury those issues which they should include in their considerations, that abuse was not considered relevant. The judge's direction to the jury stated:

> The only characteristics of the defendant about which you know specifically that might be relevant are that she is an Asian woman, married, incidentally to an Asian man, the deceased, living in this country.
>
> (*R* v *Ahluwalia* 1992: 897)

The legal process decontextualised Ahluwalia's actions, eliminating the very element which gave her behaviour meaning. It was not she who could decide the characteristics that were relevant and those that were not; this is a discretion that the law reserves for itself. As part of the basis for her appeal, it was argued by her lawyers that the context and effects of abuse should be taken into account. However, that argument was rejected by the court, and the only ground of appeal accepted was the new evidence of her psychiatric illness.

> [Counsel's] argument [regarding the grounds of provocation] amounted in reality to an invitation to this court to change the law. We are bound by the previous decisions of this court . . . unless we are convinced that they were wholly wrong. Where a particular principle of law has been reaffirmed so many times and applied so generally over such a long period, it must be a matter for Parliament to consider any change. There are important considerations of public policy which would be involved should provocation be redefined so as possibly to blur the distinction between sudden loss of self-control and deliberate retribution.
>
> (*R* v *Ahluwalia*, 1992: 896)

These comments demonstrate the power of precedent in a common law legal system, for even when the prejudicial effect of legal principles is brought to the attention of judges, they are prevented from making changes.

It is ironic that the courts' acceptance of the notion of the 'disordered individual' in cases of domestic abuse has been celebrated across so many jurisdictions as a victory, given how far it is from the original vision fostered by proponents of BWS. It is now clear just how much the theory and the practice of a BWS defence differ. It simply has not produced the platform from which courts would come to view women's actions as 'reasonable rather than aberrant' (Schuller and Vidmar, 1992: 277). The central problem facing women is that courts strenuously endeavour to decontextualise behaviour, seeking to evaluate it against generalised, objective standards. In practice, this is impossible, for the meaning of behaviour necessarily lies in its relation to context. When context is not considered, the meaning of a behaviour appears to lie within the behaviour itself, or at least within the person who generated it. Legal doctrines are of course replete with contexts, but they are the contexts of men's experience, not women's experience. When men's and women's contexts are in conflict, it is the meaning of women's actions that will appear aberrant. This aberrance results from law's failure to acknowledge the contextual nature of its reasoning and to recognise those contexts as gendered. Of course women's experiences come to seem odd and misshapen, the result of forcing them into a male mould that they do not fit. The masculine nature of the mould, of law's perspective, is not marked as such. It is instead treated as if it were devoid of context: objective. It is this complicated medley of objectivity, male normative standards, and individualism, that is the implicit relation.

Conclusion

In some ways, the admission of BWS into courtrooms is an achievement that works in women's favour. It acknowledges the existence of domestic violence and serves to challenge the myths and stereotypes that often guide jurors' reasoning. It gives lawyers a basis on which to argue mitigating circumstances, thus preventing women from serving long prison sentences. But these are moderate successes. Expert testimony on BWS has not been successful in altering the fundamental situation in which battered women who kill their partners find themselves. The implicit relation has played a key role in this lethargy.

Women's actions have been made comprehensible by virtue of their disordered psychological origin. This is an entirely different interpretation from that given to actions explained through a defence of provocation or self-defence. In accepting these defences under traditional male circumstances, the law is indicating that a killing is regrettable but that it falls within the bounds of reasonable behaviour. Women's actions, as explained via BWS evidence, are unreasonable, abnormal, the result of mental malady. Men's actions can be justified; women's actions must be excused. The effect is to produce another stereotype – that of the woman who, once battered, inevitably becomes mentally disordered.

Many commentators (e.g. Ewing, 1987; Fox, 1995; McColgan, 1993; Schneider, 1980) have argued that it is futile to use BWS to try to fit women's experience into the existing law. They argue that a more effective strategy is to construct new defences which are not based on male norms, as would be accomplished, for example, by expanding or changing the definitions of self-defence and provocation. We would endorse that view, for the use of BWS will always characterise women's actions as disordered as long as it remains within the DSM. It will be extremely hard to move beyond that characterisation, for rules of evidence such as general acceptance force explanations to stay within established boundaries. Expectations of 'good practice' further reinforce the stagnation; Nicolson and Sanghvi (1993) predict, for example, that defence lawyers will develop a preference for BWS experts who are willing to diagnose their female clients as psychologically damaged, because a failure to do otherwise might decrease their chances of winning the case and thereby constitute a breach of their duty to their clients.

It is possible that an educative approach to the problem could be effective. It is possible for expert testimony from psychologists to highlight the effects of violence without characterising them as mental disorder. This approach is in keeping with the admission of social framework data in other domains (Colman, 1991; Fiske *et al.*, 1991; Loftus, 1991; Monahan and Walker, 1988), and it is a possibility we explore in greater depth in Chapter 8. Unfortunately, psychology's embrace of BWS hampers this possibility. If both psychology and law believe that the explanations offered by scientific investigations of human experience – in this case women's reactions to abuse – are objective and reliable, why should either seek other explanations? In working together, they reinforce each other's perspectives, and the possibility of further change is impeded. Real change can only result as a result of serious critical self-reflection on the part of each discipline. Until that happens, there is little chance of substantial change on women's behalf.

In the meantime, the implicit relation continues to operate powerfully and invidiously. It continues the long tradition of marginalising women by invoking explanations of madness (Chesler, 1972; Ussher, 1991). Although BWS may have achieved laudable short-term goals for some individual women, it is not helpful to the long-term interests of women as a group. It preserves institutional bias towards the male norm, nourished in a guise of scientific objectivity.

5   Rape Trauma Syndrome

Definitions belong . . . to the definers – not the defined.

Toni Morrison[1]

In this chapter we consider the operation of the implicit relation in regard to rape.[2] We will give particular attention to the growing practice of admitting evidence on Rape Trauma Syndrome in cases of rape. A more recent addition than Battered Woman's Syndrome to the array of syndrome diagnoses within the psychological and psychiatric fields, Rape Trauma Syndrome has begun to be admitted for the same general purpose: to assist judges and/or juries in making sense of a woman's actions. Unlike cases of women who kill abusive partners, and who are thus the perpetrators of the crime, in cases of rape, the woman will be the victim[3] of the crime. It is significant that the implicit relation governs the way that scientific evidence of a psychological syndrome is admitted under both sets of circumstances.

Incidence of rape

Rape is a depressingly common event in women's lives. The figures publicised in reports differ considerably, with estimates indicating that between 5% and 45% of women are raped at some point during their lives. For example, Koss, Gidycz, and Wisniewski (1987) surveyed 3187 women in the United States and found that 42% of them reported an experience which met the legal definition of rape. Similarly, interviews conducted by Russell (1984) with 930 women revealed that 44% had experienced at least one completed or attempted rape. Studies in the UK also reveal high levels of prevalence. A 1985 study carried out in London involving 1236 respondents indicated that 17% of the women had been raped, 20% had suffered attempted rape, and 31% had been sexually assaulted (Hall, 1985).

There are, of course, numerous problems in gathering information about the frequency of rape. Whose statistics should be used: those produced by the police, the government, rape crisis centres, or researchers? Each source is likely to arrive at different figures. Governmental officials can only draw together information about the instances of rape that have been reported to official agencies such as the police. The police can only provide information about those rapes which are reported to them; the majority of rapes are not. Koss and her colleagues (1987) found that only 5% of the women in their sample who had experienced rape had reported it to the police. Russell (1984) also found that only 7% of her sample had contacted the police. The figures regarding the frequency of rape emerging from support agencies, such as Victim Support and Rape Crisis, tend to be substantially larger than those reported by official agencies. The discrepancy may lie in the fact that women are much more likely to contact support centres. However, even these figures only reveal the number of women who contact such centres, and women who are raped may not choose to do so. Thus, the research studies in which a large sample of women are interviewed, such as those discussed above, may produce the most accurate figures.

Several reasons have been offered for the low level of reporting of rape, including embarrassment, fear of reprisal, self-blame, and panic. Most importantly, the treatment of rape victims in the criminal justice system is notorious, with many women so appalled at police and court procedures that they describe the judicial response to rape as worse than the rape itself (Adler, 1987; Edwards, 1996; Estrich, 1987; Lees, 1996; Temkin, 1987). Measures have been taken to improve the reception given to rape complainants (Burman and Lloyd, 1993), such as instituting special 'rape suites' at police stations for interviewing victims and making available specially trained police officers and female medical officers. However, it is clear that significant barriers remain in place to inhibit women from reporting rape, as more and more women recount their unpleasant experiences within the system and by the agencies of the system.

Statistics make it clear that, for perpetrators, rape is a 'low risk, high reward crime' (Scully, 1986). In Scotland, while the numbers of recorded rapes between 1986 and 1995 rose by 61.7%, the proportion of those prosecuted reduced significantly (Scottish Office, 1995, 1996, 1997). Thus, in 1995, only 12.1% of recorded rapes were prosecuted, and only 7.9% of rapes recorded resulted in a conviction. In England and Wales, Home Office statistics (1995) reveal that despite an almost threefold increase in the number of cases of rape recorded by the police between 1985 and 1995, the percentage of convictions for rape has fallen by more than 50% (from 24.4% of all recorded rapes in 1985 to 11.7% of all recorded rapes in 1995). UK figures produced in 1996 by Victim Support were more encouraging, as of 646 rapes where the outcome was known, the conviction rate was 19%. However, this is still a dismal outcome.

Directly comparable figures for the US are difficult to obtain. This is because the statistics for rape convictions are calculated on very different bases across the various jurisdictions in the US. Bienen (1983a) estimated that they were between 2% and 5% nationwide. In Estrich's (1986) review of the literature, rather higher figures for conviction rates in individual states are cited. They ranged from 34% (for California) to 20% (for Washington DC). Her comments (p. 1170) that such low figures 'may appear shocking to some' are ironic, given that they are the best of all the conviction rates reported here.

One of the most common complaints voiced by rape victims is the extent to which their character is attacked when they are giving evidence from the witness box about the circumstances of the rape they have suffered (Kelly, 1988; Temkin, 1987). Given that research demonstrates clearly that the majority of rapes are perpetrated by a man whom the woman knows, and in the light of DNA evidence, with its capacity to corroborate the identity of the alleged perpetrator, the majority of men accused of rape do not now deny that sexual intercourse occurred. Instead, their defence is that the woman consented (Chambers and Millar, 1983; Koss, Gidycz, and Wisniewski, 1987; Russell, 1984; for discussion see Edwards, 1996). A favoured tactic of defence lawyers trying to convince a jury that a woman is likely to have consented to sex is to demonstrate that she is sexually experienced, or even promiscuous or engaged in prostitution (Lees, 1996). Not surprisingly, women who are cross-examined on their sexual past often feel degraded and that they are the ones who are 'on trial', rather than the alleged rapist.

To combat such defence tactics, laws known as 'rape shield laws' have been enacted in many jurisdictions to prevent unnecessarily intrusive questioning into a woman's sexual history. These laws are intended to preclude defence lawyers from cross-examining a woman with questions about whether she has had an abortion, her sexual preferences, her previous sexual partners, or her choice in underwear, none of which are usually germane to the issue of whether or not a woman was raped. However, rape shield laws have not always proven effective, for there is a high rate of success for applications to waive the protection given by these provisions. In a 1987 study at the Old Bailey in London, Adler (1987) found that 66% of applications to lead sexual history evidence were granted, and Brown, Burman, and Jamieson (1993) discovered a similar level of success for waivers in Scotland. On average, between 1987 and 1990, 85% of applications were granted. Even more worryingly, Brown's team found that in 24% of cases, sexual history evidence was led by the defence despite there being no formal application to the judge for a waiver. It is abundantly clear that, as a matter of course in the UK, prosecutors and judges are lax about enforcing rape shield legislation (Brown, Burman, and Jamieson, 1993; Temkin, 1993). In the US, the removal of rape shield legislation is also at the discretion of the judge if the defence seek to have it waived. Estrich (1987) is among those who has criticised it for failing to deliver protection to complainants, especially since no evidence has been produced to suggest that the experiences of rape victims in US courts has been improved by the existence of such legislation.

Further legislative changes relating to the treatment of rape have been introduced through the abolition of the marital rape exemption (Harrison, 1991; Williams, 1992). Until remarkably recently there was no such concept as rape within marriage. By virtue of the marriage vow, a woman was deemed to have given permanent consent to sexual intercourse and bound herself to the provision of sexual services for the duration of the marriage. As a result of pressure from feminist and other campaigning bodies, during the 1970s some US states began to abolish this obligation on wives, and the law recognised that a man could indeed be charged with the rape of his wife (Caringella-MacDonald, 1991). Similar changes occurred in Scotland in 1989 (*Stallard* v *HMA*) and in England in 1991 (*R* v *R*).

Notwithstanding legislative change, the focus in societal and legal discourse of rape still 'falsely remains on the victim as an instigator of most rapes' (Allison and Wrightsman, 1993: 2) and the acknowledgement that rape can occur within marriage provides no guarantee that prosecutions will be any more common (Bienen, 1983b; Caringella-MacDonald, 1988). Well-established social myths proclaim that women are in part responsible for rape when they wear the wrong clothes, walk in the wrong neighbourhoods, go to the wrong parties, and just generally project the 'wrong' message. In fact, any activity demonstrative of a free and independent lifestyle tends to be suggestive of the sort of woman who knowingly (and therefore by choice) puts herself at risk of rape. Such prevalent societal myths inevitably influence judges, prosecutors, defence lawyers, and jury members. For example, Donald Findlay, a leading Scots criminal lawyer, was recently willing to risk 'sound[ing] harsh' when he stated unequivocally that 'women have to have a certain degree of responsibility in this . . . [when] she invites a total stranger back to her home' (*Daily Mail*, 10 November 1998). In a 1981 case tried at the Old Bailey, Judge Wild declared that:

> Women who say no do not always mean no. It is not just a question of how she says it, how she shows and makes it clear. If she doesn't want it she only has to keep her legs shut and she would not get it without force and then there would be the marks of force being used.
>
> (cited in Kennedy, 1993: 111)

In a 1995 case, Judge David Griffiths was reported as saying in Winchester Crown Court to a man convicted of indecent assault, 'If you had had the courage and good manners to say you were sorry and sent a bunch of flowers, all would have been forgiven' (*Daily Telegraph*, 6 October 1995). Attitudes such as this belittle women's experience of sexual assault, often using romantic images to transform rape from a crime of violence to a crime of miscommunication. Perhaps most astonishing in recent times was the judgement issued in February 1999 by the Supreme Court in Italy who quashed a 45-year-old driving instructor's conviction for rape of an 18-year-old pupil on the basis that she was wearing tight jeans. Their reasoning was that common experience demonstrated that it was practically impossible even partially to remove a pair of jeans 'without the effective co-operation of the person wearing them' (*The Guardian*, 12 February 1999).[4]

It is against this background of low reporting rates, falling conviction rates, failed legislative reform, and enduring acceptance of rape mythology that attempts have been made to introduce new kinds of evidence into rape trials in order to redress the balance currently so tipped in favour of defendants. Such evidence concentrates on the psychological response of 'typical rape victims' and involves expert testimony on Rape Trauma Syndrome.

Rape Trauma Syndrome

In the 1970s professionals working with victims of sexual assault began to document the types of reactions and behaviours exhibited by women who had been raped. In 1974 Burgess and Holmstrom identified a constellation of reactions which they labelled Rape Trauma Syndrome (RTS). Since 1980, the syndrome has been classified as an anxiety disorder in the *Diagnostic and Statistical Manual* (DSM). Like Battered Woman's Syndrome, RTS is a sub-category of Post-Traumatic Stress Disorder (PTSD) and comprises characteristic symptoms following exposure to an extreme traumatic stressor 'involving direct personal experience of an event that involves actual or threatened death or serious injury, or other threat to one's physical integrity' (DSM, 1994: 424).

Burgess and Holmstrom described RTS as usually conforming to a two-phase reaction.

> The first is the acute phase. This is the period in which there is a great deal of disorganization in the woman's lifestyle as a result of the rape. Physical symptoms are especially noticeable, and one prominent feeling noted is fear. The second phase begins when the woman begins to reorganize her lifestyle.
> (Burgess and Holmstrom, 1974: 982)

They pointed out that reactions to rape vary greatly. In the immediate hours following a rape, a woman may experience a wide range of emotions, including shock, disbelief, anger, fear, and anxiety, while in the later aftermath, a woman's feelings might range from fear, humiliation, and embarrassment, to anger, revenge, and self-blame. Not every woman experiences the same symptoms in the same sequence, although very few show a complete absence of symptoms. Women's frequent experience of rape as life-threatening, even if no overt threats are uttered, adds to the likelihood of trauma. Thus, RTS was regarded as valuable for its clinical implications, in particular for its assistance in developing a model of crisis intervention.

However, as we have already discussed, many women do not report the rape, either to police or to other officials. They are more likely to seek support from an informal agency that can offer crisis intervention, such as Victim Support or Rape Crisis. Such agencies do not generally offer clinical diagnosis, nor do women go to them for that purpose. Indeed, one of the reasons women may not seek help from a clinical professional such as a psychotherapist or psychiatrist is that they do not define the rape – or their reaction to it – as a clinical problem. They may seek therapeutic help in recovering, but this differs from seeking a clinically diagnostic label. A diagnosis of RTS risks victimisation, and women who have been raped have already been victimised enough. Perhaps instinctively, women resist their own medicalisation. Taking back control of their lives, a common reaction in the long-term aftermath of rape (Hall, 1985), is arguably more affirming. One potentially powerful route to doing this is for a woman to testify in court in support of the prosecution of her alleged attacker.[5]

RTS in the courtroom

In the mid-1980s RTS began to receive attention for its evidential value in rape trials (Bristow, 1984; Lauderdale, 1984; Murphy, 1992). It can serve two distinct purposes: to educate judges and juries about typical reactions to rape, and to bolster the evidence of a complainant, providing some degree of corroboration that the alleged attack occurred. With regard to education, expert testimony on RTS is introduced to provide the jury with background information regarding typical reactions to rape. It functions as social framework data (Walker and Monahan, 1987, 1988, 1994) and can be particularly valuable as an antidote to the widespread mythology that affects jurors' perceptions of the crime, including the typical circumstances within which rape occurs and the 'type' of woman who is raped. This information is intended to enable jurors to make a more informed decision concerning the credibility and reliability of the victim's account.

The need for such information to counter 'the influence of extraevidential bias' (Tetreault, 1989: 244) has been well documented (Feild and Bienen, 1980; Gerbasi, Zuckerman, and Reis, 1977). For example, it is not at all uncommon for women to delay in reporting a rape or to remove many traces of forensic evidence through vigorous showering and bathing, although jurors often believe that a time lapse or systematic cleansing weakens the credibility of a complaint. Research has revealed a high level of juror confusion, misinformation and misconception in regard to women's typical behaviour in relation to rape (Borgida and Brekke, 1985). LaFree and colleagues, conducting post-trial interviews with jurors regarding their perceptions of rape and their decision-making processes in trials, reported that even where there was explicit evidence that the victim had been forced to submit to intercourse, such as evidence of physical injury or the use of weapons, these factors did not significantly affect the verdict. Rather, jurors were primarily influenced by the moral character of the victims.

> [Jurors] were less likely to believe in a defendant's guilt when the victim had reportedly engaged in sex outside marriage, drank or used drugs, or had been acquainted with the defendant – however briefly – prior to the alleged assault.
> (LaFree, Reskin, and Visher, 1985: 397)

Even where a woman has suffered extreme violence, she risks having her experience denigrated in court. For example, Jill Saward, who was raped, buggered, and sodomised at knifepoint by three men, had her experience described by the judge, Sir John Leonard, as 'not being that great' (*Scotland on Sunday*, 19 February 1987). Such judicial and juror misconceptions can be challenged by the introduction of RTS evidence. Indeed, studies using mock jury trials to explore jurors' perceptions have revealed that admitting expert testimony of RTS leads jurors to be more likely to find the defendant guilty and to recommend harsher sentences (Tetreault, 1989).

With regard to the second purpose of admitting RTS evidence, corroboration, the rationale is that if evidence can be led showing that a woman complainant has exhibited symptoms of RTS, this should help to corroborate her allegations and/or her credibility. Complainants of rape face scepticism and doubt, the origins of which can be found in the writings of the seventeenth-century English jurist, Sir Matthew Hale, who said: 'it must be remembered, that [rape] is an accusation easily to be made and hard to be proved, and harder to be defended by the party accused, tho' never so innocent' (Hale, 1678, cited in Graycar and Morgan, 1990: 339). Graycar and Morgan (1990) point out that such attitudes die hard, for the tenor of Hale's statement was reiterated in the 1978 edition of *Textbook of Criminal Law*, by Glanville Williams, an author of major influence in the twentieth century. By the time the second edition was published in 1983, Williams's comments had been diluted to: '[s]ome (we do not know how many) complaints of rape are false, since the woman in fact consented' (Williams, 1983: 238). It might be noted that Williams was not the most liberal of lawyers and was unconvinced about the merits of removing the marital rape exemption, arguing that 'good reasons can be found for giving a first offence of rape within marriage some other legal name than "rape"' (Williams, 1992: 11). Like many others in the judicial system, Williams appears to have overlooked or disbelieved the empirical evidence showing that the rate of false complaints of rape (i.e. 2%) is no different from that of other crimes (Adler, 1987; Lees, 1996; Temkin, 1987).

The odds of proving rape are stacked against women. Sexual assaults usually take place in private. There are rarely eyewitnesses, and in the absence of significant physical injury, there is little to distinguish rape from consensual intercourse, especially if the parties are known to each other and the complainant has little independent evidence to support her assertion that she did not consent. In these situations, symptoms of RTS serve as a form of circumstantial evidence to bolster the woman's version of events and therefore her credibility. This is demonstrated very well in the 1982 Kansas case of *State* v *Marks*, which was the first US case to admit expert testimony on RTS. It was considered a landmark decision because it recognised RTS as reliable, admissible evidence. Marks had met his victim at a private club, had a couple of drinks with her, and then they had gone back to his house, where the sexual assaults had taken place. Marks admitted that sexual acts had taken place but claimed that they were consensual. This was a classic case of 'his word against hers', although there was forensic evidence of a laceration near the woman's vagina which could have supported her version of events. Crucially, the court was willing to admit the testimony of Dr Herbert Modlin, a neurologist with expertise in the field of forensic psychiatry. Dr Modlin testified about the diagnosis and treatment of PTSD, drawing attention to rape as one type of traumatic event. In particular, he stressed the symptoms of RTS, including fear of offender retaliation, fear of being alone, sleep disturbance, and a sense of shame. On the basis of his examination of the victim, Dr Modlin testified that she was suffering from the 'disorder' known as RTS. Marks was convicted of rape and aggravated sodomy. Marks appealed against his conviction on the basis that RTS should be inadmissible in a case where consent was the defence. His legal team argued that such evidence invades the province of the jury, in that it attempts to substitute an expert's opinion for the considered view of the jurors. The Supreme Court of Kansas ruled, however, that 'if the presence of rape trauma syndrome is detectable and reliable', it constituted evidence that a forcible assault did take place and was thus relevant to rebut the argument that sexual intercourse was consensual. Evidence concerning RTS would function, they indicated, like any other evidence, 'with the expert subject to cross-examination and the jury left to determine its weight' (p. 1299). On the basis of the literature available on RTS, the court judged the diagnosis to be an issue which had been generally accepted within its scientific field. Thus, it was ruled admissible and Marks's conviction upheld.

Since 1982 there has been a plethora of US cases which have ruled on the admissibility of RTS, although there is considerable inconsistency in judicial reasoning and decisions. In keeping with the decision in *Marks*, expert testimony was allowed in the California civil case of *Delia S* v *Torres* (1982), the court holding in regard to RTS that: (a) the subject matter was not within the common knowledge of the jury; (b) the qualifications of the expert, a clinical social worker with experience of rape crisis centres, were acceptable; and (c) the testimony relating to the common reactions of rape victims was relevant in so far as it showed the complainant's behaviour was consistent with such reactions (cited in Frazier and Borgida, 1985: 987). In *People* v *Reid* (1984) the court allowed RTS testimony on the basis that an expert could 'express an opinion that the complainant suffers from [RTS] but cannot testify as to whether she or he *believes* the complainant' (cited in Frazier and Borgida, 1985: 988, emphasis in original).

Decisions that run contrary to *Marks*, and reject the admission of RTS, include *State* v *Saldana*, a 1982 Minnesota case. Saldana was convicted of criminal sexual conduct. It was agreed he was known to his victim, Martha Fuller. Unsurprisingly therefore, like Marks, Saldana did not deny that the intercourse had occurred, but claimed that it was consensual. Lynn Dreyer, director of the local Victim Assistance Program, testified about the stages of recovery that a rape victim typically goes through (i.e. RTS) and stated that, on the basis of her ten-week period of counselling with Fuller, she believed that Fuller had not fantasised or 'made up' the attack, but that she was the victim of a sexual assault. The Supreme Court was asked to rule on whether or not the decision to admit Dreyer's testimony was proper. Their decision was that it was not. They considered that RTS had not yet reached a level of reliability and accuracy that assisted the jury in evaluating the facts in the case and that its admission would therefore add confusion rather than clarity. Moreover, they considered that suggesting that a rape had occurred, on the basis that the complainant exhibited some of the symptoms of RTS, was 'of no help to the jury and produces an extreme danger of unfair prejudice' (Justice Scott, *State* v *Saldana*, 1982: 229). Thus, they reversed the conviction and the case was remanded for a new trial. At the retrial RTS evidence was not admitted and Saldana was acquitted.

In *State* v *Taylor* (1984) the Supreme Court of Missouri also ruled expert evidence of RTS inadmissible. The scientific status of the evidence was challenged, and the court held that the evidence carried too great a prejudicial effect. In *People* v *Bledsoe* (1984) the California Supreme Court ruled against RTS evidence where used to prove a rape had occurred, though it acknowledged such evidence might be acceptable for the purpose of educating the jury (Frazier and Borgida, 1985: 987).

Since the 1980s, the rate of recording of cases concerning RTS in the official US law reports has slowed considerably. This appears to be because the issue of its reliability has been settled. For example, in *State* v *Hines* (1997: 784), the court observed that

> [t]he State does not dispute that the phenomenon of PTSD is generally accepted within the field of psychology and consequently has sufficient reliability to satisfy the . . . test of admissibility identified in [the case of] *Kelly.*

Searches of legal databases in 1999 for RTS cases reveal that, where cases containing a reference to RTS are reported, it tends to be for a reason marginal to the central issues in the case. Overall, this shift suggests that in general both psychology and law now consider the diagnosis to be a reliable, generally accepted, scientific phenomenon (but see Jonakait, 1994, and our discussion in Chapter 2 for a contrasting view).

In the UK there have to date been relatively few reported cases that deal directly with the admissibility of expert RTS testimony. Two recent cases are of most relevance. The first of these (*R* v *T*, 1990) concerned a 23-year-old woman who was charged with robbery. At the time of her arrest she was described as 'passive and indifferent', and only subsequently did it emerge that she had been violently raped three days prior to her arrest. Psychiatric evidence indicated that she was suffering from PTSD and, at the time of the robbery, had entered 'a dissociative state' such that the offence had been committed during 'a psychogenic fugue and [thus] she was not acting with a conscious mind or will' (pp. 256–257). The court held that this was the first time in which the defence of non-insane automatism (see Chapter 6 for a discussion of this defence) was allowed to be used on the basis of a rape (and the pathological mental state which followed it). They noted that it still remained a matter for the jury to decide whether or not the evidence supported her claims regarding that defence.

The second of these cases concerned the granting of refugee status. In *R* v *Secretary of State for the Home Department ex parte Ejon* (1997), an appeal was made on behalf of Molly Ejon, a Ugandan refugee who had been refused political asylum in the UK. The appeal was based on the grounds that material information relating to her experience of kidnap and multiple rape had not been available to the Secretary of State when he decided to reject her asylum application, and that had such information been available her application would have been determined differently. It was claimed that the information had been unavailable because Ms Ejon suffered from RTS arising from the rapes and had not been able to disclose her experiences for some considerable time afterward. The Secretary of State, on behalf of the British government, opposed the appeal, arguing that despite the medical evidence of perineal scarring consistent with very violent sexual abuse, it was not accepted that this gave rise in Ms Ejon to a well-founded fear of persecution meriting political asylum. Additionally, government counsel argued that the failure of Ms Ejon to provide details of the multiple rapes at earlier stages in her asylum application indicated that her accounts were inconsistent and not credible. The court upheld the appeal, preferring the arguments of Ms Ejon's lawyers that severe RTS prevented her from earlier disclosure.[6]

The limited presence of RTS in the UK courts is not surprising, in that this is in keeping with the general reluctance in the UK jurisdictions to admit expert psychological and psychiatric testimony (see Chapter 2). The fact that it has been admitted so far only as part of a defence, where the woman is accused of a crime (in contrast to the US where it is used mostly in relation to a woman's role as witness), is arguably a reflection of that resistance, for the pressure to admit it under such circumstances will be greatest. It is, however, only a matter of time before RTS begins to play a stronger role in UK decisions, given that UK trends tend to follow US trends. The increased commitment professed by the UK Labour Government (elected in 1998) and the Scottish Parliament (established in 1999) to improving the treatment of witnesses is also likely to encourage a shift in this direction. We fully expect that RTS will, before long, come to be used in the UK in the more expansive capacity that it has played in the US and other countries: as applicable to women in their legal roles as witnesses, victims, and defendants.

Thus, it is useful to summarise the US position by noting that the available caselaw has tended to resist admitting expert testimony on RTS in a corroborative role, because it is seen as being unfairly prejudicial to the defendant. The decisions in *State* v *Saldana* and *People* v *Bledsoe* are good examples of this reasoning. Expert testimony is more likely to be admitted when confined to the role of educating the jury. This was the subtext in *People* v *Bledsoe* and has also been seen in other cases such as *People* v *Reid* (1984) and *Henson* v *State* (1989).[7] Expert testimony on RTS clearly presents the court with a conflict of interests. There is a need to weigh the interests of a fair trial for the defendant against the victim's difficulties in producing corroboration in a crime generally committed in private. Ironically, RTS tends to be excluded in its corroborative capacity precisely because it is so convincing. It is more acceptable to courts when it is used in a general (less threatening) sense to bolster the victim's story and thus, indirectly, her credibility. As Frazier and Borgida (1985: 991) have observed, 'there is a very fine line, psychologically, between corroborating and bolstering testimony in this context'.

The implicit relation

The emergence of RTS in the courtroom reveals the implicit relation at work. The difficulties faced by women complainants in the criminal justice process have naturally made those concerned about problems in the prosecution of rape cases attentive to any strategies that might enhance the success rate of prosecutions. The use of evidence on RTS is an enticing possibility, for it appears to counter problems inherent in the rule of corroboration and the difficulty of demonstrating lack of consent. However, the strategy of introducing RTS evidence is successful only to the extent that the implicit relation allows it to be, for it harbours the three key characteristics we have identified. Ultimately, these factors militate against women's interests, and judicial processes are not altered in the fundamental sense that reformers would wish.

Objectivity

The veneration of objectivity can be observed in two aspects of the way that rape cases are handled by the legal system: in the legal definition of rape and in the type of evidence that is considered to be acceptable proof of non-consent. Psychology is able to make its contribution to the implicit relation by providing accounts of RTS that are based on accepted scientific methodology and which meet the courts' demands for objectivity.

At the centre of any incident of rape lies the issue of definition. What constitutes rape? Who should make that determination? What if opinions among individuals, groups, agencies, and official institutions differ? The definition adopted in most legal systems is penetration of the vagina by the penis without the woman's consent. In some jurisdictions, such as England and Wales, the definition has recently been extended so that rape now includes penetration of the anus by the penis (hence widening the scope of the crime to include male victims), but other jurisdictions, such as Scotland, confine rape to vaginal penetration. None of the UK jurisdictions classifies penetration other than by the male sexual organ as 'rape'. Thus, assaults in which bottles, broomsticks, knives, or other implements are used to penetrate any of the woman's orifices do not constitute rape, but are classified as sexual or indecent assault. (For a comparative discussion of definitions within the UK jurisdictions, see Ferguson, 1993.)

In the US various definitions of rape apply in the separate states, but fundamentally rape is the crime of sexual intercourse without the consent of the victim (for discussion see Muehlenhard *et al.*, 1992). It is acknowledged that consent is vitiated if there is force or threat of force. Since the 1970s most states in the US and the federal government have amended their rape laws to broaden the definition of rape (Largen, 1988), extending the offence to include anal as well as vaginal penetration and to include penetration by either objects or the penis (which now makes it possible for women to commit rape). The primary focus remains, nevertheless, on penetration of the vagina, usually by the man's penis.

The definition of penetration by the penis has generally been seen as unproblematic, in that it offers a singular, precise, and ultimately objective denotation of the act. The law demands such objectivity in determining the standard against which actions are to be evaluated. However, the problem is that this narrow, linear standard reflects only one possible perspective on rape. It is formulated as a physical assault; the emotional terror which is part of a woman's experience of rape is disregarded. The possibility that a sexual assault by an instrument other than a penis could cause equal or greater harm to a woman is overlooked. The degradation, humiliation, and powerlessness inflicted upon the woman is invalidated. In effect, a woman's subjective experience of the invasion of her body and integrity is marginal to law's objective definition of rape.

Law also demands objectivity through its preference for tangible evidence in the proof of rape. Given that penetration of the vagina by the penis constitutes the core of both consensual and non-consensual sex, the issue of consent becomes the pivotal issue in legal considerations of rape (MacKinnon, 1987). In order to prove a case of rape, the law demands to see evidence that no consent was given. For this purpose the law seeks tangible evidence: torn clothing, cuts, bruises, bodily fluids. A woman's verbal assertion that consent was not given is rarely sufficient, for if there is no visible damage, the law asks, how is the reliability of her statement to be judged? It is merely her subjective account of the act. Tangible evidence is preferred because it is observable, measurable, concrete, and ultimately perceived as objective.

Evidence of RTS is intended to assist in challenging both of these factors. If evidence of a woman's emotional experience of rape is introduced into the case, some insight is offered as to how rape can be characterised in other than strictly physical terms. One of the most distressing aspects of the trial process for women is the concentration on 'real' evidence. Lees has reported that 'the majority of women found their experiences in court humiliating and distressing', with a common complaint being that 'they were not allowed to explain fully what had happened to them, or how they *felt* during the rape' (Lees, 1996: 31, emphasis in original). Because feelings are regarded as subjective, not objective, they are typically deemed irrelevant to law's purpose (Matoesian, 1993, 1995). However, RTS begins to provide a way in which women's feelings can be introduced into the courtroom. Indeed, they serve as a type of 'circumstantial evidence' that the alleged crime in fact took place. Rape, for all the reasons discussed above, is often incapable of producing 'observable, measurable, concrete and objective' evidence. If a woman's fears lead her, sensibly, to decide not to fight back against the threat of violence (whether implied or made explicit), there may be few signs of physical damage.

The difficulty in obtaining objective evidence has fuelled enthusiasm for admitting evidence on RTS, for evidence of psychological damage may corroborate the woman's allegations that she has been raped. At its most basic, the reasoning is that if a woman claims she has been raped, and then behaves in a way that exemplifies the typical behaviour and emotional reactions of women suffering from RTS, it is highly suggestive of the veracity of her allegation that she has indeed been raped. A key problem with this reasoning, however, is that those feelings are characterised as disordered, increasing the risk that any psychological damage resulting from the rape will be used against the woman, perhaps to suggest that she had a subsisting mental instability, that she 'gave off the wrong signals', or was especially vulnerable to misinterpretation of the man's intentions.

Psychology has reinforced this view, for it affirms that women's reactions to rape are indeed pathological. This is an inherent consequence of the acceptance of RTS into the DSM, given the editors' emphasis that 'each of the mental *disorders* included in the manual 'must currently be considered a manifestation of . . . *dysfunction* in the individual' (DSM, 1994: xxi–xxii, emphasis added). Moreover, the 'illness' has been discovered through the use of scientific, objective methods. 'Detailed interviews, questionnaires . . . structured observations of rape victims' behavior, cognitions and perceptions . . . [and] objective psychological inventories or scales' have been used to mirror the methodologies used in the assessment of Battered Woman's Syndrome, and to determine the presence of Rape Trauma

Syndrome (Bristow, 1984: 277). As Bristow explains, the results of these structured observations and inventories form the basis of expert opinion and accord it 'scientific respectability' (Bristow, 1984: 277). The general acceptance of these methods within the field of psychology is crucial to law: because they represent standardised, objective psychological science, they have become acceptable to the courts.

This is the power of the implicit relation. Psychology does not encourage law to examine its assumptions about women and about rape, but instead reinforces pre-existing views. Correspondingly, law rewards psychology for consistency and certainty in its analysis of women's behaviour, and particularly for its successful application of scientific methodology to this problem. Encouraged in its use of objective methods, psychology is relieved of the need to look again at its own presumptions. This has led to calls for even greater use of objective methods, involving studies that are 'methodologically and psychometrically more sophisticated' using 'control groups of non victims, adequate samples, long-term assessments and objective assessment measures' (Frazier and Borgida, 1985: 990). The problem with this approach is that it does not address the fundamental problem of discounting women's experience. Laboratory-driven findings are incapable of highlighting the elements of power, intimidation, and brutality that are the embodiment of rape.

Once RTS has gained a place in the courtroom as a scientifically accepted syndrome, additional problems follow. Women's psychological reactions to rape can begin to be used against them in precisely the same manner in which rape law and societal opinion has traditionally disadvantaged women. There is already a long list about what constitutes 'real rape'. Why was the complainant dancing so provocatively? How short was her skirt? Why did she accept the accused's invitation to have coffee in his room? Why didn't she stop him when he kissed her? She's known to sleep around, isn't she? These are the benchmarks which society and law routinely use to appraise allegations of rape. RTS updates and expands the catalogue, for RTS evidence renders a woman's psychological reaction to rape one more criterion by which to evaluate her account of events.

Does she feel fearful about going into public? Does she feel scared to be alone in her own home? Does she seem to feel humiliated? Does she blame herself for what happened? Does she talk about revenge? Does she manage her life less effectively? After what period of time was she able to return to her 'previous level of functioning'? RTS simply supplements the list of expectations placed on women. A focus on her psychological state *following* the rape is added to the focus on her demeanour, behaviour, language, and dress *prior to* the event. It is psychology's contribution that makes possible this extended legal consideration of her behaviour, for it is what psychology has objectively determined happens after a rape. Law can thus further encourage scrutiny of a woman's behaviour, having gained from psychology affirmation of its existing presumptions and expectations.

It is not only judges, jurors, and lawyers who are likely to incorporate these new standards into their evaluations about what constitutes rape, but also women themselves. Research shows that women often have difficulty in defining an experience as rape, or are at least reluctant to classify it in this way (Warshaw, 1988; Wood and Rennie, 1994). In particular, when a woman is raped by a man whom she knows, there is uncertainty about how to formulate the attack. Was it rape or just lack of communication? Could he have intended to be so casual or brutal? What did she do to contribute to it? Wood and Rennie (1994: 145) have pointed out that '[i]t is usually men who name the woman's experience and they name it from their perspective'. Their research shows that women are more likely to report rape if their circumstances correspond to the classic rape situation: that is, if the rape involves a stranger, there is a high level of force, there is threat from a dangerous weapon, and significant injury occurs. If victims are given and accept the idea that particular psychological consequences such as recurring bouts of weeping or agoraphobic feelings ensue as a result of rape, they will seek to identify those symptoms in themselves. If they do not succeed, they may well doubt that what they experienced was, in actuality, rape. Certainly they might doubt whether others would believe them, and it is precisely such doubts that already contribute to women's reluctance to report rape incidents to the police (Estrich, 1987).

Ironically, as the psychological consequences of rape become more widely recognised and such knowledge is put to work in women's favour within the courtroom, there is a danger that it also gains more power to work against their interests. Rape mythology and victim stereotyping remain deeply embedded in our culture. Lees has identified some of the new myths that have recently become manifest in the courtroom. 'A common tactic used by the defence to support the idea that a woman is making a false allegation is to suggest that her reactions are *not typical* of a rape victim' (Lees, 1996: 121, emphasis added). RTS evidence has already begun to fulfil its potential for generating new myths about women's behaviour, based on the determination that professional scientific opinion has made about 'appropriate' reactions to rape. Indeed, in *Henson* v *State*, a 1989 case considered by the Supreme Court of Indiana, it was ruled that a *defendant* should be allowed to enter evidence of the *absence* of symptoms of RTS in a complainant to support his contention that rape had not occurred. The court stated that '[t]here is little doubt that an alleged rape victim's conduct after the fact is probative of whether a rape in fact occurred. . . . It would be fundamentally unfair to allow the use of [testimony regarding RTS] by the State, as was the case in [a previous judgement] and then deny its use by a defendant here' (*Henson*, 1989: 9–10 and 11). In short, the court is saying that if a victim does *not* demonstrate the psychological pathology now deemed to be 'normal' in a case of rape, that fact can be adduced as evidence that rape did not occur (see also Dobbin and Gatowski, 1997).

It is not hard to see the attraction of the use of RTS as a defence strategy. There are signs that such an approach is escalating in Canada, where it has been permissible since the 1980s for defence lawyers to gain access to a woman complainant's medical records, including details about any therapy or counselling that she might have had (Gotell, forthcoming). This is based on the argument that such records may contain information relevant to her credibility: is there evidence of a tendency to make false accusations, or of previous sexual abuse, or indeed of any sexual history? Such details are considered to be pertinent to her motive and her character, leaving the defendant's right to a fair trial at risk without them. As Busby (1997) argues, the strategy is primarily designed 'to attack complainants' credibility, motive, and character' (p. 151), with lawyers searching for any information about her that would 'reflect and deepen existing biases based on sexism, racism, ablism, homophobia and class differences' which could serve to discredit her (p. 173). This shift toward accessing personal records may reflect the effect of rape shield laws, which have constrained traditional forms of attention to the victim's sexual character. Kelly (1997) has pointed out that most complainants have at least some relevant records, which might include police reports of their involvement in victim-witness programmes, medical and hospital records, child protection information held by social service departments, and school records. Access to such documents permits defence lawyers broad scope for challenging a complainant's credibility. Kelly (1997: 187) reminds us, that the mechanisms law will use to distinguish 'facts' in conflicting accounts have been constructed, 'within the context of patriarchal discourses about sexual assault, gender, and mental illness'. This does not bode well for the women who 'own' the records. It is not only adult women's privacy that the law has failed to safeguard, but also children's, as we will see in Chapter 7.

Women have always faced immense obstacles in making heard their own experiences of rape. The law remains particularly stalwart and powerful in denying them a voice. The attempt to deliver an objective assessment of rape is a key component of such denial, and law is now ably aided in its aim by psychology.

Male norm

Catharine MacKinnon (1987: 87) argues that '[t]he crime of rape focuses more centrally on what men define as sexuality than on women's experience of [their] sexual being'. The male perspective is so embedded within the concept of objectivity that it is difficult to discuss the two separately. It is important that the two elements be disentangled, however, for otherwise the depth of what must be faced in tackling the issue of rape cannot be comprehended. We have already pointed out how the legal definition of rape as a physical act excludes women's experience of the act. How is it that this particular definition was selected? Not simply because it is a measurable one, but because it is an account which closely fits men's view of rape. Traditional rape mythology is founded in male constructions about the meaning of women's behaviour. By who else's standards could she be said to have worn a skirt that was 'too' short, danced 'too' suggestively, drunk 'too' much, slept with men 'too' promiscuously?

Generally, the operation of the male norm within law is obscured, precisely because the male perspective is not labelled as male, but as objective, neutral, and non-gendered. Occasionally, however, the propriety of the male perspective is explicitly endorsed, as in the 1975 English case of *DPP* v *Morgan*. In that case, an RAF pilot named Morgan and three of his friends had intercourse with Morgan's wife. When charged with rape, the three friends[8] claimed that they had 'honestly believed' she had given her consent, despite her protests and struggles. Morgan had told them that she would behave in that way because she liked 'kinky' sex. They sustained their claim in the face of evidence of significant resistance on her part, including screaming, calling to her 11-year-old son to get the police, and begging her husband to make them stop, all while her arms and legs were being forcibly held down and pulled apart. They were convicted of rape, a verdict they appealed on the grounds that, as they had honestly believed she was consenting, they should not have been convicted. The appeal court affirmed that a man was not guilty of the rape of a woman if he *honestly believed* that she was consenting to intercourse, *even if those beliefs were not reasonable.* The court ruled that, in this particular case, they did not consider the beliefs of the three men to have been honestly held, so their convictions were upheld. While the decision to reject the appeal may seem, at first glance, to be a victory, the standard of a man's honest belief was endorsed. This is not a victory.

The rule laid down in *Morgan* still applies in English law, and its reasoning is followed in Scots law. Even if a woman's actions indicate she did not consent to sex, provided a man can argue he believed that she did consent, there can be no offence of rape. His belief does not even have to be based on reasonable grounds; it need only be honestly held. In the Scottish cases of *Meek* v *HMA* (1983) and *Jamieson* v *HMA* (1994), the High Court reinforced the *Morgan* decision. In *Meek*, the High Court affirmed that they considered *Morgan* to be a suitable precedent to follow, and in *Jamieson* the Court of Appeal affirmed that *Meek* properly represented the law in Scotland. Specifically, the Court stated that

> [the crime of rape] includes the intention to have intercourse with the woman without her consent. The absence of a belief that she was consenting is an essential element in it. If a man has intercourse with a woman in the belief that she is consenting to this he cannot be guilty of rape.
>
> (*Jamieson* v *HMA*, 1994: 92)

The Court did recognise that a jury might find it more palatable to accept that an accused man had believed that the complainant consented if he had reasonable grounds for his belief (for discussion see Ferguson, 1993), but this did not alter their view of the appropriate standard. The subordination of a woman's wishes to a man's beliefs, of her spontaneous actions to his subsequent claims, has thus been endorsed by the courts.

Before looking at the role of RTS in reinforcing the male norm, it is useful to consider one further example of the way in which the male norm already operates in cases of rape. Special rules of evidence apply in rape trials, designed specifically to safeguard against wrongful conviction. Whereas the general rule in a criminal case is that character evidence of a witness is irrelevant, there is scope in rape trials to make the complainant's character a key issue, as we have already seen. This circumstance is peculiar to rape, for, as Hall (1985) has pointed out, there is no other serious crime in which *victims* spend their whole time in the witness box on the defensive and justifying their actions and experiences. The corroboration warning is another rule of evidence that applies specifically in rape cases. In England

and Wales, until the passing of section 34 of the Criminal Justice and Public Order Act 1994, judges were *obliged* to give a detailed warning to juries of the danger of convicting a man accused of rape on the strength of the woman complainant's testimony alone and in the absence of other material corroborative evidence. The corroboration warning owes its origins to early jurists such as Hale and Blackstone, both of whom were influential in Western legal tradition. While the requirement to give such a warning has now been removed, it is still open to judges, at their discretion, to offer it. Of course, even the option of permitting judicial discretion maintains the idea that women who complain of sexual attacks are somehow less credible than victims of other crimes.[9]

These examples demonstrate the masculinist perspective inherent within rape law. The use of syndrome evidence has done little to abate the force of that perspective. That is in large part because RTS characterises a woman's behaviour and experience as disordered. It undermines her credibility and marginalises her testimony. Credibility lies at the heart of a rape charge, for if a jury is to be convinced that a woman did not consent to intercourse, then she must appear as a credible witness. Although introduced into the courtroom in the hope that evidence of psychological symptoms would enhance women's credibility, RTS actually creates the opposite outcome. Women's credibility is diminished, for a diagnosis of RTS officially classifies her mental state as pathological. This is very meaningful for law, for a diagnosis of this sort renders it more possible for defence lawyers to attack the reliability of a woman victim's credibility on the ground that she is suffering from a mental illness.

The depiction of the woman complainer as 'incredible' and untrustworthy has a long history in law. Psychology's reinforcement of that view, augmented by the use of objective scientific methodologies and explanations, displays the implicit relation in operation. Wigmore declared that

> [n]o judge should ever let a sex offense charge go to the jury unless the female complainant's social history and mental make-up have been examined and testified to by a qualified physician.
>
> (Wigmore, 1937b: Para. 924a)

Through the use of RTS evidence, psychology has begun to do precisely what conventional legal theorists have asked. Psychology is not challenging the male normative assumptions of law but is fulfilling the call to 'examine' women's 'mental make-up'. Moreover, psychology is confirming that women who are raped become mentally disordered. They are not coping with an abnormal *event*, in the context of which their actions are reasonable and expectable. Rather, they are judged to be demonstrating a 'manifestation of a behavioral, psychological . . . dysfunction' occurring *within* themselves (DSM, 1994: xxi–xxii, emphasis added). To classify a woman's attempts to come to terms with the horror of rape as mental pathology is patently male normative reasoning.

Once the woman has been rendered officially 'ill', it is natural that a professional would be required to explain her experience and behaviour. Her behaviour must be legitimised by others. Her voice is insufficient on its own, and her contribution to a judicial process that will have a significant influence on her life is relegated to a peripheral role. In requiring the endorsement of a professional opinion, the medicalisation of women's experience is accomplished and the silencing of her voice achieved. The victims of theft, fraud, or forgery do not require professional sanction; their story is legitimated through their own articulation of it. Wigmore can be thanked for so firmly fixing this gender-specific legacy within the Anglo-American legal system. It was not the intention of the original advocates of RTS to reinforce his views. Like those who introduced BWS into law, Frazier and Borgida (1985) and others saw RTS as a way to introduce women's voices into the courtroom. Grievously, but not surprisingly, the outcome was the same as for BWS: that introduction was 'accomplished' only through the perversion of women's accounts. Women (via their professional 'representatives') may now be allowed to speak up more often in rape cases, but only if they do so in an irrational, pathological register.

It will always be in the interests of the defence to seek to cross-examine the woman on issues of character, and in so doing, to undermine her credibility. Dependence on RTS carries risks that could be exploited by clever lawyers defending alleged rapists. Given that behavioural science appears to have affirmed that women are innately 'biologically labile' and generally susceptible to syndromes (Chesler, 1972; Showalter, 1987; Ussher, 1991), then the fact that a victim currently exhibits symptoms of trauma cannot be assumed to stem from the particular sexual attack under consideration. Violence against women is endemic, occurring in forms from child abuse to domestic violence to rape. There is a statistical likelihood that a rape victim has experienced at least one previous incidence of traumatic violence. The problem is, how is one to know that this most recent attack is the one to which the trauma symptoms can reliably be attributed? A woman's symptomatic behaviour could arguably be rooted in a previous incident. Indeed, in the *Saldana* case described earlier, the court stated that 'the characteristic symptoms [of PTSD] may follow *any* psychologically traumatic event' (*State* v *Saldana*, 1982: 230, emphasis added), and it was concluded that such a general pattern could not therefore help the jury in deciding whether a rape had happened in this particular case. There is an inexorable logic to the legal reasoning which argues that, since we cannot attribute the trauma to any specific incident, we must discount it. Of course *previous* experience of trauma does not negate the validity of *this* particular event, but when questions are raised under cross-examination in the witness box, it may have that effect. If the symptoms cannot be shown to be attributable to this particular event, the argument goes, it is unjust to admit them as evidence against this particular defendant. Once again, attention to the violence of the rape act is deflected by questions about the (female) victim's biology, history, and character.

RTS must be viewed not simply in relation to its potential influence in any individual rape charge, but with regard to its impact on the conduct of rape trials as a whole. If RTS becomes an accepted and standard ingredient of the prosecution's case, then in any case where evidence of RTS is not led, its omission could draw adverse comment from defence counsel and judges. Its absence could lead to a presumption of a lack of sufficiency in the evidence. That is, if evidence was not entered to show that the woman complainant had suffered from RTS, then it could be assumed that she did not suffer from it. And if she has not suffered from RTS (i.e. if she has failed to show the symptoms prescribed by psychology), then it may create doubt that she was indeed raped, because science has 'shown' objectively that rape should result in those symptoms. The use of RTS in the courtroom presents women with novel, insidious male-normative expectations about what they must do in order to have their account of events believed. This is indeed a far cry from the vision of those who first fought so hard to have it admitted into court cases.

Individualism

The legal system treats rape as the embodiment of an individual and private ordeal. Psychology conceptualises RTS as an internal pathology, to be diagnosed and treated in the individual person. This independent but corresponding focus on the individual level allows the two fields to join together with a non-reflexive faith about their ability to account for what happens in cases of rape. The problem with this myopia is that it negates the social context within which rape occurs and within which a woman copes with its aftermath.

Law's concentration on the individual is a feature of the public/private dichotomy which, some argue, lies at the heart of law as a tool of patriarchy (Smart, 1984). When law operates within the public domain, it is subject to transparent checks and balances that reflect the broader interests of modern political society. However, once law enters the private arena of the interpersonal relations of individuals, this transparency is lost and with it the level of accountability that is demanded in the public context. Thus, it is far harder to intervene to control abusive behaviour when it occurs within the family home than when it takes place on the street corner. Rape, like so many forms of violence against women, is a very private and personal matter. The event is rarely witnessed by anyone, and it frequently occurs in a private dwelling house. The reaction from some quarters to the removal of the marital rape exemption, such as that of Glanville Williams (1983, 1992) whom we considered earlier in this chapter, underlines the tendency to privatise and individualise rape.

Ironically, efforts to 'protect' a woman once she is involved in the public criminal justice system as a victim can serve to keep rape (literally) behind closed doors. For example, the statutory reporting restrictions in place in jurisdictions within the UK were developed to protect the woman's identity and to avoid her further exposure to unpleasant media attention. In some ways, these restrictions have the converse effect of minimalising rape. It is interesting to note the number of women who choose to waive anonymity in particularly horrific cases and go on to make public statements about their treatment by the law. Recent UK examples include 'Judy' who spoke out very critically at the Conservative Party Conference in 1995, gaining prime television coverage and much public sympathy, and also Jill Saward, whose experience, previously described, of being raped at knifepoint by three men in 1987 became known nationally as the Ealing Vicarage Rape. Since the rape, she has written her autobiography and campaigned to raise awareness about the treatment of rape victims (Saward with Green, 1990). More recently, in 1996, Julia Mason, a woman rape victim in England waived her right to anonymity to criticise a criminal justice system that had effectively permitted her to be raped a second time 'in front of judge and jury in a British court of law' (*The Lawyer*, 3 September 1996). The man accused of attacking her, Ralston Edwards, had dismissed his lawyers and proceeded to cross-examine her in lurid and extensive detail about the rape, wearing, throughout his six-day interrogation of her, the same clothing he had been wearing when he had raped her. An unusually positive outcome is that the UK government has since introduced legislation – the Youth Justice and Criminal Evidence Act 1999 – to remove the *right* of a rape defendant to conduct his defence in this way. However, this protection is, as ever, subject to the overriding interests of justice, thus retaining judicial discretion to permit it. Such discretion has, of course, been shown to be exercised primarily in favour of defendants, not the victims of rape.

In Scotland, protective measures exist in the common practice of clearing the court of non essential personnel when a woman complainant is giving evidence (authorised by statute: section 92(3) of the Criminal Procedure (Scotland) Act 1995). While this practice is intended to be undertaken in the woman's interests, it also maintains the privatisation of rape, because by excluding the public from the heart of the rape trial process, the full realisation of how badly women are treated remains hidden. The wider public thus remain relatively uninformed about rape victims' experience of court, so it is hardly surprising that calls for reform make little headway in general society.

Reliance on RTS evidence in the courtroom merely reproduces the problem of individualism by narrowing the focus to a single woman's actions, and in the process, decontextualising them. The focus remains firmly on the behaviour of the individual woman. Just as her actions prior to the rape have always been scrutinised, her actions following the rape now come under inspection as well. She will be judged not only by her immediate response to the rape, but also by her long-term reaction, because both the immediate and the extended periods after the attack are relevant to a diagnosis of RTS. Thus, if the woman seems to be coping with her life, returning to work, and continuing with her previous activities, she risks giving the impression to a judge and/or jury that she has recovered, and if she has recovered, then her trauma can be interpreted as not very substantial.

In other areas of the criminal law where syndrome evidence has been admitted, experience suggests that the woman's psychological condition becomes a para-mount evidential issue, diverting attention from the actions of the man involved. For example, when a battered woman kills her partner and then relies on a defence of diminished responsibility (see Chapter 4), attention comes to focus on her actions and her mental state, rather than the behaviour of the abusive partner. Jurors' prejudices are renewed and reinforced that the behaviour of the battered or raped woman is of prime relevance in explaining what happened to her. The assault and its consequences become in large part her responsibility, for some explanation of the event seems to be possible if sense can be made of *her* behaviour. But this conclusion occurs because the law and psychology refuse to allow her experience to be placed in its context. The focus must be kept on the (decontextualised) actions of the individual. She cannot give her account of what happened; rather, she is allowed to call attention only to those aspects of the context that *law* has already decided are relevant. When the context of what she felt and believed and understood is critical to understanding the story, the expulsion of these elements prevents her from telling a sensible story. Of course her account appears irrational, given that it is missing key elements. Law and psychology create gaps in her story, and then fill those chasms with interpretations that change her story so fundamentally that she cannot recognise herself within it.

Indeed, a focus on the pathology of individual women diverts attention from the wider societal context of pervasive male violence toward women. This is a key element of the context within which rape occurs. Feminist analysts argue that taking account of the cultural context is essential for explaining and tackling the problem of rape (e.g. Brownmiller, 1991; Estrich, 1987; Kelly, 1988). Women's attempts to cope with male violence need to be conceived as a 'conflict [that is] primarily between the individual and society' (DSM, 1994: xxii) – precisely the type of conceptualisation that is *excluded* from consideration in the DSM's explanation of behaviour. Thus, psychological and psychiatric explanations, as currently conceived, can provide little in the search for a more expansive understanding of sexual violence against women, for they characterise it within traditional individualistic boundaries, emphasising internal pathology rather than any sociological dimension of the violence. The power of that model to endorse the traditional practices of law becomes far more than an unexamined shortcoming in psychological theory. Burgess and Holmstrom (1985) warned that RTS should not be dismissed as a private syndrome, arguing instead that it should be a societal concern and that treatment should be funded through public expenditure. However, psychological explanations are fundamentally unsuited to societal application or analysis precisely because they adopt an individualistic model. As Koss argues:

> the problem of violence against women cannot be fully understood, let alone solved, by focusing exclusively on individual psychology. Only by changing the social and cultural institutions that have given rise to the problem can a lasting solution be achieved.
>
> (Koss, 1993: 1055)

The implicit relation ensures that the individualistic nature of societal and legal conceptions will remain. Law seeks individualistic accounts of human behaviour, and mainstream psychology supplies them. These disciplines do not offer one another independent or neutral opinions; rather they serve to confirm joint biases. They have been able to satisfy each other that there is no need to look for an alternative way to understand or address the issue of rape.

Conclusion

We have shown in this chapter that the use of RTS evidence, which was originally introduced in rape cases to compensate for the evidential difficulties of establishing a woman's lack of consent to sexual intercourse, has been diverted to other purposes – ones which work against women's interests. Testimony from experts about a woman's mental, emotional, and psychological state following rape can be used against her as easily as they can be used in her favour. Women have always been regarded by law as incredible witnesses in allegations of rape, and RTS provides defence lawyers with a new strategy for endorsing that view. How can a woman whom science confirms is in a disturbed mental state be regarded as a fully competent witness against a (rational) man, especially if there is no physical evidence to support her subjective claims? Historical patterns of responding to women's claims have been refurbished with modern terminology and concepts.

It is important to stress that the efforts of those legal and psychological professionals who originally endeavoured to have RTS admitted into the courtroom stemmed from a motive to make a difference to the treatment of women in the courtroom. The strategy they adopted (i.e. promoting RTS evidence) was a sophisticated one, given the legal strictures within which they were operating. The admission of psychological syndrome evidence can appear, on the surface, to be an effective way of altering women's place within the legal system. We would argue there may be some role for psychological syndromes in the courtroom, if they are limited to an educational capacity. This is a theme we will take up in more depth in Chapter 8. At this point it is sufficient to emphasise that, to whatever extent one advocates the use of syndrome evidence in the courtroom, this approach needs to be pursued with a consciousness of its limitations and with the awareness that it can be manipulated to work against the original aims. In the US case of *State v Jackson* (1982), for example, the defence obtained a court order ordering the rape victim to undergo a mental health examination to ascertain whether or not she exhibited symptoms of RTS.[10] The implicit relation is a powerful force, rendered even more so by its hidden nature. Short-term strategies need to be undertaken with a cognisance of long-term consequences.

6   Premenstrual Syndrome

The sting that this remark was vaguely felt to conceal was almost neutralised by the satisfaction of being addressed in such technical language.

Edith Wharton[1]

If asked to name areas in which the law is likely to treat women inequitably, it is probable that topics covered in other chapters – rape, domestic violence, childhood sexual abuse – would come to mind most immediately. The topic of this chapter is one that is perhaps unlikely to appear on that list at all, for this chapter examines Premenstrual Syndrome (PMS). It is understandable why PMS would not feature on any such list, for PMS is not a crime, nor is it associated with any particular crime. Indeed, many people may be surprised and sceptical to learn that PMS is relevant to law at all.

Yet PMS, or its historical equivalent, has been used in the courtroom for over a century to explain a variety of criminal activities committed by women, ranging from shoplifting to homicide. It was the appearance of PMS within the legal arena that played a key role in bringing the syndrome to popular attention. As part of a defence, PMS is intended to function similarly to Battered Woman's Syndrome, serving to explain women's actions as the result of a psychological (or perhaps physiological) disorder. As such, it is argued that sufferers should be excused for criminal actions they commit while subject to its symptoms. Some observers may feel this is outrageous reasoning because then 'any woman could use it to get away with a crime'. Others may feel that the acceptance of PMS into the courtroom is a positive step, if it contributes to an understanding of (some) women's behaviour and prevents them from serving unjust prison sentences. We would argue that both responses are too simplistic, for when one looks a bit deeper, a pattern similar to that which we have seen in previous chapters becomes apparent. PMS constructs women's normal experience and behaviour as *ab*normal. At best, PMS may serve the interests of individual women, but it is deleterious to the interests of women as a group.

The organisation of this chapter will differ slightly from that of earlier topic chapters. Previously we have begun by reviewing statistical information about the frequency with which certain crimes, such as rape or domestic abuse, occur and the proportion of such crimes that eventually result in conviction. Structuring the discussion in that way helped to create a framework within which the emergence of the associated syndrome could be understood. In the case of PMS, however, there is no single crime, set of statistics, or event to which the syndrome can be attached – except, of course, menstruation. The phenomenon that is central to PMS is a phenomenon that is central to women's lives. To analyse PMS is then, in some sense, to analyse constructions of womanhood. This being a rather broad topic, we will narrow the discussion here by first reviewing the origins and growth of the syndrome and thereafter summarising some of the key legal cases in which PMS has featured. Within this initial scene-setting, the operation of the implicit relation's three key characteristics – objectivity, male norm, and individualism – will become apparent, and in the later sections of the chapter, as in other chapters, we will disentangle and elucidate their effects in more detail.

Premenstrual Syndrome

PMS was first described in 1931 by Robert Frank, a gynaecologist in the United States. In a publication in the *Archives of Neurology and Psychiatry*, he recounted patients' complaints of 'unrest, irritability, "like jumping out of their skin" and a desire to find relief by foolish and ill considered actions' (Frank, 1931: 1054). He labelled the condition 'Premenstrual Tension', hypothesising a hormonal cause of excess oestrogen. Although the condition received some attention in the medical literature, it was not until 1953 that that interest began to escalate. This shift was led by Katharina Dalton, a British general practitioner who co-authored a publication in the *British Medical Journal* (Greene and Dalton, 1953). It was she who introduced the term 'Premenstrual Syndrome', on the basis that tension was only one of the symptoms displayed by women with this condition. Dalton continues to be considered a leading expert on PMS, publishing in medical journals, writing self-help books, and offering expert testimony in court. She too believes the condition to be hormonally based, although she blames progesterone deficiency.

In 1987, PMS entered the *Diagnostic and Statistical Manual* (DSM-III-R) under the title Late Luteal Phase Dysphoric Disorder (LLPDD). In the 30 years that had passed between Dalton's first publication and this decision, medical attention to the condition had increased significantly. So also had critiques of the related research. Feminist scientists pointed out that much of the work had been poorly conducted and insufficiently theoretical (e.g. Laws, 1985; Parlee, 1973). They also challenged the link between menstruation and disease states, as well as the postulated symptoms of PMS. The proposition that any menstrually related phenomena should be classified as a *mental disorder*, by including it in the DSM, was vigorously contested by numerous individuals and groups.[2] A campaign of opposition persisted throughout the three-year DSM decision process, as Anne Figert (1996) recounts in her sociological analysis of PMS discourse. A compromise of sorts was reached, in which LLPDD was confined to the appendices of the DSM-III-R. However, in the next edition of the manual, DSM-IV, published in 1994,

PMS was listed in the main body of the text, this time under the revised title Premenstrual Dysphoric Disorder. Thus, the controversial debate over whether there is a link between women's reproductive processes and mental abnormality was apparently settled. PMS was indeed 'real', having been accorded an official title and a standard set of diagnostic criteria.

The link between women's reproduction and abnormality did not originate in the 1930s with Frank. It could be said to have arisen in whichever prehistorical era was originally born the idea that woman's nature made her inferior to man (Miles, 1993). Certainly during the nineteenth century, an obsession had developed with the female body: its sexuality, reproductive capacity, secretions, and particularly menstruation. 'Menstruation acted as an external instrument, a barometer by which doctors could read the internal health, mental as well as physical, of their patients' (Shuttleworth, 1990: 47). Taking such readings was important, for the reproductive organs were considered to be responsible for women's health, morality, sensibility, and even the buttressing of social order. In 1854, for instance, Maddock observed that the reproductive organs were 'closely interwoven with erratic and disordered intellectual, as well as moral, manifestations' (quoted in Ussher, 1997: 331). Hollick (1847) agreed with these sentiments, for, he reminded readers, the uterus was 'the controlling organ in the female body, being the most excitable of all, and so intimately connected, by the ramifications of its numerous nerves, with every other part' (quoted in Tuana, 1993: 98).

Today, such beliefs sound fanciful and misguided, especially when considered in conjunction with medical treatments, such as electric shock, cervical cauterisation, and the use of leeches, which were used to correct menstrual 'interference', 'blockage', and 'stoppage' (Shuttleworth, 1990). However, these statements represent the leading medical opinions of their day. Victorian women's lives were governed by such edicts, with medical assistance deemed necessary not only for abnormal menstrual functioning but also for *normal* functioning. 'Proper performance' was best accomplished by the 'careful attention of both the woman and her medical adviser' to her bodily functions (Shuttleworth, 1990: 62). In short, 'disordered menstruation' was seen, in the nineteenth century, as a problem of general blood circulation. 'If the menstrual flow were obstructed and thence denied its usual exit, it would, doctors warned, be forced to flood the brain and thus lead to irreparable psychological breakdown' (Shuttleworth, 1990: 48).

The twentieth century has seen the development of more sophisticated theories about the functioning of the human body and mind. The driving force behind the menstrual cycle is now understood to be the hormones produced by the ovaries. Comparably, the driving force behind women's 'abnormal' reproductive functioning is also believed to be hormonal, although the experts – gynaecologists, psychiatrists, psychologists, and other medical researchers – cannot yet offer any detailed account of PMS: what causes it, which hormones are involved, what its precise symptoms are, how to recognise it reliably, or how to treat it. Just as nineteenth-century experts did not really understand menstruation, twentieth-century experts do not really understand PMS. But the conclusions both have reached are similar: there is a causal relationship between women's reproductive cycle and their emotional and behavioural states. Frank's identification of PMT, and all the relabelling that has occurred since, is merely the contemporary instantiation of an ancient and timeworn (but unfortunately not worn out) view that women are incapacitated by their reproductive capacity and, thereby, their biology. As Jane Ussher (1997: 331) puts it: '[T]he sophistication of the categorization may appear to have increased yet, arguably, the process is the same.'

The lack of a clear contemporary understanding of PMS can be discerned at a variety of levels in the study of the condition. There is, for example, little agreement about the symptoms of PMS: what they are, how they should be measured, or where their origin is to be found. Budieri and her colleagues (1994), reviewing the literature relevant to 350 clinical trials, found that a total of 65 different questionnaires and scales have been developed to assess PMS. Among them, they include 199 different symptoms, not one of which appears in all of the scales. Irritability was the symptom that appeared most frequently, and it was still included in only 44 of the 65 questionnaires. Other common symptoms included sadness, anxiety, anger, insomnia, lethargy, libido change, indecision, rejection sensitivity, suicidal ideation, nausea, sweating, vertigo, bloating, decreased motivation, decreased efficiency, decreased concentration, social isolation, breast tenderness, muscle pain, acne, greasy hair, and dry hair. Despite the lack of agreement amongst professionals, and the flexible reasoning about symptomatology, it is still generally accepted in the field that some sort of premenstrual condition exists. Inclusion of that condition in the DSM is a very effective suppressor for any remaining dissension.

The techniques through which PMS is measured and defined lead to further gaps in understanding women's menstrual experiences. The scales used to assess women's symptoms rarely permit women to cite positive changes. The majority of questionnaires are constructed such that it is impossible to report changes such as increased happiness, contentment, sexual interest, or energy. Instead, it is generally possible to report only negative symptoms. As Anne Walker (1997) points out, this results in the impression that positive feelings are either not possible during the premenstrual period or that they are not worth measuring. A critic might argue that the purpose of the medical profession is to explain and treat distress – rendering the investigation of happiness and well-being is a superfluous consideration. However, if investigators ignore or negate some aspects of a phenomenon by concentrating exclusively on others, it can easily result in a misleading impression of that phenomenon. 'If women can experience both positive and negative feelings but are able to rate only the negative ones, then they may appear to be depressed all the time . . . when in fact they are not' (Walker, 1997: 202). Ultimately, a biased account of women's experience is created.

It is significant that that bias operates in the negative direction. A pattern of change can be interpreted in various ways, depending on the baseline one uses. Current discourse tends to emphasise the negative changes that occur between the early and middle stages of the cycle. A woman's patience and restraint are said to decrease, her anger and hostility to increase. Such changes could just as validly be characterised positively, with an increase in patience and a decrease in anger evident between mid-phases of one cycle and early phases of the next. This point was made in a 1981 editorial in the *Lancet*.

> With some exceptions, the data seem equally consistent with the hypothesis of a mid-cycle syndrome of lowered crime, fewer epileptic seizures, increased self-esteem and elation, and increased sexual desire and activity. It would be incomplete to say only that women perform worse at certain times in the cycle than others; their performance may at all times be better than the average performance of males on the task in question.
>
> (*Lancet*, 1981; quoted in Laws, 1985: 57)

Indeed, just as women's behaviour can be characterised as 'less feminine' during mid-cycle, it could also be said to become 'more masculine'. The binary construction of gender in contemporary society dictates that men are (still) seen as less sensitive and aware, more aggressive and violent. Women are the loving, patient, and even-tempered ones. Women's behaviour appears to be 'bizarre' when it does not match their gender role. Thus, if PMS 'causes' women to be more aggressive and 'less amenable to discipline' (Dalton, 1961), it could be said, rather amusingly, to lead women to behave more like men.[3] For a few days each month, women can behave in a masculine fashion, driven (or liberated) to such a state by their unruly hormones. Such an account is striking only because social norms dictate a particular baseline for women's behaviour, and when they fail to meet that expectation, illness provides a convenient explanation.

One final way in which the medical profession's poor understanding of PMS manifests itself is in the variety of opinions available concerning prevalence rates and treatments (see Walker, 1997). Estimates of sufferers range from 5% to 100% of women, depending on how PMS is defined. Proposed treatments include progesterone supplements, progestins and oral contraceptives, androgens, lithium, sedatives, dietary restrictions, diuretics, prostaglandin inhibitors, and hysterectomy. The range of opinion on these issues is, in part, so broad because gynaecology and psychiatry are the two medical specialities that have contributed most to the contemporary framing of the condition, and they strongly disagree concerning its aetiology and effects. Gynaecologists concentrate on the physiological features of the condition (e.g. abdominal cramps, bloating, swelling, breast pain, and headache), while psychiatrists are much more interested in the psychological nature of menstrually related experiences, such as anxiety, tension, irritability, mood swings, and depression (Jarvis, 1994; Walker, 1997). Differences in the emphases of the two fields often lead to very different conclusions concerning the definitions, symptomatology, and treatment of PMS. Indeed, it has sometimes been asked whether PMS is 'really' a psychiatric or a gynaecological condition; are the two fields even referring to the same concept? The raging array of disagreements about PMS led Rubinow and Roy-Byrne (1984: 169) to conclude, in their review of PMS, that '[d]espite 50 years of study, there is still surprisingly little known about menstrually related mood disorders; questions of etiology and treatment are largely unanswered'. The more recent texts by Figert (1996) and Walker (1997) make clear that the passage of more than a decade has brought no greater clarity to the issue; all that has really been accomplished is some shifting of labels.

Despite such inconsistencies and disagreement, PMS has become a household term in Western homes, and PMS discourse has become a powerful social and political force. It has been given as reason for preventing women from entering professions ranging from boxing to the clergy;[4] it continues to be cited as a source of child abuse, marital strife, and criminal behaviour; it drives a lucrative trade in self-help books, medical treatments, and greeting card merchandise; it is said to cause industry colossal financial loss due to employee absenteeism and inefficiency. (For discussion of these themes, see Figert, 1996; Jarvis, 1994; Reid and Yen, 1981; Quilligan and Zuspan, 1990.) It is the power of such discourse that has led feminists to critique the diagnosis and that has embedded them in the dilemma we have already seen in other chapters. Is PMS helpful to individual women? Is it helpful to women as a group? What if the two categories are in conflict? Interestingly for our purposes in this book, it was key legal cases in the early 1980s that brought PMS, and feminist criticism of it, fully into societal awareness.

PMS in the courtroom

Legal cases in which medical evidence about menstrual disorders is introduced in order to explain women's behaviour go back at least as far as the nineteenth century. As we saw earlier, during the Victorian era 'disordered menstruation' was believed to cause temporary insanity. It is not surprising that such insanity would have been used to explain women's commission of violent and criminal acts. Legal records of the period reveal precisely that outcome, with crimes ranging from murder to shoplifting.

For example, Martha Brixey, a domestic servant, gained the illustrious title 'The Greenwich Murderess' when she killed her employer's infant son in 1845 by slashing his throat. She was acquitted on grounds of insanity probably arising from the 'temporary suspensions of the action of nature' (*London Medical Gazette*, 1845: 169). In 1865, Constance Kent confessed to killing her infant stepbrother, whose death had initially been blamed on a nursemaid. Disordered menstruation and the 'peculiarities of her constitution' were believed to have played a role (*Journal of Mental Science*, 1865: 431). Amelia Snoswell strangled her infant niece and was acquitted on the basis of medical evidence relating to disordered menstruation (cited in Hull *et al.*, 1997) At the other end of the criminal spectrum, historical records show that when Ann Shepherd stole a fur boa in 1845, it was accepted that she suffered from a 'stoppage of her courses' which made her 'act oddly at times'. She was acquitted on the basis of temporary insanity caused by suppressed menstruation (*London and Edinburgh Monthly Journal of Medical Science*, 1845: 634). Mrs Castle, a wealthy American tourist, was caught shoplifting in London in 1896. Her kleptomania was thought to be a result of suppressed menstruation and she was acquitted (cited in Shuttleworth, 1990). (For contemporary sources in which these cases are cited, see Hull *et al.*, 1997; Smith, 1981; Walker, 1997.)

It is interesting to observe that in all of these cases, the women's behaviour was explained as being due to some degree of insanity stemming from menstrual disorder. Medical opinion was used to substantiate such claims, and, indeed, many of the cases were reported in lurid detail in the medical journals of the time. This was because the biological and medical explanations of the crimes had made them a 'matter of scientific interest' (*Journal of Mental Science*, 1865: 430). The women's 'dysfunctions' in these accounts were explained in terms of menstruation *per se*, as would have been in keeping for that point in medical history. Contemporary views hold that the dysfunction results from disordered hormones, and this view is reflected in more recent legal judgements.

Menstrual dysfunction dramatically re-entered the courtroom in its modern guise of PMS in the early 1980s, when it was used as part of the defence in two UK murder cases. In 1980, Sandie Smith (then known as Craddock; *R v Craddock*, 1981) stabbed a co-worker to death in the bar where they were both employed. She was charged with murder. Aged 28, Smith already had a long history of violent behaviour, having more than thirty previous convictions for criminal assault and damage. She had also attempted suicide on a number of occasions and had repeatedly been diagnosed by psychiatrists as having an unstable personality. Her condition did not, in their view, constitute a mental disorder, but neither was it considered treatable. While Smith was on remand awaiting trial, her father observed that all the offences had occurred in 28-day cycles, leading to an investigation of the possibility that her violent outbursts were related to her menses. Hormonal testing indicated that Smith suffered a deficiency of progesterone, and it was suggested that with hormone replacement therapy, her personality swings might stabilise. Thus, sentencing was delayed for three months to monitor the effect of such treatment. 'Excellent' positive results revealed precisely that outcome: with regular injections of progesterone, Smith's violent outbursts subsided. She pled guilty to manslaughter, and, in view of the medical evidence supporting her case supplied by Dr Katharina Dalton (whose key contributions to the PMS debate were described earlier), her plea was accepted by the prosecution. The trial judge sentenced her to three years' probation, subject to her continuing to receive the progesterone treatments.

About a year later, Sandie Smith again came before the court (*R v Smith*, 1982). This time she was charged with carrying an offensive weapon and threatening to kill a police officer. At the trial, it was maintained that the officer had insulted her some three years previously, that she bore a grudge against him, and that this was the motivation for her actions. Evidence showed that she had threatened him in writing, by telephone, and finally in person, when she appeared at the police station in possession of a knife. During presentation of the evidence, it became clear that Dalton, who had continued to act as Smith's treating physician, had decreased the dosage of her progesterone treatments, and this had apparently led to a renewal of her violent behaviour. Following her arrest, the larger doses were reinstated, and her violent personality swings were again subdued. This time, Smith chose to plead not guilty, arguing that a special defence based on PMS should be allowed by the courts. This argument was rejected however (by both the trial and appeal courts), and Smith was convicted. Once again, she was sentenced to three years' probation on the condition that she continue with the higher doses of hormone treatment.

Only one day after the news of Sandie Smith's (second) probationary sentence was announced, another 'PMS case' came to the attention of the British press and public (*R* v *English*, 1982). This was the 1982 case of Christine English who had killed her lover, Barry Kitson, by driving her car at him. He had been drinking in a pub, and when she picked him up, they began to argue about his drinking and his 'other women' (*Daily Mirror*, 11 November 1982). The newspaper reports stated that Kitson slapped and punched her and, at some point, left the car saying he never wanted to see her again. When he gestured rudely at her, English said she 'just snapped' and she drove her car against him, pinning him against a telegraph pole and killing him. Medical and psychiatric evidence was introduced at the trial to show that English suffered from PMS. Although she had not previously been diagnosed with PMS, she had a long history of PMS pointers, including postnatal depression, sterilisation, and hypoglycaemia. On the basis of the medical evidence, again supplied to the court by Dalton in her role as expert witness, English's plea of guilty to manslaughter, due to diminished responsibility, was accepted. She was given a one-year conditional discharge and banned from driving for a year. This was a more lenient outcome than even Smith had received, for English was not required to undergo medical treatment or even to report to a probation officer. Thus, these cases gave PMS legal status and, through the media coverage accompanying them, brought PMS to wider public attention in the UK.

The prominent entrance of PMS into the American courts occurred with the case of *People* v *Santos* (1982). The case involved Shirley Santos, who was arrested in 1982 after emergency medical staff had determined that the cause of her 4-year-old daughter's injuries was child abuse. She was charged with assault and endangering the welfare of a child, both of which are serious crimes (i.e. felonies) under New York State law. She was reported, at the time of her arrest, to have repeated continuously, 'I don't remember it, but I would never hurt my baby. I just got my period' (quoted in Chait, 1986: 269). In pre-trial hearings, her counsel attempted to use PMS as a complete defence. That is, Santos adopted a strategy similar to that attempted by Sandie Smith in her second case (but which was rejected by the British courts). Santos's lawyer argued that because she had not known what she was doing at the time that the abuse occurred, she could not have formed the necessary criminal intent to commit the crime, and therefore she should not be held responsible for her actions. However, no legal test of this defence was achieved in the end, because Santos agreed to abandon the PMS defence in return for a reduction in the charges. She eventually pled guilty to the lesser charge of harassment. There was some disagreement about the implications of this decision for a PMS defence. As noted by Carney and Williams (1983) in their summary of the case, the District Attorney's office claimed that the plea bargain showed the frailty of a PMS defence. Santos's defence argued the converse, asserting that the plea bargain had only been offered because the strength of the defence was clear. Although Santos did not receive a sentence or a fine for the conviction (she was given a discharge on the stipulation that she continue with a counselling programme she had already begun), in family court proceedings she did lose custody of her child.

The cases of these three women are the ones that have received most attention in the literature, but PMS has featured in a range of other cases. For example, a road traffic offence was at issue in the 1991 Scottish case of *Thomas* v *Lowe*. In that case, Carol Thomas had driven into the back of a car waiting at a set of traffic lights. Although she left the scene immediately, she was traced due to information provided by a witness. She pled guilty to careless driving and to failing to stop after an accident, arguing in mitigation that she was suffering from PMS at the time of the accident. Her doctor submitted a medical certificate confirming that she suffered from very severe premenstrual tension. Thomas was fined £150, her driving licence was endorsed with penalty points, and she was disqualified from driving for six months. She appealed against the disqualification on the basis that insufficient weight had been placed on the medical evidence, and the appeal court agreed. While noting that 'it is necessary to drive home to the appellant and others that this type of conduct does constitute a serious offence' (*Thomas* v *Lowe*, 1991: 945), the appeal court felt that disqualification was not appropriate, and penalty points were substituted instead.

The US case of *Lovato* v *Irvin* (1983), involving bankruptcy and debt recovery, provides an interesting contrast with the cases previously described. In this civil case, the court did not accept PMS as a valid explanation for behaviour. In 1979, two women, by the names of Jamie Irvin and Betty Lovato, were involved in a fight with each other. The stab wounds that Irvin inflicted on Lovato required medical treatment, and Lovato subsequently sued for the cost of the medical bills. The judges ruled that Irvin was responsible for the costs. However, she appealed the decision on the grounds that she was suffering from PMS at the time of the stabbing and should not therefore be held responsible for her actions. '[E]xtensive testimony' on PMS was taken from expert witnesses, including a psychologist, a psychiatrist, and an obstetrician (Benedek, 1988: 499). None of them supported the argument that PMS was an exculpatory factor in violent behaviour, however, and Irvin's arguments were consequently rejected by the court.

This survey of cases illustrates that PMS has featured in a range of legal matters. Indeed, the scope also extends to shoplifting (e.g. *R.* v *Beer*, 1985; *Reid* v *Florida Real Estate Commission*, 1966), receipt of disability benefits (e.g. *Crockett* v *Cohen*, 1969), and child custody (e.g. *In re H*, 1983; *Tingen* v *Tingen*, 1968), as well as other cases of homicide (e.g. *R* v *Reynolds*, 1988), assault (e.g. *R* v *Morris*, 1988), and road traffic offences (e.g. *Scott* v *Hamilton*, 1988). It is likely that courts have dealt with a great many more cases that have not been listed in the official law reports (see, for example, Dalton's 1982 discussion of cases of dangerous driving, shoplifting, and infanticide).[5] Even this brief review has shown that the extent to which PMS is accepted by courts as a valid explanation of behaviour varies. In some cases a discharge has been granted, in some cases a mitigated sentence awarded, and in others the validity of evidence on PMS entirely rejected. Such breadth does not prevent us from discerning the operation of the implicit relation.

The implicit relation

The influence of the three characteristics of the implicit relation can be identified in the discourse of judges, expert witnesses, and researchers surrounding PMS. Concern is expressed by them, for example, about the consequences of women's premenstrual behaviour for society as a whole, judgements about women's morality are harboured within their reasoning, and discussion about the cultural construction of abnormality is forestalled on the basis that those who question the notion of PMS are not dealing with 'objective facts' or are 'anti-woman'. The range of views that exist about how the law should deal with 'PMS cases' highlights particularly well the conflict between the needs of individual women and women as a group, which so frequently arises in the use of syndrome evidence. It can be difficult to detect such themes, given the biological concepts and medical terminology within which explanations of women's menstrual functioning are cocooned. With the application of a wider historical, epistemological, and medical perspective, however, it becomes easy to see the deeply problematic nature of these discourses.

Objectivity

PMS is of interest to the courts because it has been, like the other syndromes we have surveyed, classified as a scientific diagnosis. Its identification and treatment by members of the medical profession initiated this impression, and its inclusion in the DSM reinforces its scientific status. These practitioners use scientific methods to study the condition and technical terminology to explain it. The objectivity that is deemed to accompany its classification as a science is meaningful to law.

This point is evident in the importance placed on medical testimony in all of the PMS cases described earlier. In the cases of Sandie Smith and Christine English, for example, it was Dr Dalton's expert testimony that was crucial to the judge's decision in each case that PMS was a valid explanation of the women's behaviour. Her testimony was also significant in the case of *R* v *Reynolds* (1988), in which a defendant who had killed her mother pled PMS as a mitigating factor. Dalton's arguments stressed the reliability of the diagnosis in these cases, a factor which was compelling to the court. In the bankruptcy case of Jamie Irvin, medical opinion was just as important – in reaching the *converse* decision that PMS was not a valid explanation of behaviour. None of the medical experts testifying on that occasion endorsed the PMS diagnosis, leading the judges to determine that the acceptance of PMS 'as an explanation for improper conduct has not yet been established either medically or legally' (*Lovato* v *Irvin*, 1983, cited in Benedek, 1988: 499). In particular, they pointed out that

> [t]he Diagnostic and Statistical Manual, DSM, relied on by many psychiatrists and regarded by the obstetrician [who testified in the case] as important, does not even list PMS. The latest edition appears to be DSM-III published in 1980. It does not recognize PMS as a mental illness, as a mental disorder, or as a personality disorder. It does not record PMS as a medical problem. The explanation for [the actions considered in this case] was a diagnosis of PMS

and its impact on the human psyche is not fully known and there is little information on that subject. It is clear from the testimony that PMS and its effect on human behavior is still the subject of medical debate.

(Benedek, 1988: 499)

Although PMS was, indeed, not a category in the DSM at the time this case was heard, it has of course since been accepted. This alters entirely the reasoning that would be available to judges now.

The DSM is pivotal because it is taken as representing the objective opinion of the medical community, including psychologists and psychiatrists. The existence of a diagnostic category within the DSM communicates the message that it has become generally accepted amongst experts that menstrual functioning is (at least sometimes) the cause of pathological behaviour. Widespread professional acceptance is, as discussed in Chapter 2, central to evidential rules such as the *Daubert* guidelines and the *Frye* rule, for invoking the use of concepts such as 'general acceptance' implies that expert knowledge is accurate, reliable, and ultimately objective.

However, the medical community does not, of course, have such a firm basis for its conclusions about PMS. General acceptance has failed to be achieved in regard to any aspect of PMS: its definition, symptomatology, treatments, or rate of manifestation. Disagreement continues to rage about each of these issues. The casual discussions of PMS 'behaviour' and PMS 'treatment', both within legal cases and professional publications, make these issues sound unproblematic and simple. Even if explanations of PMS *had* achieved general acceptance within the medical community, this would not ensure that those explanations were *accurate*. It ensures that they are *popular*. General acceptance by the medical community would be most likely to endorse the view that women are impaired by PMS, because this fits with historical and contemporary views about women's biological functioning. This is the fundamental problem of using general acceptance as a guide to admissibility of evidence in the courtroom. Consensus does not ensure accuracy. When alternative explanations about a phenomenon are not found within the scientific literature, one cannot automatically assume that those explanations are 'wrong'. It is more likely that they fail to fit with the views of the more powerful mainstream community.

For there are alternatives available to the medical account of PMS. The model promoted by many feminist researchers is one that emphasises the social construction of 'reality'. This explanation directs attention to the processes by which women's menstrual experiences come to be classified as abnormal. It is possible to acknowledge the existence of menstrual phenomena without defining those symptoms as illness. Indeed, medical textbooks sometimes identify PMS as a Western illness, noting that it 'is a feature of modern conditions of life in Western civilized communities and is rarely encountered in, or complained of, by women in Eastern countries' (Jeffcoate, 1987: 542). The issue becomes one of how cultures *construct* what it means to be ill and what it means to be healthy. The fact that certain events occur together or recur in a predictable pattern does not necessarily mean that they are linked or that they are an illness. Hilary Allen (1990: 203–204) illustrates this point splendidly by proposing the 'Pre-Breakfast Syndrome', which would 'lump together all the various complaints which could ever, in any individual, be shown to appear regularly in the first hours after waking and then to subside'. The symptoms of Pre-Breakfast Syndrome would cover a diverse set of symptoms, including 'habitual hangover, morning sickness, smoker's cough, lethargy or excitability, reduced or increased libido, irritability, intellectual impairment, and numerous others'. All of these events are real, are undesirable, commonly occur together, and have a regular pattern. Yet neither society nor medicine considers them symptoms of an illness.

It is by using analogies such as this one that feminist critics have tried to highlight the processes by which menstrual changes have been categorised as disease in our Western, twentieth-century culture. This analysis has been extended not only to PMS, but also the menarche, postpartum period, and menopause, among other reproductive stages. Unfortunately, the subtlety of the social constructionist argument is easily lost. When feminists argue that a premenstrual syndrome does not (or may not) exist, they are frequently taken to mean that menstrual-related changes do not exist. It is alleged that feminists deny the existence of PMS, preaching that the symptoms are 'all in women's heads'. Feminists' wish to contest the *classification* of the changes, rather than their *existence*, is a point that is frequently missed, drowned out in the professional shouting match.

For example, Joann D'Emilio (1985: 586), arguing in favour of PMS as a criminal defence, remarks in one of her papers that '[s]ome feminists, because of the possible deleterious effects that would result from the acceptance of PMS evidence, deny the very existence of the syndrome'. In support of her comments, she cites Elizabeth Holtzman, the prosecuting attorney in the *Santos* case, as saying 'that there is no scientific evidence proving the existence of a syndrome that causes women to become insane or violent in connection with their menstrual periods' (D'Emilio, 1985: 586). In a rejoinder that Holtzman wrote to D'Emilio's article, Holtzman reiterated her view, emphasising that 'there is no single well-defined medical condition which can be called "premenstrual syndrome"' (Holtzman, 1986: 712–713). Holtzman is absolutely correct. As we saw earlier, there is no single well-defined medical condition – there is a tumultuous jigsaw of hypotheses, evidence, and interpretations. Whether or not the final product resembles a 'real' syndrome depends on how one fits the pieces together.

Dalton, too, specifically targets feminist objections to PMS. The following statement is taken from the introduction to her most recent text on the syndrome.

> The other major group of people who refuse to accept PMS [besides psychoanalytic psychologists] is to be found among the more extreme feminists. As they see it, the existence of PMS means that women are not the equals of men; their political beliefs revolve around the article of faith that women are equal to men in all respects, and if anything conflicts with this belief then it must be wrong. . . . *We have to accept the world as it is*; instead of bewailing or rationalizing away *the fact of PMS*, the authors of this book are

trying to do something constructive about it; by freeing women from PMS we seek to remove this 'inequality' (if that is what it is). We would like to feel that we are doing more than some other (more politically motivated) people to help women.

(Dalton, 1994: xv, emphasis added)

Dalton's reference to the 'the world as it is' and 'the fact of PMS' implies that the world is an objective place and our experience of it an objective process. We must 'take the world as we find it', rather than seeking to understand how we participate in creating our understanding of and response to it. By highlighting the political position of feminists, but failing to acknowledge her own, she engages in the custom of treating the unmarked position as a neutral one. It is precisely this practice that maintains the façade of objectivity.

The presumption that an objective position is achievable and desirable contributes to an 'either–or' impasse. Either PMS exists or it does not. Either it is real or it is made up. Either women have it or they do not. Such rigid dichotomies do not allow for discussion of the subtle, but vitally important ways, in which PMS is constructed as an illness. The message of those critiquing PMS is exactly that: there does not have to be a choice between non-existence and pathology. It is possible to recognise menstrual experiences without categorising them as illness. However, because scientists and lawyers and society seek an answer that appears to be generally accepted, factual, and objective, the nuances of this line of reasoning are lost. Amidst the fracas, it is understandable why, as Laws (1990) observes, so many women have been driven to see those who promote the notion that PMS is an illness as a 'pro-woman force'. As PMS inches its way into the legal system, the medical account becomes further legitimated, for law's acceptance accords the diagnosis even greater reliability and reality. There is less need, and less scope, to question it.

Male norm

An attraction of the 'diagnosis' of PMS, for many women, is that it appears to legitimise their experience. Their cramps, irritability, mood swings, headaches, nausea, and lack of concentration are real. They cannot be accused of making up these things, for medical science has accorded their experience an official label. The weakness in this argument is that legitimisation does not solve the key problem. It simply affirms what the law, psychology, medicine, and societal norms have always surmised anyway: that women are emotional, unstable, and frail. Legitimising women's experience by labelling it as illness does not move the debate forward. It leaves women where they started. It is in realising this that it becomes easy to see the degree to which objectivity and the male norm are intricately entangled.

It is not uncommon to hear women say that if science confirms the reality of their symptoms, then no one can say that they are making it up. For example, Figert (1996: xix–xx) recounts the occasion on which the grandmother of a friend contacted her to say she favoured the inclusion of a PMS-related disorder in the DSM-III-R because 'she thought that it would prove that what she felt as a young woman was "real", even though nobody would believe her at the time'. Kingston (1980: 63) makes the following remark at the beginning of her PMS self-help book.

> In those days people thought there was something magic or evil about menstrual blood. Now we know that it's chemistry that's doing the damage. We're clumsy and accident-prone because the chemical balance of our bodies is upset.

Laws, too, points out that '[m]uch of the thrust of the pro-PMT lobby's argument is that women *want* it to be defined as a medical problem' (Laws, 1985: 32, emphasis in original). The assumption is that validation of women's experience will occur through 'proving' that it is real. Such reasoning is amiss, however; legitimising menstrual experience in a way that is positive for women can only be accomplished if the menstrual changes are characterised as normal. PMS does not do that, and thus it is ultimately detrimental to women. It may confirm the *existence* of the symptoms, but it does not change their *characterisation* as abnormal. This is a crucial distinction.

Finding a scientific label for the inferior aspects of women's nature offers no intrinsic benefit to them. The term 'PMS' serves only to confirm what powerful groups and institutions have always maintained – that women are problematic, impaired by their physiological nature. Leading gynaecological textbooks,[6] for example, still advise that

> [disorders related to PMS are] especially common in women aged 20 to 60, who often have a background of marital stress, sexual frustration, depression or anxiety. . . . Treatment is unsatisfactory and many patients have to learn to live with their disorder, until their domestic problems are resolved.
>
> (Llewellyn-Jones, 1990: 61)

> The [PMS-]affected individual is often full of restless energy, cleaning the house when it is already spotless, fussing and nagging the children, worrying when there is no need.
>
> (Jeffcoate, 1987: 542)[7]

The label PMS also confirms what men have always believed. Laws's interviews with men led her to conclude that 'many men had held for a long time that periods made a woman a bit odd, cross, unpredictable, and that PMT was to them just a new name for something they knew about all along' (Laws, 1990: 193).

Most importantly for our purposes, PMS confirms that law's traditional perception of women's behaviour (as irrational) is valid. For example, the inconsistent application of legal defences that we saw in regard to cases of domestic violence (Chapter 4) can be observed in the case of Christine English. Her partner,

Barry Kitson, was described in the press as an alcoholic, with stories relating details of the argument they had been having, in which he had 'punched her when they quarrelled . . . about his drinking and his other women' (*Daily Mirror*, 11 November 1981). Another recounted that 'he slapped her and pulled her hair' (*The Sun*, 11 November 1981). English said that she had 'just snapped'. She had 'only wanted to frighten him' (*Daily Mirror*, 11 November 1981). English's account is very similar to accounts offered by men explaining that they have killed their female partners as a result of 'snapping', especially if confessions regarding sexual promiscuity were involved. It is for such circumstances that the defence of provocation was devised. When this defence is accepted (as the review of cases in Chapter 4 reveals it often is), the law is indicating that the defendant's actions, while unfortunate, were understandable. Any 'reasonable man' might have reacted in this way to these circumstances, and thus the behaviour needs no further explanation. Christine English, however, did need a further excuse for her actions. Her defence involved pleading mitigating circumstances. Thus, her 'snapping' was excused by the law not because it was considered 'reasonable' but because she had an illness which explained it. That is not to say that we are arguing English's actions would necessarily be considered 'reasonable' in laypersons' terms. Rather, we are trying to highlight the gendered nature of what the law considers to be 'reasonable'.

That this 1980 view continues the traditional legal view is illustrated by reference to a 1969 US report, emerging from the President's Commission on Law Enforcement and the Administration of Justice. Noting that 'the single greatest cause of homicides in the US' was 'intra-familial quarrels', and concerned that 'every fifth policeman who is killed in the line of duty dies in the process of breaking up a family fight', the Commission made the following recommendation.

> In the case of the woman who kills or maims her husband, lover, child, or other relative or who is killed or maimed, this study suggests that it is important to ask the question: What was her menstrual condition at the time of the event?
> (Ellis and Austin, 1971; quoted in Wallach and Rubin, 1971: 229–230)

The authors are suggesting that for every instance of violence in which women are involved – whether committed by her or against her – there may be a menstrual connection. Women are accorded the responsibility both for committing violence and for provoking it in others. *English* is far from being the most recent legal decision to reflect this view. The 1998 case of William Gallacher brings it up-to-date, when the court accepted Gallacher's explanation that he had punched his wife because her menopausal mood swings had provoked him (*The Scotsman*, 10 December 1998).

By focusing on women's behaviour, the context of male violence within which their actions so often occur can be ignored. By blaming intra-familial violence on women's menstrual cycles, the President's Commission relieved themselves of the need to consider how male violence formed both a private and societal context of women's experience. This restricted view, commonplace in the 1960s, was part of what the women's movement of the 1970s sought to address. Christine English's

1980 case demonstrates that continued efforts are required. The media coverage of her trial de-emphasised Kitson's violence, treating it as if it were 'merely incidental' (Hey, 1985: 77). His 'provocative gestures, language and demeanour, as well as his physical assaults, retain[ed] the status of background "colour"' (Hey, 1985: 78). The focus of the story remained on English's actions, with no serious attention given to the setting within which they occurred. The same restricted focus would have existed in the courtroom, for Kitson's general violence would have been deemed irrelevant, and thus inadmissible, to the specific issues under consideration in the case. The rules of evidence would have prevented the court from even considering how Kitson's long-term behavioural patterns might have contributed to English's actions that evening. Surprisingly, the limited focus has even been retained in academic discussions of the case (e.g. Chait, 1986; D'Emilio, 1985; Luckhaus, 1985; Sommer, 1984), thereby rendering the 'background colour' of male violence a completely bland, irrelevant, unnoticed one. Like so many other cases in which women kill abusive partners (see Chapter 4), discussion about the *English* decision has come to focus on the merits or limitations of the specific defence used. The context which frames women's actions has not been illuminated. While such context is often present in cases of men's violence, as for example when the court accepts that her irrational menstrual behaviour provokes him to violence, syndrome explanations such as PMS and BWS have not been successful in drawing attention to the context of women's actions. Indeed, by stressing the (disordered) characteristics of the individual woman, they have been successful in helping that context to remain hidden, protected, and unexamined.

Robert Carney and Brian Williams argued in a 1983 publication that the decisions in the *English* case in England and the *Santos* child abuse case in the US indicated a trend toward recognising PMS in criminal cases (see also Sommer, 1984). They urged that American courts needed to decide how they would respond, and the purpose of their article was to explore what they viewed as the three most realistic responses. Although their predictions of a strong trend have not been borne out, it is useful to examine the responses they propose because the operation of the male norm is so clearly demonstrated in them. One response identified by Carney and Williams was the establishment of a substantive defence which would allow PMS to stand on its own, and the other was allowing PMS to serve as a mitigating factor in sentencing following conviction of a crime.

If PMS were recognised as a substantive defence, Carney and Williams suggest it would be analogous to an insanity defence, in that a defendant who was successful in pleading that defence would be acquitted (i.e. found not guilty). In order to be convicted of a crime, it must generally be shown that the defendant was able to form the intent to commit the alleged crime, a concept known as *mens rea* in legal terminology. If it can be shown that the defendant was not able to form that intent, perhaps because of a failure to understand the consequences of that behaviour or because s/he was unaware of the behaviour or could not control it, then it is the view of the law that such a person ought not to be held responsible, for s/he is not morally blameworthy. Of course, a defendant who is found not guilty by reason of insanity is likely to be committed to a mental institution (if the crime is a serious one). Carney and Williams argue that this would not be an appropriate outcome for a PMS defence, because incarceration in a mental institution would serve no rehabilitative function.

Thus, they suggest that, as a substantive defence, PMS fits more closely with the defence of automatism, which is a narrowly defined but accepted defence in many jurisdictions, including England, Scotland, and the US. Indeed, automatism is precisely the defence for which the counsel of *R* v *Smith* (1982) and of *People* v *Santos* (1982) argued. Automatistic behaviour refers to that committed while a defendant is in an unconscious or semiconscious state, and can be caused by somnambulism, delirium from fever, hypoglycaemia, diabetic shock, epileptic seizures, and the ingestion of drugs, among other factors. For Carney and Williams, if a defence of automatism were successful in PMS cases, it would acknowledge that the 'PMS sufferer . . . is no more able to control her actions than the automaton or the legally insane' (1983: 265).

In order for this defence to gain recognition by the courts, however, a mechanism needs to be in place to allow PMS sufferers to be treated and supervised. 'Without such a mechanism, the courts could not ensure that . . . society is protected from future antisocial behavior' (p. 266). While this type of mechanism is available in the UK courts,[8] it tends to be absent in US jurisdictions. Where it is not available, Carney and Williams suggest that PMS should be treated as mitigation, thus providing 'a workable compromise between completely rejecting PMS as a legal issue and recognizing it as a substantive defense to crime' (p. 266). The mitigated sentence should stress treatment, rather than a reduced prison sentence, for 'under no circumstances' do Carney and Williams believe that 'PMS-induced conduct' should be punished by courts (p. 267).

The outcome of this reasoning is that women are placed in a double bind: they can either be guilty or they can be crazy. They can be wicked or they can be controlled. But they cannot be reasonable and autonomous, and they cannot engage in criminal or violent activity for rational reasons, as men can. Thus, in the case of *R* v *Beer* (1985), a woman who stole a joint of beef worth £4.10 could not explain her theft as a (reasonable, if illegal) strategy for coping with poverty, but as a consequence of her PMS. In *R* v *Morris* (1988), a woman who wounded her partner, by stabbing him after hearing that he was making advances to a neighbour, could not successfully argue that she had done so because she was provoked into doing so by his behaviour, the basis on which many men have explained murderous behaviour and been awarded suspended sentences (see Chapter 4). Rather, her argument that she was under treatment for PMS enabled the appeal court to reduce her 30-month sentence to a 24-month sentence. PMS explanations take away women's ability to be responsible for their own behaviour. 'Its crude biologism allows for women's different and therefore "dangerous" bodies to be disqualified' (Hey, 1985: 66). While this may be useful in dealing with an unjust legal system, as Laws (1983: 21) observes, 'the consequences for women struggling towards a positive view of themselves are worrying'. The consequences for women's treatment under the law are also worrying, for the use of PMS arguments simply reinforces the deviance with which Woman has been traditionally characterised by the law, by medicine, and by science.

Finally, the operation of the male norm becomes apparent when one realises that there are judgements about the morality of women's behaviour residing within the PMS debate. Expectations about how women *should* behave are voiced, and when they do not live up to those expectations, suggestions are made about how women might be controlled. Such judgements are particularly clear in legal commentary.

For example, the outcome of Carol Thomas's road traffic offence, described earlier, was sufficiently notable to cause the editor of the *Scottish Criminal Case Reports*, in which the case was reported, to remark upon it. If editors consider the outcome of a case to be particularly unusual, they may include some commentary upon it. The editor of the 1991 *Reports*, Sheriff Gerald Gordon, a widely respected and influential writer in Scots law, states in regard to *Thomas* v *Lowe* that

> [a]lthough the recognition of premenstrual tension as a mitigating factor will no doubt be welcomed in many quarters, one is left wondering whether people should *be allowed* to drive at times when they are known to be likely to behave irrationally. [The relevant sections] of the Road Traffic Act 1988, which deal with removing driving licences because of *disability*, do not provide for the restriction of a driving licence to certain times. It is probably reckless driving to drive at a time when one knows one is likely to behave *irrationally*. . . . [A]lthough [reckless driving] can be committed by driving a vehicle known to be unsafe, it does not apparently extend to driving when one knows oneself to be *unsafe*.
>
> (Gordon, 1991: 945, emphasis added)

There are undoubtedly millions of times per day that cars are driven by people in aggressive, irrational states (a majority of them men, if road rage incidents are any measure – Joint, 1995). Yet, Gordon does not appear to be concerned about these aggressive individuals. It is the appearance of irrational states in women with PMS that worries him here. Although he uses the term 'people', he means women, given that he is commenting on a PMS case. He perceives them to be in a 'disabled', 'unsafe' state, and recommends that they therefore not be 'allowed' to drive. Given that by some definitions all women suffer PMS and, further, that PMS sufferers are, necessarily, expected to become irrational and disabled on a monthly basis, this implies that perhaps all women should be restricted from driving for those crucial few days each month. (What a novel traffic calming measure that would be.) It also shows how, once a diagnosis is verified as 'real', it can just as easily be used to undermine and control women as it can to help them, a pattern which has been observed in other domains such as Rape Trauma Syndrome (Chapter 5).

The comments of the judges in the case of Sandie Smith (1982) are even more moralistic in tone. They declared that 'the dark side of her nature appeared as a result of being unable to control the impulse, which she would not have allowed to dominate her normally'. Her hormones were said to have turned her into a 'raging animal each month and forced her to act out of character' (quoted in Lacey and Wells, 1998: 587), an image that the media made much of. Similar character-isations of the effect of PMS can be found in *R v Morris* (1988), whose act of stabbing was said to have occurred because she 'lost her self control', and in *Lovato v Irvin* (1983: 1), where the judges observed the defendant's contention that the assault was 'the result of uncontrollable conduct . . . as if someone else took over her body'. In *Scott v Hamilton* (1988: 264), the trial judge accepted that the appellant's moods were 'uncontrollable when she was at the relevant stage of her menstrual cycle but that otherwise she was a normal, rational person', and in *Thomas v Lowe* (1991: 945), PMS was said to lead to actions like those of 'a completely different person; she can become almost aggressive and acts irrationally'. In short, these women had within them monsters, demons that could jump out and cause havoc when not controlled.

The language used in these cases is uncannily similar to that used over a century ago to explain women's behaviour. Bucknill and Tuke, in their 1858 edition of *A Manual of Psychological Medicine*, discussed the various forms of insanity which women suffered as a result of 'puerpal mania'. This condition was associated with women's confinement during childbirth, making it somewhat equivalent to today's condition of Postnatal Depression. They remarked that

> [e]very medical man has observed the extraordinary amount of obscenity, in thought and language, which breaks forth from the most modest and well-nurtured woman under the influence of puerpal mania. . . . [R]eligious and moral principles alone give strength to the female mind; and . . . when these are weakened or removed by disease, the subterranean fires become active; and the crater gives forth smoke and flame.
>
> (quoted in Smith, 1981: 151–152)

Victorian women clearly had monsters hiding within them too. Such reasoning is identical to that used by the judges in more contemporary cases. Both consider that the medical condition suffered by the woman renders her unable to control the smouldering cauldron of unacceptable social behaviours that lurks beneath her respectable exterior.

Even the common societal pressure on girls and women to 'be nice' is revealed as a moral injunction. At the time of the *Smith* and *English* cases, Dalton was quoted in the *Coventry Evening Telegraph* as saying

> I think women have a duty if they know they are going to break something and going to be irritable to be treated and to look after themselves. They owe it to themselves and to women in general. Otherwise they will get what they deserve from men.
>
> (quoted in Laws, 1985: 31)

These comments are ominously similar to those that crop up so frequently in legal and lay discourses about rape, abortion, domestic violence, and other areas of women's lives about what women 'ought' and 'ought not' to do. In Dalton's view, treatment becomes a duty on the part of women, and if they fail to fulfil that obligation, they get what they deserve. Certainly a male norm is operating when anyone (regardless of their sex) construes women's 'failure' to seek treatment for a naturally occurring event as punishable.

In short, the diagnosis of PMS provides a contemporary vehicle through which women's behaviour can be controlled and their fulfilment of societal expectations of feminine conduct can be evaluated. However, because the medical, scientific discourse driving that vehicle is believed to be objective and neutral, the moralistic quality of the syndrome is often imperceptible. It is but one more way in which PMS supports a male-normative account of women's behaviour. Whether it performs the role of label for the woman's ordinary bodily functions, defence for her crimes, or insight into her moral obligations, PMS without fail characterises women's experience as unreasonable, abnormal, and in need of control.

Individualism

Like other psychiatric and psychological syndromes, PMS is conceptualised as a diagnosis of the individual. It is a condition that an individual woman experiences. It is a condition which can (ostensibly) be controlled through treatment administered to an individual woman. Indeed, as a key characteristic of the implicit relation, individualism is displayed in PMS perhaps more obviously than in any other syndrome we consider in this book. That is because the disorder is characterised as biological in origin. Unlike all of the other disorders we have considered, PMS is not a psychological reaction to a traumatic event (e.g. domestic violence, rape, childhood sexual abuse). It is considered a result of physiological, bodily forces. A biological explanation is the ultimate form of individualism.

One consequence of characterising a condition as individualistic is that this relieves the need for courts, and for society in general, to consider the social circumstances that contribute to its existence. It was a common charge, for example, that the suffragettes' actions, in their pursuit of the vote for women, were due to menstrual dysfunction and 'chronic spinsterhood' (Kennedy, 1993: 24). (Yes, indeed, if those troublesome suffragettes had just found themselves a good man . . .) If a woman's problems can be shown to be due to her internal state, there is no need to look at how wider social circumstances may influence, or even 'cause', her condition. The political, economic, and societal contexts within which illnesses are experienced by women and 'identified' by professionals can be ignored. If a condition is biological, then society can certainly be relieved of any responsibility for its origin. Society cannot cause a woman's biological disorder. But can Woman's biology cause disorder in society?

Whenever the theme of PMS and its adverse social consequences appears in the mainstream literature, the underlying message is that women's biological nature is problematic for everyone. It is troublesome not only for herself, but it is also dangerous to others. PMS becomes a concern for the whole of society; it is in the interests of everyone that women and their moods be controlled. This is the case regardless of whether that control is to be exerted at the level of the individual woman or women as a group. Either way, the old refrains calling for women's regulation and restriction continue to resonate.

PMS came to be a social concern when it was linked to murder, through media coverage of the cases of *Smith* and *English*. If popular attention to the adverse social consequences of PMS did not emerge until the 1980s, the research literature had always maintained a focus on the social problems caused by 'women's raging hormones'. PMS was originally conceived of as a problematic state. 'From the beginning the scientific approach to PMS was not concerned with the investigation of a "neutral" phenomenon, equivalent to plant growth in botany or muscle function in physiology, for example, but with the investigation of a disease or dysfunctional state' (Walker, 1997: 145). It is particularly social problems caused by PMS that have worried researchers, with the literature linking PMS and menstruation to a plethora of events that hold adverse implications for society: marital discord, family disharmony, academic performance, psychiatric admissions, suicide attempts, household accidents, factory accidents, automobile accidents, and even loss of control of aircraft. The cost to industry and commerce, through absenteeism and work inefficiency due to PMS, has been deplored. The contribution to crime, including theft, prostitution, drunk and disorderly conduct, shoplifting, burglary, embezzlement, forgery, child battering, and child neglect, has been condemned.[9] Even the behaviour of 'naughty schoolgirls', including 'talking when silence is requested, lateness, and forgetfulness', has been reproachfully attributed to the menstrual cycle, with the explanation that 'hormonal changes of menstruation probably make the individual less amenable to discipline' (Dalton, 1961: 1753). Indeed, Aleta Wallach and Larry Rubin were concerned enough to write a 104-page article entitled 'The Premenstrual Syndrome and Criminal Responsibility' that was published in the *UCLA Law Review* in 1971. (For other literature that discusses such associations without any critical analysis, see Carney and Williams, 1983; Dalton, 1960b, 1961, 1964; D'Emilio, 1985; Hull *et al.*, 1997; Jeffcoate, 1987; Quilligan and Zuspan, 1990; Reid and Yen, 1981.) It is these kinds of societal concerns that motivate researchers to conduct their work on PMS and with which contemporary gynaecological texts begin their discussion of menstrual problems. It is these kinds of concerns that mobilise practitioners to develop treatments for the condition. It is this association that is for researchers an unproblematic context within which to design experiments, interpret findings, and validate scientific enquiry into the disorder. (And it is these kinds of concerns that capture powerfully the sense in which PMS might, as pointed out earlier, be said to lead women to act more like men.)

Mary Parlee (1973) compiled a powerful critique of this research literature, pointing out that the methodological and theoretical rigour of these studies had often been 'less than sound' (p. 455). For example, researchers frequently failed to define the length of the phases they were treating as variables, and doubtful methods had been used to identify phases of the cycle (e.g. reviewing prison inmates' records). Examination of the psychometric properties of questionnaires (i.e. their reliability and validity) was frequently neglected, and the retrospective nature of many popular questionnaires shed doubt on the accuracy of the data they generated. Many studies failed to establish a baseline from which any increase or decrease in behaviour could reasonably be assessed. Control groups were not always employed, and were often of a theoretically simplistic nature when they were used. Parlee particularly emphasised the way in which correlational studies, which comprise a large proportion of research on PMS, had been interpreted as implying that phases of the menstrual cycle *cause* particular acts. Such interpretations are usually accomplished through the use of suggestive language, rather than explicit reference to causative factors. A particularly entertaining example is that of Whitehead's 1934 publication in the *Journal of Aviation Medicine*, in which he reports three aeroplane crashes, in all of which the pilots were women who were thought to have been menstruating at the time of the flight. Such an association tells us nothing, of course, about whether menstruation *causes* pilots to crash, nor whether 'women pilots tend to be boyish females, homosexuals or a normal type' (Whitehead, 1934: 48). Similarly, finding a significant correlation within a set of research findings does not allow the experimenter to draw any firm conclusions about the cause of the association. Even the suggestion of such an interpretation contravenes the basic logic of experimental design.

Problems such as these did not stop researchers from citing earlier work, however. Parlee traced the way in which myths persist within psychology, as a result of authors' failures to evaluate critically or even to check original sources before referring to them. The fact that many early papers continue to be cited uncritically in papers published since Parlee's article demonstrates that little has changed. Parlee's insightful (but, to many, irksome) observations made little impact on the field. Traditional gender politics are still being served.

The entrance of PMS into the courtroom has highlighted the issue of individualism in a particularly explicit way. It has sparked a contest between the rights of the individual and the needs of women as a group. As Mulligan (1983: 227) summarises the problem,

> [t]he benefits possibly available to the small class of women charged with crimes who would be able to raise a successful PMS defense, or use their PMS condition to mitigate their punishment, must be weighed against the potential setback to the women's movement stemming from reenforcement by the legal system of the widespread perception that all women are violent and irrational during their premenstrual phase.

If PMS provides a possible defence for women accused of crimes, should they be denied it because there are concerns about how it serves the wider interests of women? D'Emilio (1985) argues that PMS has been prevented from becoming more widely accepted as a defence by fears that the public would perceive all women as suffering from menstrually related disorders and that women would be kept out of positions of authority. These fears highlight the conundrum: which is more important – the interests of the individual woman defendant or women as a group?

D'Emilio answers that question by coming down unreservedly on the side of the individual. She contends that

> social implications place speculative and attenuated social concerns above the right of the individual defendant to a fair trial. . . . [I]t would be unjust to deny a fair trial and substantial justice because of an unfounded fear that the basis of [a defendant's] relief from criminal liability could possibly harm broader social interests.
>
> (D'Emilio, 1985: 587)

Helena Kennedy, senior counsel and member of the House of Lords in the UK, agrees in principle. She observes that 'it is the lawyer's imperative to prevent people going to jail', and she notes that in order to accomplish this, 'most defence advocates will be happy to exploit PMT, leaving aside the impact of this for women generally' (Kennedy, 1993: 24). In short, both D'Emilio and Kennedy are saying that individual rights are more important than wider social consequences of the use of PMS in the courtroom.

However, the ways in which these two commentators approach the issue indicate very different levels of comprehension of the issues involved. Kennedy frames her comments within the context of the demands of the job: 'it is the lawyer's imperative to prevent people going to jail'. She 'leaves aside' the impact for women in general. The tone of Kennedy's language implies that she realises the impasse of her choice. D'Emilio, however, downplays the risk to women in general, labelling the concerns 'speculative', 'attenuated', and 'unfounded'. She reaches her solution by denying the legitimacy of the concerns.

The concerns, however, are neither speculative nor unfounded. It is precisely such concerns that led to the vigorous campaign to keep PMS out of the DSM (see Figert, 1996). The solution is neither obvious nor easy, for the individual and the group cannot be separated. It is not sufficient to argue, as D'Emilio does, that 'PMS sufferers should be entitled to enter evidence . . . *regardless of* the serious policy concerns asserted by certain women's rights groups' (1985: 587, emphasis added).[10] The needs of the individual and the group are inextricably linked, as the vintage feminist adage 'the personal is political' sought to communicate.

It is interesting to note, therefore, that it is with awareness of this fusion that Hilary Allen (1990) and Linda Chait (1986) argue for the opposite position of Kennedy and D'Emilio. Chait proposes that '[PMS] should be treated under the law just like any other organic illness and not given special treatment as a "women's defense"' (Chait, 1986: 283). Allen states unequivocally that she believes 'there should be no premenstrual tension defense and no special judicial treatment of premenstrual tension sufferers as such' (Allen, 1990: 223). Acknowledging that this 'implies the (politically uncomfortable) advocacy of severer treatment for women than that which they might currently receive' (Allen, 1990: 223), Allen's position is based on the contention that questions of responsibility and guilt cannot be reducible to biological state and that it is not desirable to treat men and women differentially as defendants. She points out that the law already has criteria for judging a defendant's mental state at the time of an act. Because these criteria are, in principle, indifferent to disease categories, they should be sufficient to assess responsibility for all criminal acts. Both Chait and Allen offer the interesting argument that, on a logical basis, characterising PMS as increasing sufferers' propensity to crime – arguments promoted by Dalton and others – does not constitute grounds for special leniency once one has committed such crime. There are other medical conditions that increase the likelihood of sufferers' committing violent acts, such as XYY Syndrome, but no treatment has been developed that helps to prevent them from such actions. They contend that it is inequitable to accord leniency to some criminals because medical treatment is available to help curtail their behaviour while continuing to punish others who have no treatment available to them. Overall, as Allen (1990: 226) argues, the 'antisocial behaviors' of women who have featured in PMS cases have a 'relevance to the law that is irrespective of their relationship to women's hormones in general'.

The position adopted by Allen and Chait may seem a harsh one. It is, however, logically consistent, and it is one in which they acknowledge and attempt to deal with the uncomfortable consequences it generates. Their position refutes the contention of critics, such as Christina Hoff Sommers, that radical feminists support women at any cost: 'The message is that women must be "gynocentric", that they must join with and be loyal only to women' (Sommers, 1994: 22). Feminist analysis has often highlighted the conflicts that can arise between the needs of individual women and those of women as a group, a contrast that is particularly illuminated in the PMS domain. When such conflicts are not easily solved, there is a tendency to deny or ignore or simply despair of them. The contributions of Allen and Chait demonstrate the possibility of alternative responses.

Conclusion

PMS has been called 'the disease of the 1980s' (Figert, 1996: 6). Official endorsement had finally arrived, after doctors had spent years telling women that it was 'all in their heads'. Our aim in this chapter has been to show that such affirmation has not served women particularly well, however. The irrationality and deviance traditionally ascribed to Woman had simply been relocated – from her womb to her hormones. Women, via their biological inheritance, continued to be blamed for economic mishap, family breakdown, and criminal mayhem. It is notable that interest in PMS should have increased at a time when women were gaining economic independence and power, as a result of the women's movement in the 1970s. 'Discussions of PMS were published at a time when women were not only participating in increasing numbers in the paid labor force but were also proving themselves to be quite capable within this context' (Rittenhouse, 1991: 419). As we have argued throughout this text, consideration of the socio-historical factors that give rise to a syndrome diagnosis are as important in making sense of it as the professional discourse that sustains it.

Why, though, has the use of a 'PMS defence' not escalated, as was predicted by a number of authors in the years following the cases of the early 1980s (e.g. Carney and Williams, 1983; Mulligan, 1983; Sommer, 1984)? The entry of the diagnosis into the DSM certainly might have been expected to facilitate an explosion of cases, given that the message had finally been sent of the medical profession's general acceptance of the syndrome. We would suggest that this has not occurred because the legal system, and society in general, is instinctively aware of the contradiction that resides within a PMS explanation. If all women are subject to its emotional and cognitive ravages, then it seems they should indeed be controlled. Such a conclusion may have been acceptable to Victorian society, but as an explicit objective, it is of course incompatible with late-twentieth-century attitudes.

This could help to explain why the legal debate has largely been confined to discussions about only a few women – those who appear to lie at the end of a nebulous spectrum. If that restriction can be preserved, the proverbial apple cart will not be upset. But legal decisions always have implications for a much wider group than the specific defendants to whom the decisions pertain. Thus, each time that a legal decision involving the diagnosis of PMS is taken, the spectre is raised that all women are tarred by this diagnostic brush. It is harder in the domain of PMS, than in any other discussed in this text, to separate the individual woman from women as a whole. With domestic violence, rape, and child sexual abuse, it is possible to find some way of discriminating between those women affected and those exempt: their behaviour, their dress, their self-worth, their seductive qualities, their dysfunctional family. It is impossible to erect such safety barriers when hormones are the discriminating factor. All women are at risk of inclusion. Law must take on that mantle if it wishes to acknowledge a PMS 'defence', but even with the assistance of psychology and the medical profession, it may not wish to risk such fury.

Such an account may also help to explain why attention to PMS has thrived in a different, less public sphere. Rittenhouse (1991: 417) discusses the way in which, over the course of the 1980s, PMS became 'something to be managed'. Premenstrual changes became problematised, rather than the women who suffered from the changes. That is, PMS became privatised. Women could control it, through self-help techniques such as eating the right diet and 'putting their feet up' (Kingston, 1980). Women were being afforded the means by which to gain control of their hormones, suggesting that perhaps societal institutions could relax. The battleground thus shifted from that of society to that of the home, which was arguably the primary sphere of concern in the PMS discourse in the 1990s. Contemporary merchandise and jokes tend to focus on the effect of PMS on a woman's personal relationships: her husband, her children, her family, and her friends (Figert, 1996). It is the effect of her hostility, mood swings, 'crying jags', and unpredictability on these recipients that now features in the popular press. This shift relieves law of the need to concern itself with PMS, for the privatised, domestic domain has always been outside the realm that law sees as its primary responsibility.

This shift does not extricate women from their double bind, however. PMS only attains the privatised sphere, and any protection from women's legal regulation that that may bring, by virtue of its capacity for management. This implies that women are obligated to control their PMS and their behaviour, an obligation that is evident in many of the comments we have included in this chapter. If they fail to exercise such dominion, they fail in their moral duty and are once again subject to law's authority. We argued earlier that women's choice was either to be guilty or to be crazy. It appears they have a third option: to manage their craziness. This leaves the implicit relation intact, for women are encouraged to seek the assistance of professionals in managing – in treating – their 'natural' pathology. The law can draw on professional evaluation whenever it needs. The normalising of women's experience has not been achieved through the discourse of PMS. Instead, as the 'legacy of a patriarchal heritage' (Jackson, 1985: 13), the diagnosis will always carry with it the stain of women's deviance.

7   False Memory Syndrome

With so many versions to choose from, the task of disentangling the truth . . . is not an easy one.

Caroline Gonda[1]

Unlike the syndromes featuring in previous chapters, False Memory Syndrome has only very recently emerged. It has yet to gain an 'official' status within psychological or psychiatric discourse, such as entry into the *Diagnostic and Statistical Manual* would bestow. It has, however, already become a very 'real' entity, in that it is a label increasingly used to describe and account for adult women's recollection of sexual abuse committed against them during childhood. Supporters of this diagnostic category urge caution in accepting women's allegations, particularly under the conditions where the abuse had been forgotten for some time. They charge that such memories can be implanted by therapists who employ improper techniques when helping the women to recover from alleged childhood trauma. The False Memory Syndrome movement, emerging only during the 1990s, now embraces a wide range of supporters, including academic psychologists, therapists, clients, journalists, authors, family members, and lawyers. Many of those involved in the debate pursue a distinctly populist path, harnessing the media and internet to promote their cause, while others contribute through conducting scientific research on the properties of memory. The emergence of False Memory Syndrome provides a prime illustration of the way in which psychological syndromes are culturally situated and politically inspired (Lee, forthcoming; Scott, 1990; Young, 1995). It is not therefore surprising to find the implicit relation already at work, even in the early stages of the growth of this syndrome.

Child sexual abuse

Any reflective examination of False Memory Syndrome (FMS) needs, at the outset, to highlight its connection to the phenomenon of child sexual abuse. Several commentators have depicted the FMS movement as a backlash to the shame and guilt aroused through the uncovering of endemic child sexual abuse in the Western world (Armstrong, 1996; Follini, 1995; Schuman and Galvez, 1996; Webster,

1996). 'Child sexual abuse' is a generic term for a range of sexual offences, labelled variously by the criminal law as rape, incest, indecent assault, sodomy, and lewd and libidinous behaviour. This abuse usually occurs in the family home and is perpetrated by a trusted family member, often the father. The feminist movement has played a significant role in the insistence that such abuse be taken seriously and that its aetiology be researched and addressed (e.g. Armstrong 1978, 1996; Bell, 1993; Hall and Lloyd, 1989; Kelly, 1988).

The scale of child sexual abuse has always proven difficult to estimate. The difficulties encountered in assessing the scale of the problem include the secret nature of the act, making it hard to gauge its full extent, and the wide range of behaviours that embody child sexual abuse, from inappropriate touching to rape and sodomy. The problems in gathering statistics are those that we have seen already in regard to rape, domestic violence, and PMS. The statistics that are collated depend on how the issue is defined and measured, the sources of information and methods of research used, and also the purpose of the figures (La Fontaine, 1990). The statistics for child sexual abuse may reveal the number of offenders but do not reveal how many victims were affected by an offender or how many times the offence was repeated. The offence may have been committed against one child or several children, on one occasion or numerous times over a period of years. The figures, of course, provide no information about the vast numbers of offences that remain unreported.

It is only in the last two or three decades that Western society has begun to be able to grasp the frequency with which child sexual abuse occurs. In 1969 the American Humane Society estimated that some 200,000 to 300,000 female children were molested annually in the US (Helfer and Kempe, 1987: 11–12), which, in the context of the overall population, permitted Finkelhor to comment that in the mid-1970s child sexual abuse was 'regarded as a rather uncommon problem' (Finkelhor, 1984: 1). By the 1980s, the picture looked very different, with Russell (1984) estimating that 28% of San Francisco women (based on a sample of 930 women surveyed) revealed having suffered unwanted sexual touching prior to age 14, and 38% suffered such touching prior to age 18. A wide diversity in prevalence estimates began to be produced in studies in both the US and the UK, varying from 5% to 62% for females and from 3% to 31% for males (Finkelhor, 1986: 19; Ghate and Spencer, 1995: 3; Hall and Lloyd, 1989: 22–23; Renvoize, 1982: 42–69). The possible scale of the issue sent shock waves through most social circles, resulting in a variety of reactions. At one end of the spectrum there was the conviction that only the tip of the iceberg had been uncovered (e.g. Finkelhor, 1986; Kelly, 1988; Renvoize, 1982), while at the other end of the spectrum there was utter disbelief, reflected in comments that it was 'simply "impossible" that such a high proportion of women [are] sexually abused' (cited in Freyd, 1996: 35).

Disbelief, first of the frequency of the occurrence and then inevitably of the veracity of the complainant, underscores much of the reaction of the legal system to child sexual abuse. The frequently cited comments of Lord Justice Salmon provide an exemplary illustration of this view. In a 1969 case in which two men appealed against their convictions of raping a 16-year-old girl,[2] he commented that:

> [H]uman experience has shown that in these courts girls and women do sometimes tell an entirely false story which is very easy to fabricate, but extremely difficult to refute. Such stories are fabricated for all sorts of reasons, which I need not now enumerate, and sometimes for no reason at all.
> (*R* v *Henry and Manning*, 1969: 153)

Like the comments in rape cases (see Chapter 5), such statements reveal much about judicial perceptions and attitudes. Although one might hope that such views of 'girls and women' had become outdated since 1969, when Justice Salmon offered his views, Lise Gotell's research (forthcoming) indicates that is not the case. She found similar views being expressed in the 1997 Canadian case of *R* v *NR*, where the court permitted a rape victim's medical records to be released to the accused's lawyers in order to assist in the preparation of his defence. The permission was granted on the basis that the records contained details of when she had lost her virginity, a piece of information that the judges accepted would have a bearing on her credibility 'in the sense that she has both a motive and a propensity to fabricate' (cited in Gotell, forthcoming). In summary, evidence strongly suggests that sexual abuse of children is very common, but there is a reluctance to accept this, even amongst the judiciary, some of whom still believe girls are making it up.

Recovered memories and False Memory Syndrome

Since the early 1990s a further dimension to the debate surrounding child sexual abuse has developed, through reports of recovered memories of childhood sexual abuse. These reports originate from adults who have made allegations of sexual abuse, based on incidents which occurred during their childhood, the memory of which they have forgotten for a period of time and only later recalled. The recollection of these memories may be triggered by a variety of events, including a further trauma, media accounts of sexual abuse, reading accounts of abuse, joining an incest survivors' group, or the death of the abuser (Bass and Davis, 1994; FMSF Website, 1999; Freyd, 1996; Hall and Lloyd, 1989). The memories may also occur during a period of therapy, and it is this route that has become a critical issue within the literature. There are many who argue that, rather than being 'recovered', the memories are 'false', having been implanted by therapists using improper therapeutic techniques (e.g. Gardner, 1992; Hochman, 1994; Pendergrast, 1998; see Prozan, 1997 for review). A variety of labels now exist in the literature for memories that have apparently been remembered after a period of quiescence, and the distinctions in terms are important because they embody different perspectives on the accuracy of the memories. Terms such as 'repressed memories', 'recovered memories', and 'delayed memories' imply that the recollections are accurate, while the term 'false memory' implies that the memories are fabricated, either partially or entirely. The term that an author chooses to use is in part dependent on her or his perspective on the phenomenon. One of the difficulties with such a breadth in terminology is that it encourages interchangeability to the detriment of precision. The danger is that *any* memory of childhood sexual abuse risks being classified as a false memory – a point to which we shall return.

On one side of the debate are those who view delayed memories of child sexual abuse as a credible occurrence (e.g. Armstrong, 1978, 1996; Bass and Davis, 1994; Hall and Lloyd, 1989; Hester, Kelly, and Radford, 1996; Kelly, 1988; Russell, 1984; Schuman and Galvez, 1996). Many of these commentators bring a feminist perspective to the issue, and they consider the reports consistent with women's experience[3] of what Kelly (1988) has termed the male 'continuum of violence'. Sexual abuse of children is characterised by secrecy. 'The child is expected, told or forced by use of threats to keep the secret of sexual abuse' (Hall and Lloyd, 1989: 45). This 'conditioning' of the child's consciousness by an abuser who is usually in a position of trust and power over the child acts as a cogent deterrent to disclosure of abuse. That may be why it is often not until children reach adulthood, with its attendant autonomy, that they are able to face such memories and to break their silence. A loss of memory for the events may be a strategy for coping with early traumatic betrayal (Freyd, 1996). Certainly immense emotional difficulties face survivors of child sexual abuse. At worst, the result is severe, chronic psychological and/or psychiatric dysfunction; at best, survivors are likely to experience continuing bouts of low self-esteem, guilt, anxiety, and depression (Hall and Lloyd, 1989). It is unsurprising that women who try to tell their stories of childhood abuse can appear to be confused, distressed and hesitant.

On the other side of the debate are those who are sceptical about the recovery of previously forgotten memories (e.g. Ceci and Bruck, 1993, 1995; Ceci and Loftus, 1994; Goldstein with Farmer, 1992; Hochman, 1994; Lindsay and Read, 1994; Loftus, 1993; Pendergrast, 1998). Many of these critics are cognitive psychologists, for whom the key issue in this debate is the memory process itself. The phenomenon of recovery breaches current scientific understanding of the way that memory works. Because memory retrieval is always subject to a host of influences including retrieval cues, suggestibility, and source monitoring (i.e. the initial experience of the event and subsequent reaction to it), these scientists urge substantial caution in accepting the accuracy of long-forgotten and incomplete memories. In particular, they distrust many of the techniques allegedly used by therapists in exploring childhood experiences, such as hypnotic age regression, 'truth drugs', guided imagery, dream interpretation, and Rorschach tests. Cognitive psychologists prefer the use of laboratory techniques such as word association, recall tests, and neuroimaging (e.g. Payne *et al.*, 1996; Roediger and McDermott, 1995; Schacter, 1996; Schacter and Curran, 1995) because these allow for control, replication, and verification. Those most sceptical of the notion of repressed memories (e.g. Underwager and Wakefield, 1994) consider women who claim to recover memories of childhood abuse to be suffering from delusions. These 'delusions' or 'mistaken memories' are categorised as 'false memories', and those who have them are said to be suffering from a pathological condition: False Memory Syndrome.

The term 'false memory' and the label of 'syndrome' are, in large part, the currency of the organisation called the False Memory Syndrome Foundation. It was set up in 1992 in the USA by a group of accused families and interested professionals, including Ralph Underwager and his wife, Holly Wakefield, and Pamela Freyd, following a well-publicised case of repressed memories of alleged incest. It has a Scientific and Professional Advisory Board of over thirty members, including prominent academic and clinical psychologists and psychiatrists such as Aaron Beck, Henry Ellis, Rochel Gelman, Henry Gleitman, and Lila Gleitman. According to its supporters the remit of the False Memory Syndrome Foundation (FMSF) is 'to document and study FMS, to disseminate the latest scientific information on memory and to help families' (FMSF Website, 1999). According to its critics, the aim of the False Memory Syndrome Foundation is to 'form an advocacy group' for those accused of abuse (Schuman and Galvez, 1996: 9).

By the early 1990s 'False Memory Syndrome' had become a household term in the United States (see Pendergrast, 1998, for discussion of its history). Newspaper and magazine articles regularly appeared describing the condition. Victims and alleged perpetrators appeared on television talk shows and in documentaries to detail their experiences. Victims spoke of the devaluation of their lives as their recollection of childhood abuse was dismissed as fanciful, the product of a sick mind. Those accused of abuse described the ways in which the allegations cost them their families and relationships, resulted in job losses, and brought about the destruction of professional reputations and personal integrity. All participants in the debate sought to raise the awareness of the American public of the potentially spectacular damage FMS could do.

The profile of FMS in the UK has been more muted. The British False Memory Society (BFMS) was founded in 1993 by Roger Scotford, a former naval officer who claimed he had been wrongly accused of sexual abuse by his daughter, memories of which she recovered while undergoing therapy (*Sunday Times*, 10 July 1994). The BFMS was set up to mirror the activities of its sister organisation in the USA. It too has an Advisory Committee, consisting of eminent British psychologists such as Janet Feigenbaum, Elizabeth Newson, and Larry Weiskrantz. It has cultivated a media profile commenting on the few relevant legal cases that have been reported in the national broadsheet press, television documentaries, and talk show discussions. The Society also actively engaged in the debate surrounding the British Psychological Society's 1995 survey of therapists concerning their experience of recovered memories, as well as the Royal College of Psychiatrists' 1997 recommendations arising from their Working Group on *Reported Recovered Memories of Child Sexual Abuse*. Although the number of cases of 'false memory' handled by the BFMS and the degree of press coverage of the Society's activities has never yet reached the level afforded to its US counterpart, it is an active association within the UK.

Pendergrast has put forward several explanations concerning why the profiles of the UK and US associations should differ as much as they do. He has suggested that British parents are 'too embarrassed, frightened, and depressed to come forward' (Pendergrast, 1998: 562) and that allegations of abuse are not being pursued in the UK because the perpetrator is dead, the woman does not want publicity, or the therapist advises against it. While it is probably accurate to say that in general the British public does not have the taste for litigation that the American public exhibits, it could equally well be the case that prosecutions are being pursued, but because the perpetrator pleads guilty, publicity is avoided. It could also be that the British culture encourages women to resolve their anger and trauma in ways that do not involve use of the courts. (Depending on one's point of view, this could also be described as cultural norms discouraging them from doing so.) There is certainly no evidence to support the conclusion that Pendergrast draws, on the basis of a statistical calculation, that since 1990 'well over 100,000 [FMS] cases have been fomented' in the UK (Pendergrast, 1998: 561–562).

Although there is, to date, no entry in the *Diagnostic and Statistical Manual* for FMS, it seems that proponents of the syndrome would be keen to see it included there. The 1999 website of the False Memory Syndrome Foundation contains a commentary written by the Executive Director of the Foundation, Pamela Freyd,[4] in which she makes the following remarks in regard to the absence of FMS from the DSM.

> It quite properly takes many years for the official recognition of a medical diagnosis. The fact that the major professional organizations have issued statements about FMS is an indication of its seriousness.

Advocates of FMS already discuss the syndrome in language indicative of factual reality. John Kihlstrom, Professor of Psychology at Yale University and a member of the Foundation's Scientific Advisory Board, offers the following definition of the syndrome in the introductory comments of the website:

> When the memory is distorted, or confabulated, the result can be what has been called the False Memory Syndrome; a condition in which a person's identity and interpersonal relationships are centered around a memory of traumatic experience which is objectively false but in which the person strongly believes.

Kihlstrom draws explicit parallels between FMS and Multiple Personality Disorder, a disorder that has been listed in the DSM since 1980, explaining that 'the analogy to personality disorder is intentional'. These statements make clear that the False Memory Syndrome Foundation views the syndrome as a clinical condition and that DSM recognition of FMS would be regarded as desirable.[5]

The argument that FMS is inextricably linked to the phenomenon of child sexual abuse is less common than might be assumed. When it is put forward, it tends, unsurprisingly, to come from those situating their analysis within a feminist perspective (e.g. Armstrong, 1996; Bass and Davis, 1994; Benatar, 1995; Brown and Burman, 1997; Schuman and Galvez, 1996). Because much of the psychological community regards the issue as one of cognitive function and general human memory processes, many articles on recovered and false memories make little or no reference to the social context of child sexual abuse (e.g. Groff, 1994; Kihlstrom, 1997; Memon and Young, 1997; Schacter, Norman, and Koutstaal, 1997; Yapko, 1997). Where acknowledgement is given, it is often residual to the main argument, detached from any purposeful attempt to set FMS within the context of child sexual abuse (e.g. Lindsay and Read, 1994; Ofshe and Watters, 1994). Thus, in one of the most influential papers on repressed memories, Elizabeth Loftus (1994: 443) begins by observing that '[m]ost of us . . . have nothing but the deepest sympathy for victims of the crime of child abuse', but devotes the remainder of the paper to warning of the dangers of implanted false memories.

Richard Webster provides respite for those who wonder whether the only criticism of the FMS movement has emerged from a feminist base. Webster is author of *Why Freud Was Wrong: Sin, Science and Psychoanalysis* (1996), a text which analyses Freud's theories in an attempt to develop a better understanding of contemporary cultural trends. In an Afterword to his book, written specifically in response to the rapid evolution of FMS in the US, Webster firmly places responsibility for the FMS movement on Freud and the psychiatric establishment, as well as on the uptake of Freud's ideas within the legal system. Webster considers that

> the extensive denial of the reality of child sexual abuse which has reigned both among lawyers and among mental health professionals throughout most of the twentieth century . . . provided the essential conditions without which the recovered memory movement could never have grown and flourished in the way that it did.
>
> (Webster, 1996: 512)

The link between repressed memories and Freud's psychoanalytic theories plays a key role in the recovered memory debate. It causes particular concern for cognitive psychologists. Freud was one of the earliest proponents of trauma theory, originally believing that the source of much adult neurosis was due to the psychic response to childhood trauma, including sexual abuse, created when the psyche erected a barrier to 'block out' or repress unpleasant memories. Professional reaction in the early twentieth century to Freud's theory was so hostile that he retracted it, retreating to the alternative theoretical position in which the associations between sexual abuse and hysteria were denied.

The debate surrounding recovered memories and FMS has become very heated. In her 1997 summary of the area, Christine Courtois commented that

> [t]he positions taken in the controversy have often been extreme, overdrawn, and caustic. A rational middle ground that incorporates the legitimate issues of each side is lacking and is much needed.
>
> (Courtois, 1997: 206)

Others have characterised it as a bitter contest to determine 'whether analysis and analytic psychotherapy are objective, scientific enterprises or subjective, hermeneutic disciplines', with the winner claiming authority to speak for the psychological community (Levine, 1997: 9). In contrast, some commentators regard the contest as a backlash against radical feminism, which continues to expose incest and other forms of male abuse of power within the family and society (e.g. Armstrong, 1996).

Certainly the divisions over FMS derive in part from the contrast between experimental psychology's classification of the issue, which is primarily one of memory and cognition, and the classification preferred by those within the clinical and therapeutic field, who prefer an experiential, person-centred approach to understanding the phenomenon. In an attempt to deliver a definitive, scientific explanation of memory and to define that as the key to the dilemma, experimental psychologists have marginalised the phenomenon of child sexual abuse. Therapists counter that no real understanding of the FMS movement can be achieved without placing the prevalence of sexual abuse at the centre of explanations, just as they argue that no understanding of memory for sexually abusive events can be gained without putting traumatic abuse at the centre of investigations of those memories. This divergence of opinion surrounding the role of child sexual abuse in relation to memory and FMS has significant consequences once the syndrome enters the legal domain.

FMS in the courtroom

FMS arises in both criminal and civil matters. We are particularly interested in this book in the former, where a man[6] who is charged with sexual abuse argues that he has been wrongly accused and FMS is integral to that defence. The operation of FMS in civil suits is also important, though, because it was this type of litigation that first helped to thrust the issue of recovered memories into societal awareness and because there is often a connection between the filing of a set of criminal charges (of sexual abuse) and a related civil suit. FMS tends to arise in the civil arena when a man is being sued by the woman for damages, as a result of the harm caused by the alleged abuse and its long-term consequences. He may use FMS to discredit the plaintiff's claims and even file a counter-suit against a therapist or health authority (or both) for undertaking therapy of a type that is alleged to have induced false memories in the woman concerned.[7]

The phenomenon of FMS first entered the courts in 1994 in the US civil case of *Ramona* v *Isabella*, when Gary Ramona, a Californian wine executive, successfully sued his daughter's therapist, whom he accused of implanting memories of sexual abuse. Ramona's daughter, Holly, had alleged that he had committed incest over a period of years during her childhood. Her memories of the abuse were recovered after two therapists treated her using hypnosis in conjunction with the drug sodium amytal. Ramona's strenuous denials of the abuse were believed by the jury, who awarded him $475,000, although that was a sum considerably less than that for which he had sued (Follini, 1995: 14). The Ramona case became a *cause célèbre* within the United States, propelling psychotherapy into the limelight and placing practising therapists on the defensive. It made public the division within the psychological profession, with celebrated experts ranged on either side of the recovered/false memory debate. Elizabeth Loftus testified for Gary Ramona, while Lenore Terr, a psychiatrist who has supported the possibility of repressed memories, testified in defence of the therapist Richard Rose who was being sued. The False Memory Syndrome Foundation welcomed the eventual decision, arguing that it supported their claims. Feminist commentators criticised it, arguing that it trivialised the issue of child sexual abuse and perpetuated the characterisation of women as victims (Armstrong, 1996).

Although some commentators argue that the issue of recovered memories is separate from that of child sexual abuse (see Loftus and Ketcham, 1994; Robbins, 1995) the caselaw suggests a different interpretation. In *United States v Rouse and others* (1995) the appeal court allowed a retrial for four defendants who had been convicted of a series of sexual offences against various children. The grounds for this decision were that the trial judge should have allowed expert testimony showing that the children's testimony had been tainted by suggestive questioning in the investigation process, thereby raising the possibility that false memories might have been induced by the questioning. Moreover, the appeal court criticised the trial judge for refusing to permit an independent psychological examination of the children to test their credibility, which the defendants had requested. This shows the elision of the two issues. The allegations of sexual abuse made here were treated as necessarily possibly tainted. The mere nature of the claims (i.e. sexual abuse) rendered them in the judges' eyes as questionable, in need of particular scrutiny. This is the routine response to claims of sexual abuse and rape (as discussed in Chapter 5), to which victims of other crimes are not subjected, demonstrating that the issue of recovered memories cannot be separated from that of child sexual abuse, particularly in the courtroom.

In the UK, whilst there have been numerous prosecutions based on childhood sexual abuse alleged to have occurred many years previously, there have, as yet, been no criminal cases reported in the official law reports based on a defence that formally raises FMS (Lewis and Mullis, 1999). There have, however, been covert references to it. In *R v Jenkins* (1998), a man who had been charged with various sexual assaults on children nearly 30 years in the past was allowed to appeal his conviction. Reference was made to the fact that the allegations of abuse had been raised only after one of the complainants had undergone counselling in adulthood and that 'there were unexplained delays, inconsistencies, and instances of "improved memory" and some evidence of "contamination"' (*R v Jenkins*, 1998: 411). In her commentary on the case, Diane Birch (1998: 412) observed that the Appeal Court seemed to be particularly influenced by the issue of delay in reporting and was suspicious of the 'recovered memory' of the women. Although she concluded that it was the 'mysterious and dramatic improvement' in the details that one of the women could recall that most concerned the court, rather than the risk of FMS *per se*, this is precisely the concern that many people retain in regard to recovered memory therapies. How does one tell whether the now-detailed memories are *recovered* or are *false*, implanted by dubious therapeutic techniques?

A handful of criminal cases citing FMS have been reported in the newspapers (as opposed to official law reports). In July 1994, the *Sunday Times* reported that a

61-year-old merchant seaman was acquitted of charges of rape and assault based on uncorroborated evidence emerging from his daughter's regression therapy. On 29 March 1995 *The Times* reported that a 48-year-old shopworker was freed after the prosecution dropped charges of sexual assault against him. The charges had been based on allegations from his daughter, then 22, that she had suffered abuse since she was 7, the memory of which had arisen during regression therapy. The report states that evidence gleaned from recovered memory therapy has increasingly been used in British trials although 'few convictions have resulted'. In November 1996, a 44-year-old man, prosecuted for sexually abusing his daughter some years previously, was acquitted at Manchester Crown Court (*The Independent*, 30 November 1996; *Daily Telegraph*, 30 November 1996). The prosecution dropped the case once presented with expert psychological testimony that stated the woman complainant might have been suffering from FMS. The defendant's barrister, Stephen Meadowcroft, claimed that it was the first time the defence[8] of FMS had been used in Britain in response to a criminal prosecution.

As in the US, some of the most well-publicised cases in the UK have been civil matters. In 1997, for example, Jim Fairlie, a local politician in Perthshire, Scotland, was accused of sexual abuse by his daughter after she spent a period in a mental hospital as a patient undergoing recovered memory therapy. Fairlie was never prosecuted and his daughter has now withdrawn her claims, but he has since sued the local health trust and the social services responsible for his daughter's care while in hospital (*The Scotsman*, 15 October 1997). This case received extensive media attention in Scotland.

In some jurisdictions legislative changes have been made as a result of the recovered memories movement, suggesting that there is a political inclination to take recovered memories seriously. The changes have amended statutes of limitations, that is, the legislation that sets out time limits preventing cases from being pursued after a specified time period. The rationale behind establishing such limitations is that it minimises the risk of unreliable witness testimony, because witnesses' memories fade with the passage of time. There is also a belief that those who could potentially be sued or prosecuted are entitled, at some point, to have a line drawn under their activities. The statutes of limitations for filing civil claims of sexual abuse have been relaxed in a number of US states (for discussion see Mullis, 1997; Pendergrast, 1998). By relaxing statutes of limitations in such cases, the normal time limit is extended to permit applications to be made to the courts from the point at which memory of the abuse is *recalled* rather than the point at which the abuse *occurred*. While this shows that (some) politicians have been willing to take the possibility of recovered memories seriously (an action which some observers applaud and others deplore[9]), opening a procedural door does not guarantee that women's claims will receive better treatment within the legal system. Other legislative changes, such as the institution of rape shield laws, have not proven very effective in improving women's position with the law (see Chapter 5). While changes to law's framework are an important first step, it will take much more to alter the suspicious attitude with which it approaches women's and children's claims of sexual violence.

While no other jurisdictions have yet witnessed the number of cases involving FMS as have those in the US, precedents have already been established in the UK and Australia (Guilliatt, 1996) for admitting into court evidence relating to recovered memory therapy and FMS. The discussions within the British Psychological Society regarding these issues suggest that the door has been sufficiently opened to permit further introduction of expert testimony in appropriate cases. Given the established antipathy in law towards the credibility and reliability of women and children as witnesses, it is a small step to envisaging enterprising lawyers constructing a defence to assist men accused of committing childhood sexual abuse, which would be based on the implausibility (even fabrication) of the complainant's recovered memory. Indeed, Gotell's (forthcoming) review of Canadian sexual assault cases reveals that this is already happening. She points to the decision of the Alberta Court in the case of *R* v *Mills* (1997) which involved the alleged sexual assault of a 12-year-old girl by a 29-year-old man, where defence counsel applied for access to the child's counselling, therapeutic, and medical records. The court upheld the defence application, and in so doing challenged the legislative provisions of Bill C-46 which offers privacy and protection to victims of sexual assault.[10] Gotell comments that 'the spectre of "false memory syndrome" . . . lurks just beneath the surface' of the court's decision and is apparent in some of the observations by the judge, Belzil J., regarding the risk of therapy. As Gotell observes, it is striking to note that the judiciary are raising concerns about the risks posed by the 'dubious' nature of recovered memory and the 'contaminatory' practice of therapy even where 'no expert testimony or other evidence was entered specifically on repressed memory' and, notably, where the case involves a child and not an adult woman. This pattern, while alarming, is not surprising, given the way in which law has traditionally characterised women and is indicative of the implicit relation.

The implicit relation

It is within this climate of distrust, suspicion, accusation, and counter-accusation, that the two polarised sides of the recovered/false memory debate have constructed their arguments. Controversy rages around the essential characteristics of memory, and the arrival of FMS in the courtroom may appear to provide an opportunity for some resolution of the issue. Many in psychology continue to seek a definitive answer to the fundamental question of whether a memory can be repressed and subsequently recalled. Judicial opinion can act as an external validation (or invalidation) of the available research findings. It is in this way that law has helped to reshape the issue of recovered memories, driving it to the forefront of the psychological debate and giving it new impetus.

Objectivity

The critical element in the recovered memory debate is the nature of human memory. How does it work; how well are its processes currently understood; how much trust can be placed in any specific memory? Psychologists have, since the birth of the discipline, considered the study and explanation of memory to be one of their areas of expertise. The work of Hermann Ebbinghaus (1885), for example, in which nonsense syllables were first employed to study patterns of forgetting, is considered fundamental to the field. The debate surrounding recovered memories has become so heated because it reveals divisions within the psychological community concerning the nature of memory. A deep rift exists between academic and clinical psychologists, each side being 'anchored in a particular epistemological view of what constitutes meaningful evidence' (Schooler, Bendiksen, and Ambadar, 1997: 251). The division is, in effect, a power struggle, 'a fundamental paradigm clash between clinical and experimental views regarding the status of recovered memories of sexual abuse' (p. 251). When it becomes necessary to choose between two different characterisations of memory, as law is forced to do in cases of sexual abuse, who is chosen as the spokesperson for psychology? The implicit relation ensures that it is experimental psychologists, due to their alignment with the discourse of objectivity.

Experimental psychologists study memory through the use of empirical, quantitative, laboratory procedures. These include the repetitive recitation or viewing of series of letters, words, or numbers, the recall of which is assessed over some period of time. Such methods are favoured because they permit controlled, measurable, replicable findings. Methods that draw on more naturally occurring events (e.g. recalling when you last went to a postbox) would not permit such control and so are of less use and interest to experimental psychologists. Given that memory is a function of the brain, it seems the natural preserve of cognitive psychology, whose models of human functioning are the most esteemed in psychology today (in contrast with, for example, behavioural, psychoanalytic, or social constructionist models). Indeed, cognitive psychology has become particularly aligned with experimental paradigms, it now being very difficult to separate the two. It is cognitive psychologists who are considered by themselves and others to be guardians of contemporary explanations of memory.

With the advent of claims concerning repressed/recovered memories, alternative accounts of memory function to those offered by cognitive psychologists have emerged. These are derived in large part from the perspective of clinical psychologists, whose 'raw data' are the narratives and observations of the interview room. This community often objects to the charges laid against therapeutic practices, pointing out that laboratory investigations cannot assess the validity of sexual abuse allegations, that sex offenders are notoriously manipulative, and that, in the absence of corroborative evidence, just as a memory cannot be proven to be historically true, neither can it be proven to be historically false (Courtois, 1997: 210–211). Moreover, because the primary goal of therapists is the recovery of a client to good health, clinicians sometimes argue that it is immaterial whether recollections of childhood events are deemed objectively 'true'.[11] The recollections themselves are valuable tools in a client's recovery (Levine, 1997). The memory has therapeutic value regardless of whether it meets the criteria of scientific objectivity. For the experimental school, however, the lack of the objective status of memories is precisely the problem. They insist that only data obtained with controlled, replicable, verifiable procedures are valid in discussions of memory function. The methods and conclusions of therapists are, in the eyes of experimental psychologists, too subjective, speculative, and ultimately unscientific. Thus, their rejection of the concept of recovered memory is in part based on their antipathy towards its aetiological and epistemological base.

One of the problems that has resulted from the sparring between the two communities is a considerable confusion and lack of precision in the debate. Winbolt (1996: 100), for example, conflates the notions of recovered memories and false memories. He defines FMS as 'the phenomenon of recovering memories, normally during adulthood and with the help of a therapist, of sexual abuse which occurred during childhood' and as a phenomenon which arises in 'situations where the victim has no memory of the event prior to the intervention of a third party to help with the recovery process'. This suggests not only that memories recovered through therapy are invariably false, but it also takes no account of memories that are recovered independently of the therapeutic process. Yet the experience of many groups who work with abused women, such as Rape Crisis, Incest Survivors, and Women's Aid, is that adult women's recall of traumatic abuse in childhood is often spontaneous or is triggered by a further trauma in adulthood (Hall and Lloyd, 1989). They are not necessarily resurrected through counselling or therapy. Indeed, the working party set up by the British Psychological Society in 1994 to investigate FMS found that 'the most common context in which memory recovery occurred was *prior* to any therapy' (Andrews *et al.*, 1995: 211, emphasis added).[12] The working party further noted that this finding was contrary to the impression gained from the public debate, which insinuated that recovered memories only occur with the aid of a therapist. Basic psychology textbooks also tend to give this impression, by making statements such as 'many of these recovered memories emerge *only* with the assistance of a therapist who is genuinely convinced that the client's psychological problems stem from childhood abuse' (Gleitman, Fridlund, and Reisberg, 1999: 290–291, emphasis added). In contrast, The Royal College of Psychiatrists' working party, set up in 1995 to consider the issue, stated in the *Brandon Report* that false memories 'usually but not always' occurred during the course of therapy (Brandon *et al.*, 1998). Therefore, categorising a recovered memory as necessarily false is misleading and unfair, as is imputing blame to therapists for invariably being instrumental in the onset of patients' claims of sexual abuse.

There is some measure of agreement between the experimental and clinical camps over recovered memories. It is widely accepted that memory is a *construction* of events rather than a *replication* or exact representation of them (Conway, 1990, 1997). This was a point stressed by Brandon.

[Memory is] a constructive and reconstructive rather than reproductive process. . . . It is fallible, altered by the passage of time and subject to error and distortion, . . . expectations and beliefs can colour people's recollections, and . . . gaps in memory will be filled to create a satisfying narrative.

(Brandon *et al.*, 1998)

The effect of variables such as the age of the person when the event occurred, the emotions surrounding the event, and the amount of active remembering undertaken at the time have been shown to affect the memory construction process. Most psychologists also acknowledge that there is scope for memories to be forgotten and subsequently remembered. The working group that the American Psychological Association established to investigate memories of childhood abuse stated in their 1994 *Interim Report* that

> [i]t is possible for memories of abuse that have been forgotten for a long time to be remembered. The mechanism, or mechanisms, by which such delayed recall occurs is not currently well understood.
>
> (cited in Pezdek and Banks, 1996: 372)

Similarly, the British Psychological Society's working party on recovered memories, which reported in 1995, concluded that

> [c]omplete or partial memory loss is a frequently reported consequence of experiencing certain kinds of psychological traumas including childhood sexual abuse. These memories are sometimes fully or partially recovered after a gap of many years.
>
> (cited in Pezdek and Banks, 1996: 373)

Despite these similarities, reservoirs of epistemological dispute remain between the two positions, of which the most irreconcilable aspect is how to determine the 'proportion' of a memory that is construction and the 'proportion' that is an accurate representation of life events (assuming it is even possible to 'separate' the two components). How can we best distinguish 'the signal of true repressed memories from the noise of false ones' (Loftus, 1993: 534)? Until this is determined, with how much scepticism should reports of recovered memories be regarded? The desire of cognitive psychologists for objective, replicable evidence of any phenomenon leads them to encourage considerable caution. The misgivings held by Elizabeth Loftus, a cognitive psychologist well known in the field of eyewitness testimony and a member of the APA's working group on recovered memories, are typical, although she is at least willing to recognise the possibility of the authenticity of a childhood memory that is recalled in adulthood (Loftus, 1993: 518–519). Holmes (1990: 70) takes a more extreme view, declaring categorically that 'there is no controlled laboratory evidence for repression'.[13] Hayes, too, has observed that, '[t]he reliability of [repressed memories of childhood sexual abuse] has not yet been scientifically proven' (Hayes, 1994: 70). In short, these researchers are arguing that until the reliability of recovered memories is proven, they should be distrusted.

Clinicians who support the use of therapy as a means of treatment and rehabilitation for survivors of trauma argue that therapists can 'objectively guide the process of narrative construction' (Byrd, 1994: 439) whilst guarding against their own biases. They point out there are procedures and principles that can be followed to minimise the risk of distorting memories, including the administration of questionnaires and other research instruments at the onset of treatment (Gold, Hughes, and Hohnecker, 1994) and avoiding group work or self-help resources until the client has established a reasonable degree of certainty that a sexually abusive event occurred 'and that there are clinically significant sequelae for which professional help is needed' (Byrd, 1994: 439). It is not even clear to what extent 'dubious techniques' are being employed by therapists, with Poole *et al.* (1995) finding that 25% of their sample of 350 psychologists endorsed the use of such techniques, while other studies (e.g. Sullins, 1998; Tabachnick and Pope, 1997) have obtained figures in the region of 1%.

The 'turf war' between the two groups (Pendergrast, 1998) has led to a power struggle over who it is that has the authority to represent the psychological community. Is it experimentalists or clinicians? Significantly, the discourse of scientific objectivity is used to challenge the authority of clinical psychologists and to assist in settling the debate. Melton and Limber, for example, maintain that

> the extant syndromes lack a firm scientific foundation. Rather than hard data, they are based on clinical intuition, which, in the present state of the art, may be useful for treatment planning but which connotes a certainty that goes well beyond current knowledge and misleads the fact finder in a legal proceeding.
> (Melton and Limber, 1989: 1229)

Holmes (1994) jokes that therapists' waiting-room doors should carry a warning sign declaring that '[t]he concept of repression has not been validated with experimental research and its use may be hazardous to the accurate interpretation of clinical behavior' (cited in Pendergrast, 1998: 62). Recall Randolph Jonakait's contention, introduced in Chapter 2, that 'the personal opinion of an expert, no matter how scientific-sounding or how backed with experiences in helping [child sexual abuse] victims . . . is not sufficient to make out a scientifically sound opinion' (Jonakait, 1994: 450). Such comments, with their emphasis on hard data, quantifiable measurement, objectivity, and scientific methodology, drive a wedge between the two sections of the psychological community. They contend that the distanced objective approach to explaining the consequences of child abuse is necessarily better than the more subjective approach employed by therapists. The scientific explanation is superior because objectivity is (regarded as) superior.

Law's reaction to the internal disagreement of the psychological community is predictable. When it must choose between two different perspectives, it will choose the one that comes closest to its own. This is, of course, those in the experimental community, especially when their objective, measurable, replicable findings are shown to be 'generally accepted' within the field. The cases of *Ramona* (discussed earlier in this chapter), *Gier* v *Educational Service Unit* (1995) and *Isely* v *Capuchin Province et al.* (1995) confirm that unless an expert can demonstrate sufficient expertise in theoretical and experimental psychology they will have difficulty in gaining admissibility for their testimony in cases involving delayed memories of child sexual abuse. This presents barriers for those in the clinical community. In

Gier v *Educational Service Unit* (1995) the court excluded testimony from a psychiatrist and two psychologists on the grounds that the methodologies that they had employed in examining seven mentally retarded plaintiffs who had been allegedly abused were unreliable, in part because the experts were not trained in line with any standardised interview protocol or methodology. In *Trear* v *Sills* (1999: 285), Holmes's work was cited to affirm the court's view that 'it appears highly unlikely that [repressed memory] evidence commands anything close to the necessary general acceptance within the relevant scientific community'. In *Isely*, the court echoed *Daubert* (see Chapter 2), declaring that an expert who was to proffer testimony regarding repressed memories

> must be able to assure the Court that his/her theories have some degree of scientific validity and reliability. In particular . . . whether that theory can be, or has been, tested or corroborated and . . . whether the theory has been proven out or not proven out under clinical tests . . . and whether the theory has been subjected to other types of peer review.
>
> (*Isely* v *Capuchin Province et al.*, 1995: 8)

The scepticism which some commentators have expressed in regard towards *all* memories recovered during the therapeutic process (e.g. Holmes, 1990; Pendergrast, 1998; Winbolt, 1996) suggests that they believe the views of clinicians and therapists to be generally inappropriate for the legal setting. Because it is fundamental to good therapeutic practice that the practitioner accepts and supports the client's account from the outset, critics charge that this stance prevents clinicians from being useful to law precisely because they are insufficiently objective and non-partisan. If they are regarded as unsuitable, there will be further propensity to discount, and even disallow, the testimony of those who have even fewer professional qualifications, such as workers in rape crisis centres and facilitators of incest survivor groups, because they lack the credentials and authority of the 'expert'. The ability that they might have to describe women's experience more accurately or more fully to the court will be regarded as immaterial.

Through its associations with child sexual abuse and FMS, memory has become part of a highly politicised campaign. It is not confined to the decontextualised scientific laboratories within which many cognitive psychologists would be comfortable containing it. It is this process of politicisation that has led to the public characterisation of the issue as one of 'false' memory and to its being ascribed the descriptor of a 'syndrome'. It is notable that of the range of terms now in use in this area, including 'recovered memory', 'recalled memory', 'delayed memory', and 'repressed memory', it is the term 'False Memory Syndrome' that has captured popular and, increasingly, legal attention. If the issue of recovered memories had not entered the legal arena, it is unlikely it would have attracted such a striking political configuration. Nor would the need for objective accounts of memory have seemed quite so strong. It was really only with the escalation of public awareness which results from legal cases that it became clear what was at stake, legally and financially, for psychology.

The male norm

The discourses surrounding FMS are not new. They are embedded within a historical context which has traditionally regarded women and children as unreliable, incredible (i.e. not believable, in-credible) witnesses. Special rules of evidence and legal procedure have even been constructed on the basis of that belief, a practice examined in our discussion of rape (Chapter 5). Legal, psychological, and societal attitudes continue to be influenced by a bias toward women and children as unreliable witnesses. Although there have been assertions that children's claims are now believed too readily (e.g. Ceci and Bruck, 1993; Pendergrast, 1998; Williams, 1987), the bulk of the evidence indicates the contrary. When contemporary judicial comments and research paradigms are considered in relation to their historical context, it becomes surprisingly easy to identify the presence of a male norm.

The child as temptress, seductress, and a willing sexual partner, is a myth firmly embedded within law. A survey of cases of incest in the US during the late nineteenth and early twentieth centuries reveals deeply ingrained views of the child as seductress. This perspective was reinforced by the psychoanalytic views of Freud, in their heyday during this period. The legal position in force was that if a child[14] complained that she had been raped by a male member of her family (generally her father), the man could defend the charge by showing that the child had consented to the act or had voluntarily had sexual intercourse with him. If consent was demonstrated, the child was deemed to have been a willing accomplice to the crime of incest. If she testified to the contrary, her testimony had to be corroborated from another source to prove the crime. The readiness to view the child as complicit in the act, and the requirement that she corroborate her position if proclaiming her innocence, perversely placed her 'on trial'.

Such a survey can be found in *American Law Reports Annotated* (1960: 707–717). In the US case of *Ratliff* v *State* (1901), a young woman alleged that she had been raped repeatedly by her father, explaining that she had only submitted through fear and that she had delayed leaving home out of concern that her sister would then be similarly abused. She was held to have 'willingly and voluntarily consented to incestuous intercourse with the same object and intent that her father did and was an accomplice in law' (p. 711). In *Gillespie* v *State* (1906), a woman aged 30 who alleged rape by her father was held to have consented on the ground that 'she failed to make any opposition whatsoever' (p. 713), even though the court acknowledged she was an unwilling partner and did not in fact consent. In *Dodson* v *State* (1887) a young woman's allegations that her father had raped her were discounted on the grounds that her 'reputation for truth and chastity was bad long before the birth of the child which she alleged was the result of the alleged incestuous intercourse', resulting in a finding that she was an accomplice to the crime of incest (p. 713). It is apparent from these cases that a child's consent could be easily 'established' by the courts if no consideration was to be given to the threats and intimidation used to obtain such 'consent'. Although power differentials between adult and child are now recognised as a key element of the *commission* of child sexual abuse, the issue of power has rarely been considered in theories about the *memory* for such abuse. We will return to this point shortly.

The presumption of the child–woman as a seductress, who bears some responsibility for the abuse, or as a story-teller who makes up fibs, has not been halted with the passage of time. The journalist Alan Massie exhibits this view in his comments on a Scottish 1999 case, in which a woman who was arrested for drunk driving argued that it had been necessary for her to do so because she was trying to escape a man who had just raped her. Massie made the following objections to this defence.

> She did not mention the rape to the police who first stopped her. . . . She did not mention the rape when she was breathalysed; nor did she do so when she was charged. . . . It was only nine days later that she spoke of it to her lawyer.
>
> (Massie, *The Scotsman*, 14 September 1999)

According to Massie, there was no evidence to support the woman's story except for her GP's report that his examination of her ten days later found injuries consistent with rape. He therefore believed that it was the responsibility of the woman to prove her innocence of involvement in the alleged rape. As Pamela Ferguson (*The Scotsman*, 16 September 1999) noted in her rejoinder to the article, Massie treats the woman's behaviour as if an (alleged) rape was being prosecuted, wherein the defence would seek to show why her testimony was not credible. In the case in question, however, she had been charged with a criminal offence (i.e. drunk driving), and was thus the defendant. She was therefore required only to raise a reasonable doubt in the mind of the judge as to the reason for her behaviour, in order to entitle her to an acquittal. She was not obliged by the law to provide corroboration of her story.

Law's response to allegations of child sexual abuse can also be traced to historical presumptions about women's and children's seductive and deceptive tendencies. We saw this in the case of *R* v *Henry and Manning*, discussed earlier in the chapter, where Lord Justice Salmon charged that girls and women fabricate stories that are difficult (for men) to refute. Similarly, the 1976 comments of Judge Sutcliffe are well known to those familiar with the feminist literature on rape and child sexual abuse. He stated, in reference to a case he was trying at the Old Bailey, that '[i]t is well known that women in particular and small boys are liable to be untruthful and invent stories' (cited in Pattullo, 1983: 18). More recently, during the 1997 trial (and subsequent convictions) of Gordon Knott and Brian MacLennan for indecency, rape, and sodomy of numerous children in their care in homes run by local authorities in Scotland, witnesses recalled the occasions when they had tried to report the men but had been branded 'liars' by the police and other officials (*The Scotsman*, 25 November 1997, 13 January 1998). In the Scottish case of *Black* v *Ruxton* (1998), a 15-year-old girl whose father was convicted of engaging in lewd sexual practices with her was asked repeatedly in cross-examination why she had not reported the matter to anyone during the fifteen-month period when the offences were occurring. The accused's solicitor was clearly trying to infer through the use of this strategy that either she was a willing participant or that she was making it up. Glanville Williams, a leading English academic lawyer, wrote in 1987 that

> it has been known for children to invent elaborate fantasies and tell rank falsehoods. Children can be extraordinarily precocious, well versed in sexual language and quite capable of making false accusations, especially when they believe this to be a form of self-defence.
>
> (Williams, 1987: 188)

In support of his claim Williams cites 'one actual example of false evidence' (p. 189) given by researchers writing in 1963. No reference is made to the over-whelming statistical evidence of the incidence of accurate reporting of child sexual abuse available in 1987.

If children are not regarded as trustworthy when reporting sexual abuse, then it is axiomatic that women will be distrusted when recalling memories of abuse that occurred in childhood. Societal attitudes towards adults suspected of having false memories of childhood sexual abuse risk becoming indistinguishable from the attitudes expressed towards children who complain of sexual abuse. Since children's contemporaneous recollections of abuse are so often considered inimical to probity and accuracy, and therefore reliability, it is unsurprising that there should be a propensity to distrust adult women's recovered memories of such childhood experience. The scepticism with which such recollections are greeted is described powerfully by Ross Cheit (1994), who recovered memories of childhood abuse and was, most unusually, able to corroborate those memories through independent sources, thus contributing to the eventual success of the well-publicised lawsuit he brought against his abuser.

> [T]he fact remains that in 1994, it is extremely difficult to come forward with allegations of sexual abuse. And the external forces of denial are almost overwhelming. If a case as verified as mine meets with denial, I dread to think about the experience of people who don't have the kind of corroboration that I do. And I really worry that we're getting close to a point where it's going to be impossible to prosecute child molesters, because we don't believe children, and now we don't believe adults.
>
> (Cheit, 1994; quoted in Freyd, 1996: 59)

That is the precise effect of FMS: doubt is shed on any woman's (or man's) account of childhood abuse, regardless of how they emerge or the presence of any evidence that might be available to support them. FMS encourages the search for corrobo-ration that the alleged events occurred, just as the law of a century ago required. Independent corroboration and documentation have been obtained in a few cases of repressed memory, such as Cheit's and others that Loftus (1993) reviews. The fact that corroboration should have been found in any cases of repressed memory, given the considerable amount of time that would have passed and the immense difficulties that exist in obtaining substantiation for *any* sexual assault, is extremely noteworthy. This should give even those who are most sceptical of memory repression reason to pause before condemning the cases that remain uncorroborated as conclusively false.

Webster (1996) ascribes particular blame for the cynical legal view of women's character to John Henry Wigmore. One of the most influential jurists in Anglo-American law, Wigmore's 'old-fashioned' ideas have been 'kept alive by [his] immense reputation and authority' (Twining, 1985: 172). Wigmore's 1937 ten-volume work, entitled *Wigmore on Evidence*, contains a detailed exposition of the rules of evidence and their rationale. In regard to cases of bastardy (i.e. illegitimacy), seduction and rape, Wigmore made the following statement:

> In view of the danger to innocent men from the fabrications of a certain pathological type of feminine nature, well-known to psychiatrists, it seems desirable to give liberal opportunity for placing before the jury the entire facts as to the complaining witness' chastity.
>
> (Wigmore, 1940: Para. 133)

Later, this concern about 'the danger to innocent men' presented by women complainants is explored under the heading 'moral character as affecting testimonial veracity'. Wigmore is stating explicitly that women are not trustworthy when alleging sexual crimes and that 'innocent men' are always at risk from women, who are likely to be immoral, unchaste, and 'pathological'.

Wigmore's fear echoes clearly in contemporary FMS discourse, which also classifies women's claims as pathological. The aspirations of FMS advocates to gain DSM entry is evidence of this, for classification within the DSM necessarily defines a phenomenon as abnormality. The manual 'provides a classification of mental disorders', each of which 'is conceptualized as a clinically significant behavioral or psychological syndrome or pattern that occurs in an individual' (DSM, 1994: xxi). Explicit efforts have been made to link FMS, at the theoretical level, to Multiple Personality Disorder (renamed Dissociative Identity Disorder), a category already in the DSM. If FMS could gain entry into the DSM, that connection would be cemented and Wigmore's convictions regarding women's pathology re-affirmed.[15]

It is the appeal to science and authority, which occurs today as well as historically, that is particularly striking in a survey of this area. Wigmore (1937b) advised that any female who accused a man of a 'sex violation' (including situations where a daughter accused her father of incest) should be required to undergo a psychiatric examination to assess whether or not she was a credible witness. Subsequent editors of Wigmore's 1937 edition (Chadbourne, 1970: Para 924a) cite numerous articles in respected academic journals in support of his advice, including those entitled 'Psychiatric Evaluation of the Mentally Abnormal Witness' published in the *Yale Law Journal* (1950); 'Psychiatric Aid on Evaluating Credibility of a Rape Complainant', published in the *Indiana Law Journal* (1950); and 'Psychiatric Opinions as to Credibility of Witnesses: A Suggested Approach', published in the

California Law Journal (Juviler, 1960). Such references affirm the presence of an implicit relation between law and psychology (and, more widely, the psy professions), with its male-normative basis, even in the early years of this century. Thus, one of the key legacies left by Wigmore, a legal theorist so respected that his ideas are 'accepted and carried forward through several generations of legal scholarship' (Bienen, 1983a: 237) is a sturdy platform on which to base contemporary arguments about the need for medical/psychological evaluation of women's and children's complaints of sexual violation.

Paradigms used in contemporary research on children's memory abilities arguably fortify the male-normative distrust of children's testimony and, by extension, women's testimony concerning childhood events. According to Flavell, Miller, and Miller (1993: 229), leading theorists in cognitive developmental theory, '[c]hildren's memory is probably the most advanced area of research on cognitive development, at least in terms of sheer amount of research'. The body of this research warns against the credibility of children's testimony, highlighting the ways in which children are susceptible to leading questions and contextual cues, which results in inaccurate reporting. The suspect nature of children's answers is emphasised, on the basis that they require substantially more prompting than do adults in answering questions, especially when time has passed in relation to the event in questions (e.g. Ceci and Bruck, 1995; Pezdek and Banks, 1996). Their poor performance in laboratory recall exercises has also been stressed, as has their ability to cope with multiple interviews and repeated questions on the same topic (a technique commonly used to test consistency of children's and adults' stories in legal proceedings) (Doris, 1991). These negative characterisations of children's abilities not only echo historical patterns in law's views of children's abilities, but they also downplay the strengths that children show in their memory capacity. Researchers who defend the reliability of children's evidence have pointed out that many laboratory exercises are largely abstract and artificial, and that children's performance in exercises that ask them to recall real life events is notably better than in artificial tasks. It has also been shown that children fare better when they are able to recount their recollection as soon as possible after the event, and when they are able to repeat that process frequently in an atmosphere that encourages active and spontaneous remembering (Poole and White, 1995). According to Fivush and Shukat (1995: 6), research has 'amply demonstrated' that 'even quite young children are able to recall personally experienced events accurately over extended periods of time'. Moreover, 'most studies have found a great deal of accurate information is recalled even after long delays for both mundane and traumatic events' (Fivush *et al.*, 1997: 57).

Yuille and Wells (1991) are among those who have charged that laboratory research often lacks ecological validity (i.e. that findings bear little relation to events in the real world). Even those who are enthusiastic about the application of research findings within the courtroom (e.g. Baker-Ward *et al.*, 1995) warn that care should be taken in extrapolating laboratory findings. However, the problem is that such warnings have not changed the attitudes or behaviour of the research community in any substantial way. The information that they provide to courts (and other interested parties) pertains to children's *limitations*, that is, it emphasises the fallibility of children's accounts. An approach which focused efforts on designing techniques to *facilitate* accurate recall on the part of children would be more fruitful. The risk inherent within the present body of available research is that it lends weight to the conventional view, encouraged in jurors, that children have a propensity for suggestibility and are inherently less reliable witnesses than adults (Leippe and Romanczyk, 1987; Luus and Wells, 1992; Ross *et al.*, 1991). One consequence of this attitude is that it forces the crude question: if children can be shown to have difficulty remembering childhood events accurately, how can memories of childhood events possibly be credible when they are recalled years later? The combination of this doubt and other elements of mythology is incendiary. As Follini recounts of the *Ramona* case:

> Afterwards, many of the jury admitted to biases such as not understanding how Holly Ramona could tell her tale in such a flat unemotional voice and the defence attorney claimed that 'the jury couldn't believe that someone they had sat with for 35 days, who wore a coat and tie could be a sex abuser'.
>
> (Follini, 1995: 14)

Mainstream psychology has given little consideration to the way in which it constructs accounts of children's abilities, accounts which change across time in keeping with changing social values and concerns (Bradley, 1989; Kessen, 1979). Neither has it acknowledged its long history of biases against women, as we have shown throughout this book. Given that psychology has been so fiercely resistant to examination of such biases in a host of domains (see Chapter 3), it is not surprising that it would ignore such themes in regard to memory. For cognitive psychologists, memory is a general human process. The notion that the study of memory could encompass any gender dimension is likely to be seen by them as bizarre.

The fact that more women suffer sexual abuse than do men (and thus women, more than men, will need to develop the skills for remembering it) is irrelevant if the key component of the issue is seen as memory capacity and not sexual abuse. The socio-historical context within which memory is explored is, in their view, simply ancillary to the phenomenon itself. Such disregard need not be purposeful or malevolent; the mere absence of a self-reflective attitude on the part of psychologists in regard to the phenomena that they study is sufficient to cause harm. This lack of reflexivity can even be present within the therapeutic community. The 1995 survey of the British Psychological Society showed that male therapists were significantly less likely to believe their clients' accounts of childhood abuse than were their female colleagues. The majority of the 1083 practitioners responding to the survey believed that false memories were possible. Men were equally as likely as women to have had clients recover memories but 'they were more sceptical in their general beliefs, and about clients in their own practice' (Andrews *et al.*, 1995: 213). Similar, if more subtle, gender differences have been found by Tabachnick and Pope (1997) and by Sullins (1998). This can be interpreted as male therapists' being less willing to be 'taken in', or as female therapists' greater ability to identify with their clients on the basis of similar risk, or as one of many other possibilities. The choice depends in part on one's awareness of or willingness to believe the statistics about sexual abuse and also on the epistemological position that one adopts, either instinctively or purposely, in regard to the nature of memory.

We are not seeking in this chapter to make particular claims about the accuracy or inaccuracy of adults' claims about child sexual abuse. It is undeniably a complex, fraught topic. What we do wish to highlight is the historical, male-normative context within which the contemporary debate is situated. The characterisation of women as unreliable has a lengthy past, as does the appeal to science to substantiate that view. There is nothing novel or remarkable in the way that the current debate is framed. The speed with which FMS is now proclaimed when adult women recover memories of abuse merely demonstrates a continued willingness to promote the needs of men who may be mistakenly accused over the needs of women who may have been abused. An emphasis on the limitations of children's cognitive capacities shields abusers, and protection of their rights is given precedence over the rights of children to be protected from assault. Much is made of the vengeful female poised to prey on male vulnerability and innocence, while the widespread societal prevalence of violence against women and children is ignored. Put simply, it is this prioritisation, and the resistance of psychology and law to acknowledging that ranking, that constitutes a male norm.

Individualism

The final characteristic of the implicit relation arises in the decontextualised account that is provided of children's sexual abuse and the recall of it as an adult. One context which is de-emphasised within FMS discourse is the societal prevalence of sexual abuse, a tendency observed in regard to other syndromes we have discussed, with the focus retained on individual women who allege abuse. A second context which is resolutely disregarded in FMS is that of the power imbalance between adult and child, particularly within the family. The power dynamic that surrounds childhood sexual abuse is taken account of neither by law, in its attempt to apportion blame, nor by psychology, in its attempts to explain human memory processes. Decontexualisation at both levels is successful in achieving the persistent individualistic account of the phenomenon of child sexual abuse and its memory.

Law ignores the widespread nature of sexual abuse. When it seeks to prosecute an accused abuser, only the circumstances pertinent to the particular criminal event under consideration will be examined. There will be no account taken of the societal prevalence, and therefore likelihood, of the crime. Law would maintain that this focus is appropriate; law was not designed to tackle societal phenomena, but to consider 'each case on its own merits'. As the Court of Appeal pointed out in the case of *R* v *B* (1996), in quashing the convictions for rape and sexual assault of a man in regard to his daughter and step-daughter, '[e]ach case had to be considered on its own facts and circumstances, to which the judge's summing up must be appropriate' (1996: 407). In that particular case the judge's summing up was found by the appeal court to be defective in that he referred to the difficulties faced by complainants in child sexual abuse cases without balancing that against the difficulties of the accused in answering the charges against him. This reasoning not only carries the resonance of Wigmore's fears, it ignores the societal prevalence of sexual abuse within which 'each case' is embedded.

Psychology also ignores the societal context of sexual abuse. We noted earlier that the majority of academic papers on recovered memories of childhood sexual abuse do not seriously situate their analysis within the context of sexual abuse. Because they conceptualise the issue as that of cognitive memory processes which reside within the mind or brain of the individual, it is possible to side-step or ignore the phenomenon of sexual abuse altogether. It is, in contrast, the therapeutic community that situates their analysis within the wider context of sexual abuse. This reveals the epistemological dispute between the two communities concerning the relevant factors that need to be considered in exploring and explaining this phenomenon. Tellingly, it is the therapeutic community, with their failure to employ the accepted, objective methods of science, that is discredited by the experimental community. The status of therapists is challenged by characterising them as mental-health professionals 'who have not proved and are not asked to prove that their opinions provide scientifically credible information' (Sales, Shuman, and O'Connor, 1994: 403). The knowledge they have to offer is dismissed as 'empirical observations lacking in scientific underpinnings' (Ganaway, 1992, cited in Loftus, 1993: 519). By endorsing knowledge gained with one particular kind of tool at the expense of knowledge gained with another type (even if the tool of a distanced, objective approach is not appropriate for the goal of therapy), the cognitive psychological community can accord themselves the title of 'expert'. The law is happy to affirm their view, and the two thereby create a self-affirming orbit around the issue.

The focus on individual processes, at the expense of wider societal considerations, is a familiar pattern, which has been discussed in depth already in this book and within the critical psychological and legal literature. The second form of decontextualisation that occurs within the domain of FMS is rather more novel. This is the disregard of the power dynamic within which child sexual abuse takes place and the memory of it is formed. Law tacitly treats the two individuals involved in sexual activity as equal parties, whether they are a man and a woman or a man and a child, or indeed, two individuals of the same sex. When the two parties do not carry equivalent levels of power, it becomes important to factor this inequality into explanatory models, in order to gain an understanding of the dynamics of the activity concerned. This is particularly apparent in regard to child sexual abuse.

We have already observed that judges have historically characterised girls and women as temptresses. This was accomplished by employing language that accorded girls control and responsibility for sex with their fathers – power and independence which far outweighed the reality facing them. The terminology of 'consent' and 'voluntary action' was particularly important in this regard, as our earlier survey of twentieth-century legal cases from the US revealed (*American Law Reports Annotated*, 1960: 707–717). The case of *State* v *Clark* (1915) provides a particularly vivid example of the law's disregard for the power dynamics operating within a family. In that case, a young woman alleged that incestuous acts with her father had taken place repeatedly between the ages of 11 and 22, and in the room where her mother and/or siblings were also sleeping. Her claims were rejected, as the court said that 'it could not believe it possible that these acts could have occurred as testified to by the prosecutrix [i.e. the woman] without her consent' (*State* v *Clark*, 1915: 710). The court did not say the intercourse could not have occurred, but that the girl must have consented to it. Yet, given the impossible economic hurdles and social opprobrium facing a woman and children in leaving the marital home at the turn of the century, there is a very plausible alternative explanation, which would have been overlooked or ignored by the judges in the case. The female victim might have been silenced by fear into submission; her mother and siblings may also have lived in fear of the father and thus silenced into tolerance of the incest. In any event these were women and children living in the knowledge that they were the legal property of their husbands and fathers and that they would be treated accordingly, by the man and by the courts. What was to be gained from protesting about incest?

Other examples of historical cases which demonstrate a disregard for power dynamics include *Yother* v *State* (1904: 711), where the judge determined that consent was present even if 'reluctantly given'. In *Whidby* v *State* (1905: 712), intercourse procured 'even though some coercion be used' was not considered to amount to rape, only adultery or fornication. It is hard to square these decisions with others such as *State* v *Kellar* (1899: 709), where it was said that a woman's participation in sexual activity would only be considered 'voluntary' where it was unaffected by 'force, fraud, fear, or undue influence'.

These cases, which represent only a selection of those discussed in the leading text for the period (Wigmore, 1937a, b), make it clear that up until at least the early part of the twentieth century, courts were applying double standards. Judges used the language of legal formality, which assumes parity between the parties involved, but in practice they applied these terms in a manner that ignored the power dynamic between adult and child. Many of the legal cases during this period laid clear expectations on the young woman to resist the sexual assaults of her father, the implication being that without her compliance these assaults would not have happened. This contrasted with the power relations that were formalised in law, where children were classified as possessions of the father and women as possessions of the husband (Brownmiller, 1991). Although that formal authority has now been discarded, adults still retain the emotional and physical power which they have always had, and it is this power that is used to cajole or force behaviour on the part of the child. If an adequate understanding of sexual abuse, and its prevention, is to be achieved, this power dynamic must be taken into account.

Such cognisance is not yet occurring, as the contemporary cases we have reviewed earlier indicate. That the legal system should allow, despite the intervention of individual judges, any 15-year-old to be badgered as to why she had not reported her father's sexual abuse is evidence enough of this lack (*Black* v *Ruxton*, 1998). A key reason why insufficient account is being taken of power dynamics, especially in regard to legal cases involving FMS, is that psychology and law endorse each other's disregard of that context. Cognitive psychologists, in keeping with the conventional position of psychology in general (Kitzinger, 1991), intimate there is no need to consider any power dynamic. The issue at stake for them is one of general cognitive process, and the context in which memories are formed does not therefore appear to be of particular theoretical relevance.

> The critics [of repressed memories] hold to the position that, since data are not available to demonstrate otherwise, the accumulated knowledge about memory for *ordinary events* is applicable to memory for *traumatic events.*
>
> (Courtois, 1997: 207, emphasis added)

That is, in the eyes of repressed memory critics, the memory processes are decontextual: there is no need to take account of the circumstances within which memories are formed in order to develop an adequate understanding of them.

Jennifer Freyd (1996, 1997) has challenged this view, arguing that too little attention has been paid to how context might alter the way that memory functions, especially the context of trauma. She has developed the theory of 'betrayal trauma', arguing that intimate, abusive family relationships provide the ideal environment for childhood amnesia. Drawing on a range of respected psychological research in advancing her claims, including Harlow's (1959) work with monkeys that showed the effects of withdrawing predictable opportunities for socialisation, Bowlby's (1969, 1988) work on attachment, and Cosmides' (1989; Cosmides and Tooby, 1992) work on the evolutionary development of a mental mechanism to detect social deception, Freyd (1996: 74) argues that humans are 'exquisitely sensitive to cheating'. When cheating takes the form of sexual abuse, the pain of betrayal is extraordinarily great, motivating humans to find ways to block the pain in order to sustain the relationship(s) upon which they are dependent for survival.

> Thus for the child who depends upon a caregiver, the trauma of abuse by that caregiver . . . demands that information about the abuse be blocked from mental mechanisms that control attachment and attachment behavior.
>
> (Freyd, 1997: 27)

Freyd has argued that empirical support for betrayal trauma theory can be obtained; for example, the theory predicts that the greatest probability of amnesia would be directly proportional to the closeness of the relationship of the abuser to the person abused. This is a hypothesis that is falsifiable and can be tested, thereby meeting the demands of scientific psychology. Indeed, as she notes, there are already data available to support this hypothesis (Williams, 1994, 1995). Thus, it is possible to study memory in a contextualised fashion. Ironically, psychologists' failure to do so limits their ability to explain the very phenomenon they seek to understand. This subordination of social and political context is, however, useful, for it helps to sustain the implicit relation of psychology and law in the domain of children's sexual abuse.

Despite the distressingly large number of women who have been abused as children, perhaps as many as one in three, issues surrounding those women who recall memories of childhood sexual experiences are still analysed at the individual level. Feminism has spent more than two decades highlighting the societal power dynamics that lie at the heart of all violence directed by men against women, but there remains deep resistance to this account. Neither psychology nor law wishes to engage with this argument, preferring to believe that uncomfortable and inconvenient allegations of abuse could be due to individual women's pathological problems in constructing memories.

Conclusion

This analysis of FMS has exposed a range of issues, which mirror themes emerging in our examination of other syndromes. First, the inescapable evidence of pervasive child sexual abuse is neglected in the concern over false allegations. Second, factional professional power struggles over the function of memory and the methodology appropriate for investigating that function dominate the debate. Third, explanations of recovered memories are couched in terms of personal pathology, depicting women as weak, passive, and incredible, rather than coping with a very troublesome set of circumstances.

Armstrong (1996) charges that the lack of reference to child sexual abuse in much of the analysis of FMS, the professionalisation of the issue, and the resort to personal pathology is deliberate. She interprets it as an intentional suffocation of any causal connection between child sexual abuse and patriarchal power. She points out that the debate has neatly shifted ground to become a dispute about therapy, leaving women exposed to 'a language focused on personal pathology and recovery' that defuses the political content of FMS, serves the status quo, and offends no one (Armstrong, 1996: 38–39).

It is doubtful whether either law or psychology would acknowledge their political role in the FMS controversy. A more contentious issue is whether their contribution is indeed deliberate. Arguably, it may be due to a lack of reflexivity about the ways in which they influence, indeed lead, the debate. That they do not wish to reflect on their power does not relieve them of responsibility for its consequences. The contemporary patterns we have described of the treatment of child sexual abuse, rooted as they are in nineteenth-century reasoning, leave no doubt that there is a political and gendered core to this newest syndrome. It feeds on the psychology–law relation established more firmly in other domains, displaying even in its incipient form the damaging impact that has become familiar over these chapters.

8   Moving beyond the implicit relation

Truth is a matter of the imagination.

Ursula Le Guin[1]

The purpose of this book has been to set out our argument that an implicit relation exists between the disciplines of psychology and law and that it is one that works to the disadvantage of women. Is it possible to counter such a robust alliance? We believe so, and this last chapter will explore options for doing that. Feminist critique in any academic discipline leads almost inevitably to calls for theoretical and practice-based reform. Once epistemological assumptions begin to be reconceptualised, agitation for change at the levels of method and practice naturally follow. We will consider reformulations at both levels in this chapter, but first it is useful to reflect briefly on the themes that have emerged across the domains we have examined.

One theme is the continuing faith that is placed in the notion of objectivity. Despite the postmodern age of relativism and deconstruction into which academia and society have reputedly moved, the evidence we have presented indicates that confidence in the possibility and propriety of an objective stance remains high. Within the domain of syndrome diagnoses, this applies not only to those that have already been accepted into the DSM (e.g. Battered Woman's Syndrome, Rape Trauma Syndrome, and Premenstrual Syndrome), but also to those that have not (yet) gained admittance, but which proponents would like to see admitted, such as False Memory Syndrome.[2] Arguments for the introduction of these diagnoses into court is always based on the scientific methodology that has been employed in their 'discovery'. Arguments *against* their introduction are also typically based on the same reasoning: that the findings should be, but are not yet, objective enough. Thus, postmodern debates about the intersection of theory and method, the contextualisation of meaning, and multiple truths, have not influenced to any significant degree the construction and application of syndrome diagnoses. The rigid framework of law's evidential rules makes it even less likely this will happen.

A second theme that has been highlighted is the routine tendency with which women's experience and behaviour are characterised as abnormal. All of the syndromes we have examined construct women and their behaviour as pathological.

This is, again, the case regardless of whether or not the syndromes have yet been included in the DSM. More importantly, this is the case regardless of the intentions of those who originally commended the syndrome to the courts. Advocates for BWS and RTS fought to have the diagnoses admitted into court in order to normalise women's experiences of domestic abuse and rape. Advocates of PMS and FMS, conversely, wished from the beginning to emphasise (what they perceived as) the pathological nature of women's behaviour. It is ironic that neither the theoretical origin of the syndrome nor the intention of its promoters makes a difference to the courtroom treatment of the diagnosis. The rules of evidence operate to ensure that all these accounts portray women's behaviour as abnormal, an outcome ably assisted through DSM classification. All of this leaves women, and those seeking to defend or assist them, in a dilemma. Women's feelings, thoughts, and perceptions – the context that makes their actions understandable – can be admitted into court, but only if those perceptions are characterised as disordered.

A third theme that has become apparent in our analysis is the recognition that any power which women appear to have been granted in the courtroom has, in actuality, been assigned to experts. We are not any closer to hearing 'women's voices' in the courtroom, for it is not women who decide which aspects of their behaviour and experience are relevant to explaining what happened during the events under consideration. Rather, it is experts who decide which characteristics of a woman are (and are not) relevant and which elements of an event will (or will not) feature in an explanation. It is professionals who have been awarded the authority to interpret and regulate women's accounts of their experience. Women may appear to have achieved some degree of formal egalitarian status, but as Sheldon (1997: 10) points out, the 'micropowers of law and psychology mean that the real power remains vested in male-dominated medical professions'.

Presumptions about the adequacy and satisfactory nature of a decontextualised account of human behaviour constitute a fourth theme. A focus on the individual is identified by psycholegal researchers as one of the primary sites of common ground between psychology and law, and as the 'unique' perspective which psychology is said to have to offer law (Kapardis, 1997: 15). Thus, both disciplines not only acknowledge, but celebrate, the individualistic perspective; neither engages with the limitations that accompany it. Yet there are serious limitations, as we have demonstrated throughout this text. When actions are divorced from their context, they are stripped of their meaning. The abnormality comes to reside within the *woman*, rather than within the *situation* she is confronting. She is portrayed as unable to cope, rather than as a person coping under a particular set of aberrant circumstances. Attention to those circumstances continues to be vigorously proscribed by psychological and legal practices.

Finally, our examination of the psychology–law relationship has brought a heightened awareness of the conflict that exists between the needs of individual women and those of women as a group. While the admission of syndrome diagnoses may have served to reduce the severity of some women's sentences, it has not improved the legal situation faced by women in general. In short, the nature of the law itself has not changed. Greater account has not been taken of the biased perspectives operating within law's structures. Indeed, the admission of syndrome diagnoses has arguably exacerbated the effects of those biases, given that many of the changes that were originally instituted for the benefit of women have begun to work against their interests. For example, as we saw in Chapters 5 and 7, women have been forced to undergo psychiatric examination or disclose their medical records, in their role as *witnesses*, in order to support their claims of sexual assault. The initial admission of syndromes, such as BWS, has thus facilitated the introduction of those emerging more recently, such as FMS, which derive from a less benign base. It is not surprising that the law should endorse individual needs at the expense of women as a group, precisely because of the individualistic, decontextualised model around which law is constructed. Those seeking to change the law, and the position of women within it, must remain sensitive to this conflict, and they must ensure that they are not lulled into thinking that 'victories' in individual cases will necessarily build toward a positive outcome for women in general. The outcome of syndrome evidence's tenure within the legal system illustrates this need for caution all too clearly.

These, then, are some of the primary consequences of the implicit relation. How do we move beyond them? How do we assail such an embedded infrastructure? There are two primary routes through which change can be accomplished: the epistemological and the pragmatic. The appeal of the pragmatic route is that it provides possibilities for action, steps that can be taken immediately by practitioners and activists within the legal and psychological communities. However, pragmatic changes on their own provide only short-term solutions; they do not address the underlying structural problems. Changes at the epistemological level are necessary to tackle these deeper issues. This entails re-examining the bases by which knowledge is acquired and evaluated, but because this is a long-term and rather indirect approach, it can be more frustrating.

It is not necessary to choose between these two paths. Both can be valuable, and we would argue that their simultaneous pursuit is the most effective strategy for dismantling the implicit relation. The aim of this final chapter is to explore the possibilities offered by each of them, particularly when they are undertaken in conjunction with one another.

Epistemological change

To call for epistemological change is to call for transformation. It requires questioning the basis of knowledge, reframing the grounds for decision-making, and acknowledging the consequences that stem from any particular belief system. Engagement in such activity can be liberating, in that one is freed from established boundaries, but the easing of familiar strictures is also profoundly troubling. It is such disquiet that, in part, binds individuals and disciplines and societies to accepted practices. But it is the willingness to engage in epistemological reflection that Sigmund Koch (1981: 265), the respected historian of psychology, views as the 'saving grace of the race'. Meaningful thinking is, he maintains, made possible by the 'ability of individuals, occasionally, to climb out of [their conceptual] boxes and look around: to see around the edges of our "received" concepts, our technical constructions, our formal belief systems'. Without engagement in epistemological contemplation, disciplines drift toward hollow, and ultimately destructive, practices.

The call for transformation is not an original conception. A host of critical theorists have argued that, given the entrenched nature of science and of law, changes will need to be dramatic if they have any chance of promoting a different kind of practice or an alternative form of thinking (e.g. Aronowitz, 1988; Babbitt, 1993; Cornell, 1993, 1995; Crawford and Marecek, 1989; Frug, 1992; Jasanoff, 1995; Lacey, 1993; MacKinnon, 1982, 1983; Morawski, 1994; O'Donovan, 1985, 1998; Sampson, 1981; Smart, 1989; Thornton, 1986; Wilkinson, 1997). Amongst these authors, 'transformation' is a term and an image frequently invoked.[3] But what, specifically, would be transformed in a reconceptualised system of law or science?

Above all, it is the concept of objectivity that needs to be remade. Objectivity is the issue that lies at the core of all forms of critical theory. Critical theory is primarily an examination of and commentary upon epistemology: what counts as knowledge and how it is possible for anything to be 'known'. In science and in law, critical theory has particularly interrogated the notion of value-free, objective truth, which exerts so much influence upon the theory and practice of these disciplines. How, though, is it possible to transform this quality? It seems difficult even to imagine on what basis other than objectivity a scientific discipline or legal system might operate. It is telling that not a few theorists have borrowed the futuristic tone of a science-fiction novel to articulate their vision, arguing that we must go to such a 'liminal place' (Morawski, 1994) or 'imaginary domain' (Cornell, 1995) in order to even begin to conceptualise an alternative to an objective stance.[4] Twenty years of postmodern reflection has convincingly demonstrated (at least to the satisfaction of some) that there is no singular, objective Truth. Rather, it is common now to speak in plurals: feminisms, epistemologies, identities, truths. This shift from singularity to plurality is one response to the displacement of objectivity. Yet postmodernism itself has been criticised for offering little more than *de*construction (e.g. Bordo, 1990; Lacey, 1993, 1996; Sokal and Bricmont, 1998). It is not always clear how reconstruction is to be added to the intellectual agenda. It is here that reconceptualisations of objectivity are valuable.

Objectivity as subjectivity

One means of transforming objectivity that has been proposed by critical theorists is reconceptualising it as subjectivity. Objectivity and subjectivity are generally seen as dualistic opposites, unable to be treated in any equivalent fashion. Indeed, it is the fear that chaos lies on 'the other side' – that bedlam resides in using subjectivity as the basis for knowledge – that weds disciplines (and individuals) to the notion of objectivity. 'The specter that hovers in the background [is] . . . the dread of madness and chaos where nothing is fixed, where we can neither touch bottom nor support ourselves on the surface' (Bernstein, 1983: 18). The argument has been made, however, that subjectivity and objectivity can be united and that this can be done without retiring from rationality.

> On the contrary, clinging to the belief that such objectivity is possible inhibits the search for rational understanding. By taking into account our inevitable subjectivity, we are empowered to use it in a productive manner; it becomes a conscious and intentional component to our constructions of knowledge, rather than an unrecognized and therefore potentially an insidiously forceful contaminant to our understanding.
>
> (Bohan, 1992: 17)

That is, by reconceptualising objectivity so that it includes, rather than excludes, subjectivity, a more effective and responsible form of knowing becomes possible.

While many critical scientists have explored the idea of consolidating objectivity and subjectivity (e.g. Barnes, 1977; Bloor, 1977; Collins, 1990; Haraway, 1988; Hubbard, 1990; Rose, 1994), it is perhaps most helpful here to focus on the work of a specific few, taking their ideas as broadly representative of the wider group. Sandra Harding's work is a good example of this position (e.g. 1986, 1991, 1993). She argues that the trouble with objectivity as currently conceived is that it is *not objective enough*; it is 'too weak to accomplish even the goals for which it has been designed' (Harding, 1993: 51). She asserts that 'strong objectivity' is required to correct this pervasive fault. Strong objectivity represents the amalgamation of subjectivity and objectivity, where subjectivity is regarded as a resource rather than as a problem. The 'subject of knowledge [is] placed on the same critical, causal plane as the objects of knowledge' (Harding, 1993: 69). That is, science and scientists are accorded the same level of scrutiny as the things they study. Conducting and defining science in this expansive sense would create a science that is more democratic, more effective, and simply better. It necessarily requires members of dominant and powerful groups 'learning to listen attentively to marginalized people; it requires educating oneself about their histories; . . . it requires critical self-examination to discover how one unwittingly participates in generating disadvantage to them . . . and more' (Harding, 1993: 68). In particular, this approach removes the 'mystifactory character' of objectivity, which Harding regards as 'largely responsible for [objectivity's] usefulness and its widespread appeal to dominant groups' (Harding, 1993: 71). In effect, Harding yokes objectivity to reflexivity, the willingness to gaze upon one's own actions and assumptions with the same degree of analysis as is directed to the object of study. Harding maintains that (strong) objectivity cannot begin to be approximated without strong reflexivity.

Evelyn Fox Keller's (e.g. 1983, 1985, 1987, 1992) vision is similar to Harding's, although she takes the argument further by stressing the need for *inter*subjectivity. Intersubjectivity is the process of merging two subjects, two subjectivities. In Keller's view, the topic of study needs to be framed as subject, not object. It is only in such a *shared* space that real meaning and understanding can be generated. Keller asks 'to what other ends might a different language – of kinship, embeddedness, and connectivity, of "feeling for the organism" – be equally appropriate and useful?'

(Keller, 1992: 35). In other words, an intersubjective approach based on connection would provide a very different kind of knowledge for science and for society than that which can be obtained with the distanced, dispassionate, objective approach dominating science today. Indeed, it would offer, in Keller's view, a better kind of knowledge.

Legal theorists, too, have offered redefinitions of objectivity in which subjectivity is celebrated. Katherine O'Donovan (1993, 1997), for example, has argued that the law can gain no understanding of crime, or why any individual person has committed a crime, unless its processes begin to encompass greater subjectivity. The artificiality of a single objective standard cannot assist with this aim. She maintains that the subject of law – that is, the person who is the subject of law – need not be confined to the rational, autonomous being of liberal theory. It can be constituted as 'fluid', used 'to call attention to, and to validate, those qualities which traditionally denoted "woman"' (O'Donovan, 1997: 52). She argues that the law cannot fulfil its own aims without such an undertaking.

> As a cultural artifact law is male; yet is aspires to represent us all. If it is to do so it will have to change its practice. It will have to know, to have knowledge of, to acknowledge, difference.
>
> (O'Donovan, 1993: 434–435)

The processes by which subjectivities can be articulated and accommodated within law invariably demand greater contextualisation than the law presently permits, but such contextualisation might fairly easily be realised through an extension of the rules of evidence.

The quest for contextualisation has been questioned by Nicola Lacey, who charges that to regard this strategy as one which could achieve substantial progress for women is 'somewhat naive' (Lacey, 1998: 202). She argues that it underestimates the role of other social practices engaged in the construction of woman, such as the family, the labour market, and political policies, and indeed the kinds of inter-disciplinary forces we have highlighted in this text. While it is relatively easy to criticise law for its masculinist ordering – the reasonable man in all his guises – and to identify the way that the feminine is currently conceived, it seems less easy to find a successful strategy for a new ordering. The structure of the law appears immutable to a genuine re-ordering. Carol Smart (1995), who is also extremely conscious of law's limitations, remains optimistic, though, that making space within the legal process for women's voices would go some way towards undermining law's centralising power.

> The idea of investigating the legal construction of, for example, the raped woman, is of little value unless we are also talking to women who have been raped [for] we could not begin to conceptualize the legal construction as something quite so specific, if we did not already have other versions constructed from accounts provided by women.
>
> (Smart, 1995: 231)

By being able to compare two accounts of experience, in this case those offered by the woman who is raped and that offered by the law, it becomes possible to identify *each* account as subjective. Space needs to be made within the legal system for such competing accounts.

However, it is entirely inadequate for that space to be merely symbolic. Women have that already: in the witness box, as practitioners, in the academy. A major epistemological shift is necessary, one which acknowledges the presence, and the value, of subjectivity. In a system founded on an objective model, when two subjectivities are in competition, one must 'win'. The winner will inevitably be the male perspective in the masculinist system that operates at present. If women's voices are to be heard, scope for multiple voices must be created. This requires the adoption of a new model of truth.

Certainly these theorists' visions for objectivity represent a radical shift from traditional conceptions. It is that radical nature that creates the possibility of transformation. It is also that quality that breeds scepticism and scorn amongst mainstream scholars, the sort of reaction in which feminist aspirations are treated as bizarre, outlandish, and 'laughable' (Keller, 1992: 36). However, these ideas demonstrate that knowledge can be based on a foundation other than objectivity, and the optimism of these authors gives a strong sense that such an epistemology might be *put into practice*, rather than remaining suspended in an abstract theoretical realm. Subjectivity and objectivity do not have to remain rivals; it is possible to reframe them as partners.

Objectivity as plurality

Having taken the step of conceiving of objectivity as subjectivity, it is a small step to conceiving of objectivity in a pluralistic fashion. We observed earlier in this chapter that postmodern contemplation has led the singular to become the multiple. It is not then surprising to find that the monolithic, singular conception of objectivity has also given way to a more pluralistic one.

This shift has been reflected in psychology particularly through the advent of qualitative methods (e.g. Henwood and Nicolson, 1995; Parker, 1992; Potter and Wetherell, 1987). This type of method seeks to understand the meaning of phenomena through the discourse used by people to describe events. This approach has been applied to the same topics that psychology has tended to study quantitatively, resulting in a store of richer, subtler, and arguably more meaningful findings on topics such as the acquisition of mathematical ability (Walkerdine, 1988), postnatal depression (P. Nicolson, 1991), identity (Smith, 1999), menstruation (Marshall, 1996), social roles (Smith, 1999), and gender (Wetherell and Edley, 1999). The linguistic data that form the core of this work are frequently obtained through interviews, but they are also derived from recording naturalistic interactions and public speeches, as well as from the analysis of written documents such as political campaign materials or textbooks. Those who advocate the use of qualitative methodology argue that this is a better way of understanding the meaning which an event or topic holds for the *participants*, rather than ascribing to it the meaning that a *researcher* thinks it should have, as is a common outcome of the use of quantitative methods. It is in understanding that the theoretical focus of qualitative research is on the 'individual's particular account of reality, rather than an objective reality itself' (Smith, 1995: 122) that the operation of a pluralistic conception of truth becomes noticeable. Ultimately, the aim of scientific work practised within this pluralistic framework is to understand which perspectives are reflected in mainstream practices and which marginalised, and to create spaces within which alternative perspectives can be heard. This differs from feminist-empiricism, which seeks to 'cleanse' sexist biases from science (Morawski, 1994: 48), thereby creating a more 'objective objectivity'. A pluralistic epistemology accepts and engages with the conflict that is inherent in negotiating all forms of meaning.

A pluralistic account of truth can also be applied within law. Carol Smart's (e.g. 1989, 1990, 1992) vision of a 'refracted law' is an excellent example, although many other authors have also offered such conceptions (e.g. Cain, 1989; Frug, 1992; Harris, 1990; Lacey, 1993, 1996). Smart argues that the law does not need to bind itself to a singular mode of evaluating human behaviour. It already contains within it different goals, applications, and effects. A man charged with rape, for example, need only demonstrate that he personally believed his alleged victim had consented to sex; his belief need not meet an objective, 'reasonable' standard (see Chapter 5). Defendants who have used the defence of provocation in response to a murder charge have sometimes had their personal characteristics taken into account by courts when evaluating their behaviour (see Chapter 4). Varying cultural norms have been taken into account in constituting statutory regulation (see Chapter 3). Thus, law can and does accommodate subjectivity, if in an inconsistent and contradictory fashion. It does not – and need not – 'have a single appearance' (Smart, 1989: 164). Such contradictions require, in Smart's view, to be much more readily acknowledged, rendering them overt and available for theorising. A refracted system of law would welcome variability, regarding it as a strength, rather than as a form of weakness. 'Legislation to preserve foetal life [could – and would] coexist with legislation which provide[d] therapeutic abortions' (Smart, 1989: 164). The realisation that 'abortion law may have a different meaning for black or native women on whom abortions are pressed, than for white women who feel they can exercise "choice"' would not present a dilemma, because a refracted jurisprudence would not strive for unified aims or standards (1989: 164). Smart's vision of law discards the need for objectivity. There would be no central standard by which to judge or direct law.

The absence of the appeal to objectivity distinguishes Smart's proposal from that of feminist theorists such as Catharine MacKinnon (1987, 1989). MacKinnon argues that *law reform* is the solution to women's subordinate position within society. In pursuing an agenda of equal rights, she reflects liberal ideology's confidence in the law as a means of redressing social and gender injustices. MacKinnon believes that a *unifying* feminist jurisprudence offers the most effective challenge to the male-normative basis of law. This is the point with which Smart so strongly disagrees (see also Cain, 1989; Harris, 1990; Williams, 1991). A unified feminist jurisprudence assumes that women embody essential characteristics which permit them to be represented as a singular whole Woman, a standpoint that postmodern feminist theory has sought to move beyond. A feminist jurisprudence merely replaces one abstracted grand theory with another. This is not, Smart believes, the way to counter the problems of traditional legal structures, nor is it the goal for which feminism has been, or should be, striving.

Indeed, for Smart a unified feminist jurisprudence is not radical enough, for it continues to put law at the centre of the debate, re-confirming law's standing 'in the hierarchy of knowledge' (Smart, 1989: 68). Law uses law – legal structures, paradigms, and language – to both define the issues and seek their resolution. Yet their resolution may lie outside law, for it is law itself that is, in Smart's view, the problem. Locating the problem within law itself explains why legal reform has been relatively unsuccessful in addressing problems such as rape, violence, sexual harassment, and child abuse, which lie at the centre of feminist concerns. Ultimately, 'law reforms empower law' (p. 161), rather than foregrounding the needs of women. It is in an attempt to work beyond legal paradigms that Smart has developed her notion of 'refracted law'. Because this vision contains no appeal to any type of objectivity, it nurtures the possibility for real change. Arguably, it is precisely such a transformational, pluralistic vision that is needed in order to move beyond the implicit relation.

Objectivity as ethically based choice

However, when faced with a diverse set of subjectivities, how is a choice to be made among them? On what basis is behaviour to be explained or regulated, if competing interpretations are allowed to co-exist? These are the questions that arise from a pluralistic conception of objectivity, and they may at first glance appear to represent an inextricable dilemma. If no particular perspective reflects the *a priori* standard, then one position will have to be endorsed at the expense of another. *Which* perspective should that be? *Whose* set of values should be implemented? It is in comprehending that such a choice must always be made – and already always is made – that the relation between ethics and epistemology becomes clear. Like personal choices, the choices of society, science, and law are based on values: on notions about what is desirable and important, or unacceptable and unjust. The production of knowledge is necessarily continual and contingent.

The rhetoric of objectivity resolves the dilemma of choice by denying that the problem exists. There is no need to make a decision about *which* position to sanction if only a single one exists in the first place. There is no need to shoulder responsibility for the consequences of the choice, if it was the only option available anyway. According to Boyle (1997: 5), objectivity absolves disciplines of the 'responsibility for examining the value systems which influence choice of research questions, methods and theories, as well as attempts to put theories into practice'. Koch (1981: 268–269) goes even further in his analysis. He argues that the presumption of 'preemptive truths' is 'no mere cognitive blunder'. It cannot be 'written off as an innocuous excess of enthusiasm'. For Koch, the presumption of objectivity raises a 'grave moral issue reflective of a widespread moral bankruptcy'. Although his comments were made specifically in regard to psychology, they can be extended to any discipline that fails to consider the ethical nature of its knowledge production systems, an extension within which law would certainly be incorporated. It is such insights that have led some theorists to reconceptualise objectivity as episte-mological ethics. They argue that ignoring the ethical component of scientific and legal systems not only produces immoral outcomes, it denies the disciplines important advantages. By reconceptualising objectivity as ethically based choice, a more productive and powerful position is achieved.

The work of Jill Morawski (e.g. 1985, 1994) captures this viewpoint well. Morawski highlights the inconsistency between the theory/rhetoric of science and the actual practices of science, leading her to argue that science should be regarded as a set of social practices. This contrasts with the traditional construction of science as an activity separated from its social context and input. Morawski has sought to demonstrate this conceptual difference through the innovative use of non-traditional methods (e.g. qualitative, sociological, and ethnographic tools) and through drawing attention to the cultural context within which psychological phenomena occur. She envisions an explicitly morally and politically oriented science, an aim to which she believes feminist theory can contribute significantly, precisely because it occupies a place 'betwixt and between' mainstream science and its alternatives (1994: 53). From within such a 'vibrant space' (1994: 239), it becomes possible to look again at the received concepts and practices of science, including psychology, and to read them in new ways.

Morawski maintains that entry into this 'liminal space' forces the adoption of a new epistemology – one that she entitles 'social epistemology'. This perspective 'opens to view the full range of practices that constitute [the] knowledge making enterprise [called science]; such a conception permits us to draw the contours of how science should proceed' (1994: 66). That is, a social epistemology enables us to see not only what science *does* do, but also what it *should* do. It provides the opportunity – and the responsibility – to take account of the ethical nature of science. The power of this contention is that it not only points out that beliefs about the nature of knowledge (i.e. epistemology) do direct disciplinary practices but also contends that this is appropriate. That is, disciplinary practices and theories are inherently a matter of ethics: they are intrinsically value-laden. We must, and we can, in Morawski's 'transmuted science' choose the values we wish to endorse. A social epistemology brings to light 'the norms or politics that are embedded in science's languages, procedures, and technology' (1994: 240). As such, it does not demand a rejection of science, but simply a rethinking of how society wishes to conduct it. Morawski views this rethinking as the essential project in which feminist psychology and feminist science have been engaged.

Drucilla Cornell (e.g. 1991, 1993, 1995) has applied a similar ethically based vision to the transformation of law. Cornell seeks the equality of men and women, but, like Smart and Lacey, she believes that law reform is insufficient for bringing about the necessary change. In Cornell's view, feminism too often sets its sights on law as the 'primary arena' for changing society, but this simply 'entrenches' feminism's energy, rendering it unproductive and stagnant (1995: 27). She argues that equality between men and women can only be achieved by inhabiting what she terms the 'imaginary domain'. It is virtually impossible at present to view women and men as equals before the law, she says, because of the 'symbolic underpinnings [that] shape our reality to the extent that we are unable to truly envision the feminine as anything other than the persona of femininity' (1995: 7–8). Only within the imaginary domain can we transcend those underpinnings. Law's responsibility, she emphasises, is not to *force* individuals to inhabit that domain; rather, law's responsibility is to *protect* the bases that make such shifts possible.

> The protection of the imaginary domain provides us [i.e. women] with the space to . . . act up. We will no longer have to fight endlessly to push back the law in order to prevent it from denying us breathing space altogether; an activity that is draining in the same way that finding oneself stuck on a treadmill is draining.
>
> (Cornell, 1995: 233)

Law's purpose, in Cornell's view, is not to force people into particular positions, but to protect their ability and their right to choose from among them.

A simplistic way of summarising the complex arguments of Cornell, Morawski, and others, is that the variety of 'stories' that can be used to explain human experience needs to be taken seriously. Science, law, society, and individuals make choices, which carry serious (as well as not-so-serious) consequences, on the basis of those various accounts. These stories must be examined, and new ones imagined. In Sampson's words (1981: 742), the aims of critical work should be to 'strive toward a psychology not of what is, but of what may yet be'. It is in accepting that value-laden choices are inevitable and that making them is appropriate that societies and individuals increase their ability to make better – more ethical – choices. The dissolution of objectivity is not chaos, but freedom.

These necessarily brief accounts provide some flavour of the transformative visions that have been offered by contemporary theorists. We have presented them in order to give a taste of what might lie on the other side, to provide a sense that something manageable could lie beyond the 'edges' of objectivity. The three positions are not mutually exclusive, of course. Keller's comments eloquently capture the links between them when she argues that intersubjective knowledge would create the basis for a better form of science. We would add that it creates the basis for a better form of law, as well.

> Since uses and practices [of science] are obviously not value-free, why should we even think of equating 'good' science with the notion of 'value-free'? Far from being 'value-free', *good science* is science that effectively facilitates the material realization of particular goals, that does in fact enable us to change the world in particular ways. Some of the goals it enables us to realize are goals that almost all people might share, others are more restricted. (*Good science*

might also enable the realization of goals that most people would reject – that is, that most people would regard as bad.)

(Keller, 1992: 5, emphasis in original)

These reconceptualisations of objectivity are complex, challenging, even disturbing and 'disorienting' (Bohan, 1992: 12), but what else would we expect of transformative visions? 'Feminism . . . inevitably challenges us to re-think the very basis of civilization and its discontents' (Cornell, 1995: 27). Unless an argument takes us to unfamiliar territory, it is not transformation. To reiterate the statement with which we opened Chapter 1: 'We are not here to make ourselves comfortable.' Tinkering around the edges of science and/or of law will not be sufficient for producing the change that is needed. Some transformative projects may not work smoothly in practice; it may not (yet) even be clear how to put some of them into practice. But then neither does the current system work smoothly or fairly. It is important to know that alternatives exist, that they can be and have been envisioned, for then we know that there are options to our present circumstances.

Pragmatic change

To effect epistemological transformation, action must follow vision. The remainder of this chapter will explore pragmatic steps that might be taken to move the fields of psychology and law in the direction we have described. We will focus in particular on reforms that could be implemented within the legal system, because women's lives could be improved in direct and immediate ways as a result of such reforms. Psychology has a key role to play in facilitating the success of these proposals, which will require change on its own part.

Promoting reform is, as we have shown, a conservative position. However, given that women have 'inevitably already been entered into' the legal system (Cornell, 1995: 235), it is reasonable to challenge law (and science) both from within and from without. Reform provides a site for *action*; it generates alternative practices in which practitioners and activists can engage. That focal point is important, because identifying problems and deconstructing systems results only in frustration if paths forward cannot be illuminated. Even as an interim step, therefore, reform can be valuable.

We will focus here on three specific reforms that could be undertaken within the legal system to underpin epistemological change: (a) amending the rules of evidence and procedure, (b) making greater use of social framework evidence, and (c) reframing legal education programmes. These particular reforms are selected because they each play a powerful role in regulating and constructing women's experience within the legal system. It is also in these areas that the epistemological act of assigning meaning to evidence is accomplished. These areas therefore hold the potential to generate and apply new meanings. Thus, reforms in these areas would constitute (small) epistemological transformations in and of themselves.

Reconfiguring the rules of evidence

If any of the problems we have highlighted throughout this text are to be addressed at a fundamental level, the rules of evidence regulating the admission of testimony into the courtroom must be reconfigured. Designed to elicit 'the facts' and to determine 'the truth', it is the rules of evidence that provide the framework for the proof process. As we have seen, the orthodox view is that such rules are impartial, that they are universal and consistent in their effect. As such, they constitute a quintessential example of 'black-letter law': areas of the law that are assumed by traditionalists to be so clearly conceived that they need no (and brook no) interpretation or critique.

In contrast to this objective characterisation, a number of feminist writers have argued that gender biases are hidden within the rules of evidence and that the rules contribute to the disadvantaged position of women within the legal system (e.g. Childs and Ellison, forthcoming; Hunter, 1996; Mack, 1993). The corroboration warning (discussed in Chapter 5), which required judges to warn juries of the dangers of relying on a rape complainant's uncorroborated testimony, is an obvious example of sexist practice. The difficulty which battered women face in having evidence regarding their history of abuse admitted (discussed in Chapter 4) is another illustration of such a bias. Thus, one way of transforming the legal system is to change the rules of evidence. While this may sound like a relatively straight-forward undertaking, the very classification of the rules as impartial black-letter law renders this suggestion radical.

One rule that could be changed is the hearsay rule (Raitt, forthcoming). This is the rule that disallows witnesses from testifying in regard to things that other people have told them. For example, if a woman who was raped told a friend of the crime, the law would not permit the friend to testify about that conversation in support of the woman's allegations. Witnesses are restricted to testifying about aspects of the crime that they have directly seen or heard themselves. Specifically, the hearsay rule states that: 'an assertion other than one made by a person while giving oral evidence in the proceedings is inadmissible *as evidence of any fact asserted*' (Cross and Tapper, 1995: 46, emphasis in original). Hearsay is excluded primarily because it is regarded as unreliable. Because the maker of the original statement may not be present in court to testify as to the accuracy of the statement, there is no opportunity for cross-examination and the trier of fact cannot observe the demeanour of the witness or form an assessment as to her/his credibility.

Women are disadvantaged by the hearsay rule. The violence which women suffer is predominantly private, hidden within spaces where it cannot be publicly observed. The violence to which men are subject is much more likely to be conducted in public spaces, where witnesses will be present to comment on the behaviour that they have 'directly seen and heard'. Therefore the type of direct evidence that law prefers will more often be available in relation to crimes committed against men than to crimes committed against women. Additionally, women have a greater propensity than men to develop emotionally intimate relationships with friends (O'Connor, 1992), and the exchange of disclosures about personal violence will be fostered within such relationships. However, the testimony of friends about those disclosures is of no value to the court, for it is considered hearsay. A person might be permitted to testify that she had observed bruises on her friend or that she had seen her behaving in a very upset manner, for these observations constitute direct evidence. But the law would only permit her to give evidence about something which she herself experienced first hand, so if she had not directly observed the rape or the husband beating his wife, she could not make allegations about the man's behaviour, on the basis of what a friend had said to her. It is for the trier of fact to draw inferences from the evidence presented.

There is nothing inherently better about 'first-hand' rather than 'second-hand' evidence. The worth of evidence can be judged only against the aims of the enquiry, and the law's preference for direct evidence is a consequence of its pursuit of objectivity. Second-hand evidence might well be useful and informative to the law, but it is prevented from fulfilling its potential through the exclusion of 'subjective' evidence. For example, evidence regarding a prior account of the event, given contemporaneously, might offer a perspective on the facts that is a more accurate one than that extracted under cross-examination; certainly it might offer one more compatible with a complainant's experience. If the trier of fact were permitted to hear from a confidant about the content as well as the tone and emotional impact of the conversation(s), that could serve to reinforce the complainer's version of events and thus her credibility. Hearsay evidence could be admitted while leaving the decision about how much weight to attach to the evidence to the trier of fact – conditions that already apply to all other forms of evidence. Although such evidence risks being distorted in the courtroom (as does all testimony), its admission could not place women in a worse position than they currently find themselves, and that is the central problem we wish to address in this text.

Another set of rules that could be changed are those that govern the process by which examination and cross-examination of a witness is conducted. Various rules operate to manage and control the witness. In so doing, the real 'voice' of the witness is stifled, forced into law's ill-fitting mould. This is considerably less of a problem for those whose experience already accords with law's viewpoint (i.e. white, heterosexual men) than it is for those who hold a conflicting perspective (e.g. ethnic minorities, homosexual men, women). John Conley and colleagues (1978) have pointed out the ways in which the language and presentational tactics in the courtroom control and constrain the facts that are allowed to emerge and to be proven, thus influencing the credibility of a witness.

> [W]itnesses who speak in a straightforward, powerful and not unnaturally formal style, who testify with minimal assistance from the lawyer, and who resist efforts by opposing counsel to cut short their remarks will enhance their credibility because they will make more favorable impressions on the jury.
>
> (Conley, O'Barr, and Lind, 1978: 1395)

Matoesian also observes that: 'the ideological supremacy of male hegemony [is] threaded throughout victim cross-examination. . . . Defense attorneys ask questions; victims answer questions. Defense attorneys set the agenda; victims follow the agenda' (Matoesian, 1993: 34–35). This has led him to conclude that 'trial talk is the incarnation of rape' (p. 34). That is, the linguistic structure of the courtroom does more than occlude women's voices; it commits its own form of violence against them.

By altering the rules of examination and cross-examination of witnesses, women could be permitted to give an account of their experience in their own words and at their own pace, focusing on the aspects of the crime that were relevant to them. Thus, in a rape trial a woman would be permitted to explain why she invited a man to her house for coffee, instead of having it implied, through the technique of closed questions and selective management of the evidence, that such an invitation constituted consent to sexual intercourse. Reconfiguring the rules of evidence and procedure relating to examination of witnesses could prevent the anger expressed by so many complainants in rape cases that

> they were not allowed to explain fully what had happened to them, or how they *felt* during the rape . . . [being] confined to answering questions briefly, and often to simply answering yes or no.
>
> (Lees, 1996: 31, emphasis in original)

The present procedures were developed because they allow lawyers to maintain control of a case. They choose the way in which it will be presented; they seek to highlight those aspects of an event which will support their explanation. It is assumed that in the course of the battle between the defence and the prosecution, the truth will emerge, with attention drawn by one party to any points missed by the other. That this eventual 'truth' may bear little resemblance to the woman's 'truth' is of relatively little concern to the law. As long as the rules of evidence have been observed, a neutral, unbiased process is deemed to have transpired.

There are a number of other ways in which the rules of evidence might be amended to address women's treatment in the courtroom, included redefining the role of expert witnesses, the boundaries within which privileged status is granted to evidence, and improving the restrictions on admission of character evidence. All of the changes suggested here could be accommodated within existing legal structures. They need not cause an internal collapse of the law, and they do not require a revolutionary overhaul of existing legal structures. While we would agree with the many commentators who would argue that such reforms are insufficient, in that they will not dislodge the sexism woven so intricately throughout law's framework, they offer at least a starting place and some points of action. Moreover, the implementation of any of these suggestions would be momentous, for this would require a tacit acknowledgement on the part of law that perspectives other than its own have validity.

Greater use of social framework evidence

Another form of pragmatic change that is promising is greater use of social framework evidence. In this form of testimony, experts are called to testify about general psychological phenomena and findings. Monahan and Walker (1988, 1994), the leading theorists on this topic, specifically define the purpose of social framework evidence as providing 'general conclusions from social science research in determining factual issues in a specific case' (Monahan and Walker, 1994: 314). It thus serves an educational function, by providing a broader or alternative context within which to 'make sense' of the factual information presented in a specific case. Social framework evidence already operates in the US and to a lesser degree in the UK, so the possibilities for developing its use are auspicious.

Examples of the types of cases in which social framework evidence has been used include those concerned with confession evidence (Sheldon and MacLeod, 1991), social conformity (Mackay and Colman, 1991), juror selection (Monahan and Walker, 1994), patent offensiveness and obscenity (*Saliba* v *State*, 1985), consumer confusion (*Processed Plastic* v *Warner Communications*, 1982), racial segregation (*Brown* v *Board of Education*, 1954), behavioural traits of abused children (*State* v *Myers*, 1984), the effects of television violence (*Zamora* v *State*, 1978), and stereotyping (*Price Waterhouse* v *Hopkins*, 1989). The domain in which social framework evidence has become most established and most discussed is eyewitness memory, with expert testimony being seen as valuable in making clear the effects of stress on eyewitness accuracy, the speed with which memory decays over time, and the lack of correspondence between eyewitness confidence and accuracy (Kassin, Ellsworth, and Smith, 1989; Loftus, 1991; Penrod, Fulero, and Cutler, 1995).

Syndrome evidence, refashioned as social framework evidence, could offer substantial benefits for women, particularly in its role of disabusing jurors of common misconceptions regarding women's behaviour. Indeed, it already often operates in this capacity. In *Kelly*, for example, the court stated in regard to BWS, that social science research illuminated

> an area where the purported common knowledge of the jury may be very much mistaken, an area where jurors' logic, drawn from their own experience, may lead to a wholly incorrect conclusion, an area where expert knowledge would enable the jurors to disregard their prior conclusions as being common myths rather than common knowledge.
>
> (*State* v *Kelly*, 1984: 378)

In *People* v *Bledsoe* (1984: 457), the Californian Supreme Court observed that research findings from group studies of the typical reactions of rape victims could help jurors to evaluate the evidence in any given case 'free of the constraints of popular myths'. While expert testimony may not always be characterised as social framework evidence, that is in effect what it often is. In many ways, then, presenting psychological evidence as social framework data simply fulfils the function that was intended by those who first advocated the use of syndrome evidence in the courts. Lenore Walker's intention in having BWS admitted was 'to teach a jury about battered women . . . explaining why [old] myths did not really hold true' (Walker, 1990: 315). The use of expert RTS testimony was initially intended to compensate for the legal rules that make it so difficult for a complainant to prove she was raped. Even testimony in regard to PMS and FMS can serve as social framework evidence, where it is used to provide general information about the number of women who are estimated to suffer from such syndromes and what the typical symptoms are.

Conceiving of syndrome evidence in this fashion, though, makes it easy to identify the drawbacks to social framework evidence. A key element of our analysis has been to show the extent to which the original intentions of syndrome explanations have been thwarted by the implicit relation. The success of a social framework approach is dependent on an account that does not pathologise women. The way in which an expert chooses to characterise a woman's behaviour will govern the message that is delivered in court, and the characterisations that experts will be permitted to bring in the first place are subject to those that have gained general acceptance within the relevant scientific field. This circular reasoning captures the essence of our claims concerning the implicit relation. Moreover, there is no requirement that social framework information be used in a particular manner. Judges are as free to use the evidence in a way that is 'helpful' to women as in a way that is 'unhelpful', as the comments in the road traffic case of *Scott* v *Hamilton* (1988: 264) illustrate.

> Having regard to the evidence to the effect that premenstrual syndrome is experienced by many women and by a substantial minority to a marked degree at a particular stage of each menstrual cycle, I was not prepared to regard the syndrome as a special reason in the sense intended by the legislature. The syndrome is not special to the appellant nor special to the circumstances of this case.

Even Wigmore's observation that it is 'common knowledge that women and children sometimes lie' (discussed in Chapter 7), could be construed as a form of social framework evidence, given that it is intended to impart general information about human behaviour. Indeed, it appears that this particular 'framework' continues to be a very persuasive one, given Mack's (1994) recent finding that a form of this exhortation is still offered by judges in 50% of sexual assault cases in Australia. As we have argued, there can be no guarantee that the evidence psychologists present when giving expert evidence will be any less based on 'mythology' than the beliefs of judges or jurists. Whether or not something is a myth depends on one's perspective.

Ultimately, it is the reasoning in the diagnostic systems of the DSM and ICD that presents the greatest barrier to effecting beneficial change for women. What if psychology characterised a woman's reaction to long-term battering or rape or sexual abuse as *normal*? The DSM states that the behaviours observed must 'not be merely an expectable and culturally sanctioned response to a particular event, for example, the death of a loved one' (DSM, 1994: xxi). Just as there is no such thing as 'Bereavement Syndrome', why is it not possible to conceive of women's anger at their devalued role in society as *culturally sanctioned* or their reaction to sexual abuse as *expectable*? Were such accounts offered by psychology, law might then be forced to examine the ways in which it makes sense of women's behaviour. There is, of course, no guarantee that this would happen, for law treated women's behaviour as deviant long before psychology began to assist it in this regard. However, psychology's contribution brings an independent confirmation of this assessment, and the possibility of change is further inhibited.

It is important, though, that the two elements of the social framework approach be distinguished. Social framework evidence on psychological issues *does* hold significant potential for addressing the gendered biases of the legal system. Its ability to fulfil that potential depends on the characterisation of women which it brings to the courtroom. If the woman's behaviour is portrayed as normal, and emphasis is placed on the context within which her actions are generated, it can be very effective. It is possible for the social framework approach to achieve this, as illustrated by the case of *Price Waterhouse* v *Hopkins* (1989), in which one of the leading accounting firms in the US was found guilty of sexual discrimination when it refused to make Anne Hopkins a partner (Fiske *et al.*, 1991). Evidence was successfully presented by expert witnesses on sex stereotyping and cognitive categorisation theories, not on something called 'Sexual Discrimination Syndrome'. Where women's behaviour is explained as the result of a psychological disorder, greater admission of social framework evidence is a sterile strategy.

Reframing legal educational programmes

Ultimately, the best prospect for accomplishing epistemological transformation is education. Education always holds the power to refashion an academic discipline, social institution, or culture, through encouraging critical reasoning, intellectual curiosity, and reflexivity on the part of its members. Such activity is promoted – or prevented – through the practices applied in the teaching environment. Although it might be thought that this is the self-evident purpose of education, the illustrations we have provided throughout this text make clear that this is not, in practice, happening. Educational structures, like scientific and legal ones, can be much more rigid and narrow than they believe themselves to be.

Discussion of the possibilities for reforming the educational structures and teaching practices within colleges and universities is well known (e.g. Damrosch, 1995; Getman, 1992; Kerr, 1991). A large proportion of this literature has been contributed by feminist theorists, who have discussed the outcomes of expanding the role models, teaching styles, and course materials that are offered to students (e.g. Kupenda, 1997; Montoya, 1994; Williams, 1991; Worell and Johnson, 1997). The possibilities for change that they highlight are exciting, but because these ideas are so widely discussed within the literature, we will focus here on professional educational programmes, which have received much less attention.

The governing bodies of most professions require that practitioners undertake continuing training and development. For lawyers, the topics of such training typically include recent legislation (e.g. the Human Rights Act 1998), developments in forensic science (e.g. reliability of DNA testing), and implementation of new procedural rules (e.g. closed-circuit television for witnesses). As an educational enterprise, professional development has great potential to promote epistemological shifts. This can be particularly valuable when inter-disciplinary issues are being addressed, such as the use of science within the courtroom. Gless (1995) argues that all those participating professionally in the legal system, from students to judges, should be required to complete courses in understanding and handling scientific evidence. This should not be, in his view, a voluntary undertaking, but should be mandated. It would serve as a forum through which lawyers and judges would be informed of changes in science, and more importantly, 'through such collaborative relationships, a more complete, mutual understanding of foundational requirements could be developed' (Gless, 1995: 290). Kapardis (1997), Levine (1999) and Saks (1989) are among others who share this view, arguing that greater collaboration between lawyers and social scientists would be valuable for those practising in both professions.

A key problem arises, however, in regard to what the content of professional training and inter-disciplinary collaborations should be, as well as the range of scientific perspectives that should be reflected in such endeavours. Gless comments that the 'realm of what lawyers and judges do not even know they do not know about science must be reduced' (Gless, 1995: 291). Our concern is with what it is that *scientists* do not even know they do not know about science. The view of science which judges and lawyers would gain through participation in professional development and in collaborations is naturally dependent upon the views held by the contributing scientists.

The difficulty of promoting epistemological reflection through professional training is heightened by the reality that, for the most part, practitioners operate within a quite different framework from that of academics. They are driven by the needs of business, the market, employers, and clients, rather than the motive of testing theories and refining intellectual arguments. While attention to practical matters has at least some chance of being seen as a worthwhile use of practitioners' time, philosophical debates and theoretical critiques can appear to be a luxury or even a waste of time. It is partly for that reason that training in the UK tends to focus on practical matters such as 'the mechanics of criminal trials, the scope of new legislation and recent authorities, and sentencing' (Thornton, 1995: 97). Even in the US, novel judicial training initiatives, such as that offered by the National Judicial College (1999), tend to feature topics such as judicial writing, court management, and dispute resolution skills.

A supplemental reason that training tends to focus on practical matters is, not surprisingly, resistance to philosophical reflection. Harry Edwards (1992), a US Appeal Court judge, recently complained of the growing disjuncture between legal education and the legal profession. He was critical of inter-disciplinary work and deconstructionist approaches because these trends do not produce *practical* scholarship. Critical legal studies is, in his view, '"impractical" because it seeks to show that the existing legal system is fundamentally flawed' (Edwards, 1992: 47). Edwards does not see a value to epistemological enquiry, for he believes that the purpose of legal scholarship should be to study topics that have 'direct utility for practitioners, judges, administrators, or legislators' (Edwards, 1992: 47). He reports that his law clerks hold a similar view. As practitioners-in-training, they wanted to study practical matters – how to solve problems through the application of doctrinal rules and precedent – not to engage in 'irrelevant' discussions about the foundations of law or philosophy and political theory (Edwards, 1992: 60). If it is difficult to communicate the relevance of jurisprudential foundations to students, how much more difficult is it to accomplish this with those who have already progressed to the rank of professional.

It is not impossible, however. Innovative programmes have been developed for underlining the relevance of such issues to judges and lawyers, such as the one based at Brandeis University, in Boston, which makes use of personal narrative and works of fiction to shift judges' views, particularly in regard to their understanding of domestic violence. Martha Minow (1990) sees this as a particularly effective strategy because

> [l]iterary accounts and narratives of experience can offer new language to challenge conventional legal understandings, or misunderstandings, of domestic violence. Narratives with evocative, rich details about subjective experiences can be used to persuade people – like judges – who have sufficient power to make a difference actually to do so for people – like children and women – who face persistent risks of violence at the hands of intimate fellow householders.
>
> (Minow, 1990: 1688–1689)

Thus, narrative can serve an important educational function, because it creates a space within which the assumptions of legal and scientific reasoning can be questioned. When the stories that (can) get told – in the courtroom, in the laboratory, in society in general – begin to be examined, the biases and assumptions that they harbour begin to be revealed and the possibility of challenging them is created. Donna Haraway identifies this as a key aim of feminist theory: to alter 'a "field" of stories or possible accounts by raising the costs of some accounts, by destabilizing the plausibility of some strategies of explanation' (Haraway, 1986: 81). The goal is to replace existing stories with ones that tell a tale more closely in keeping with the experience of more of the characters in the drama.

Educational reforms provide no guarantees, however. As O'Donovan (1998: 59–60) notes, 'stories in their representation of human actors may reinforce generalisations about gender, even whilst we are reading to empathise'. The demand of an educational system, whether working with students or with profes-sionals, is that it open up spaces for thinking. What it is that should go into those spaces remains, quite properly, a matter for continual debate.

Personal transformation

The power of narrative to challenge received wisdom is a fitting note on which to end. Narratives are not only a method for transforming a discipline, but for renewing the resolution of those who are working towards that outcome. Those theorists who have been willing to 'tell the story' of their lives and their careers and their intellectual journeys demonstrate that disciplinary transformation can never occur independently of personal transformation.

Evelyn Fox Keller, for example, begins her 1992 text by reflecting on the path of her 30-year career.

> In the mid-1970s – the very early days of my shift from 'doing' science to thinking about what goes into the production of scientific knowledge – the notion that both that process and its products reflect social norms seemed very radical. . . . I too took as a given the distinctiveness of the values and the practices responsible for the growth of scientific knowledge. . . . [The ideas in my 1992 book] represent a departure from my initial confidence in the possibility of identifying certain beliefs as 'mythlike', as distinct from other beliefs that are, by implication, 'myth-free'. Such a notion now seems to me suspiciously reminiscent of the old demarcation between 'truth' and 'ideology' or between 'good science' and 'value-laden science', demarcations that are themselves residues of the copy theory of truth.
>
> (Keller, 1992: 1 and 4–5)

The extent to which Keller's early position mirrors that adopted by many mainstream theorists today is important. For example, she observes that the aim of her 1985 text had been to 'help clarify the substructure of science in order to preserve the things that science has taught us, *in order to be more objective*' (Keller, 1992: 2, emphasis added). Her wording in that excerpt bears a striking resemblance to that employed by Michael Morgan in his recent rejection of the deconstructionist account of science.

> I agree that it is very difficult to make an observation without thinking about what it means, but this does not mean that the observation and the interpretation are inseparable, like Siamese twins with only one head. . . . The claim that data are always corrupted by opinion is, frankly, bogus. Even if it were partly true, that would be all the more reason to *redouble our efforts to be objective*.
>
> (Morgan, 1996: 32, emphasis added)

The similarity between Morgan and Keller is encouraging, for it demonstrates that a critical theoretical position is not one from which scientists or legal theorists begin their endeavours; it is one to which they move. This is not to imply that in years hence, Morgan will necessarily have become a critical theorist (a possibility he would likely abhor), but simply to emphasise that his position is one which many critical theorists have themselves at some point occupied. His transformation, like all of ours, is not assured, but it is yet possible.

This optimistic view is reinforced by surveying the personal stories offered by a variety of academic researchers and teachers. For example, Susan Estrich (1987) tells the story of how the legal system dealt with her own rape in order to illustrate why the law of rape needs to be taught in law school. Jane Ussher (1990) describes the disillusionment and discontent with the psychology curriculum that she felt as a student in order to illustrate the need for and legitimacy of feminist practices. Angela Mae Kupenda's (1997) paper, subtitled 'Confessions of an African American Female Professor Who Attempted to Crash All the Barriers at Once', was written to demonstrate the merits of retaining her own (black, feminist, female) identity, as opposed to donning the 'masks' expected by a (white, male) law faculty. Carolyn Sherif (1979) examines the means by which psychology perpetuates social myths through discussing the structure of the graduate programme in which she herself was enrolled at Purdue University. Helena Kennedy (1993: 19) recounts episodes in her legal career to make clear that she 'did not come to the Bar as a feminist', but her experiences there altered her perspective. The economist Deirdre McCloskey recalls:

> I can remember a time – 1970, say – when I believed the other and older view, that Objectivity is routinely achievable. I then regarded the argument heard from leftist critics that values enter science, before or after The Test, as unfair or irrelevant or politically inspired rubbish. . . . Now that I've changed sides, my question is . . . [what kind of argument] is going to persuade the kind of person I once was?
>
> (McCloskey, 1995: 119–120)[5]

The inaugural issue of *The Psychology of Women Section Review* (1999) was explicitly designed to provide personal accounts of the paths which had brought feminist psychologists to their area of study, in order to explore the opportunities and obstacles of the past and to speculate on those of the future. Margaret Montoya (1994: 25) explored the ways in which her Latina childhood had prepared her for a law career, in which she would need to remind herself that '[m]y truths require that I say unconventional things in unconventional ways'. Perhaps it is the risks incurred that renders personal narrative so powerful – choosing to make one's self vulnerable to intimate public scrutiny and to contest so openly the boundaries imposed by one's profession.

Personal narrative is arguably one of the essential elements of achieving the kinds of changes we have advocated in this text. Narrative helps those of us seeking alternative structures and models to realise that epistemological shifts are as much a process of personal transformation as they are disciplinary and inter-disciplinary change. 'Unless individuals are aware of the ideological deception of which they are victims, they are unlikely to engage in change-promoting activities' (Prilleltensky, 1989: 799). The process of coming to terms with the social embeddedness of science and law is a lengthy, laborious one. Sharing the accounts of our individual intellectual travels is imperative, for it helps all of us to understand it as a *process*, rather than as some instantaneous moment or enduring perspective.

It seems therefore appropriate to conclude by reflecting on the route that we have, as authors, followed in the course of writing this book. Our suspicions concerning an implicit relation between law and psychology were not fully formed when we began this project; rather, we wished to see whether additional evidence would support or defuse our initial impressions. Our discovery process has been an uncomfortable one, leaving us with a sense of betrayal that the fields of psychology and law should so willingly pervert the experiences of women and so disregard their own responsibilities. Yet engaging in that discomfort has also given us a sharper sense of our own power and the contribution that individual voices can make to these fields. To fail to speak one's personal truth, whatever it may in that moment be, is to fail to meet the responsibility we each bear as a member of an academic discipline and of humanity. We hope that in speaking our truth, others will be empowered to speak their own, regardless of whether or not their view accords with the conclusions we have drawn here. Truths are more valuable when they are self-reflective and accountable than when they are merely ratified.

Notes

Preface

1 *Pythagoras' Trousers: God, Physics, and the Gender Wars* (1997), London: Fourth Estate, p. xiii.
2 For readers unfamiliar with the structure of legal systems, it may be helpful to note that the common law approach contrasts with the inquisitorial approach favoured by the Continental systems. European countries such as France, Germany, the Netherlands, Italy, Spain, and others with a civil law tradition accord the judge a much more pro-active role in the investigation and conduct of a case. Derived from the Roman legal system, the civil law approach uses a formalised code enacted by government as the principal source of law; case law functions only as a secondary source of guidance. Both common law and civil law systems allow psychological evidence into the courtroom, although the mechanisms for admitting it differ in important respects.

1 Introduction

1 *The Good Terrorist* (1986), London: Grafton Books, p. 8.

2 The explicit relation

1 *The Charlotte Perkins Gilman Reader* (1981), London: The Women's Press, p. xiv. (Quotation cited by Ann Lane in the introduction to the edition.)
2 In view of the intentional congruence between the two manuals, no significant distinction needs to be made between them for the purposes of the present project. Because the DSM is the source predominantly cited within clinical practice and psychological textbooks, we will draw from it when quotations or other specific forms of reference are required.
3 The first information with which a reader is greeted in Comer's (1998) text on abnormal psychology is the complete set of DSM-IV diagnostic categories. This is provided on the inside front and back covers of the book. While this placement may have been carried out for purposes of saving space, it serves also to communicate very powerfully that the DSM classification system is of relevance and importance to psychologists.
4 It is interesting to note that Muensterberg was a student of Wilhelm Wundt, whose founding of an experimental laboratory is celebrated in psychology's history. This association helps to explain why Muensterberg should have felt so strongly about psychological methods so early in the field's development.
5 The characterisation of *two* primary principles (i.e. reliability and helpfulness) is our own. There are other configurations available, as Raitt (1998) discusses.
6 The term 'reliability' tends be used slightly differently by psychologists and lawyers.

For lawyers, 'reliability' is virtually synonymous with 'validity', while for psychologists the two terms refer to very different, if related, concepts (see Anastasi, 1988, for discussion). In the eyes of psychologists, reliability refers to *consistency*; does a test administered at Time A produce the same outcome when administered at Time B? Validity concerns the *accuracy* of the test; what does it actually measure and how well does it do that? Reliability is the initial concern, for if a test is not reliable and consistent, it is not useful. As Marlowe (1995: 218) says, 'Validity is ultimately circumscribed by reliability'. However, reliability cannot ensure validity; it is possible for a test to produce very consistent results without actually measuring what it purports to measure. For example, it has been argued that traditional IQ tests are not a valid measurement of intelligence; rather they measure aspects of formal education (see Eysenck, 1998, for discussion). The distinction between the concepts of 'reliability' and 'validity' is important to psychologists, but it tends to become blurred when psychology is applied in other domains such as law.

7 Loftus and Monahan also provide an interesting 'idealized' metaphor to describe law: 'Law is an adversary process. The truth is believed to emerge from a brawl in which each participant pulls no punches and gives no quarter. The judge is the referee who watches for rabbit punches and keeps things above the belt. The jury does the scoring. The best man or woman – *the one with the most truth* – wins, it is hoped' (Loftus and Monahan, 1980: 281, emphasis added).

3 The implicit relation

1 *The Descent of Woman* (1972) New York: Stein and Day, p. 159.

2 Given that Wundt and James are usually identified as the forefathers of experimental psychology, it can be confusing to see them linked to an anti-positivistic position. However, both of these theorists argued strongly that the development of empirical *and* hermeneutic methods would be required to address the wide range of questions that the emerging field of psychology sought to investigate (Polkinghorne, 1983). That their support for a dual approach has been largely eliminated from psychology's 'official' history demonstrates the inherently political nature of knowledge-making.

3 The phrase 'intellectual autocracy' was first applied to Morgan's views by Robbie Cooper in 1999, in coursework for Zeedyk's course entitled 'Developmental Theories and Epistemology'. We thank him for allowing us to use it here.

4 Mark Bennett (1999: 11) illustrates developmental psychology's resistance to postmodern critiques by quoting the recent response of a 'senior and well-known developmentalist' to a query about their worth: 'Postmodernists? Pah! Someone tell them about the object concept.'

5 Research on the decision-making processes of juries is conducted almost exclusively in the US, as in the UK the provisions of the Contempt of Court Act 1981 prevent investigation and publication regarding the reasoning and deliberation processes of juries.

6 Technically, this design does not follow strict experimental design requirements, as men and women were not randomly assigned to the two gender conditions. However, it is a design that is used extensively in research, and thus captures the reasoning that psychologists use in practice, even if they are not 'supposed to' in theory.

4 Battered Woman's Syndrome

1 *The Handmaid's Tale* (1986), London: Virago Press, p. 144.

2 That is, the law considers 'insanity' to be a legal matter, not simply a medical or clinical one. A diagnosis of psychopathy will not necessarily be accepted as tantamount to the legal concept of partial insanity (e.g. Gordon, 1978: 396–397).

3 Ibn-Tamas' fears about her husband's continuing power over her are, arguably, very reasonable, given that that power would have resumed once his wounds had healed.

4 For a recent illustration of this see *Hobson* [1998] 1 Cr App Rep 31.

5 Rape Trauma Syndrome

1 *Beloved* (1988) London: Pan Books Ltd, p. 190.

2 In this chapter we focus exclusively on the rape of a woman by a man. We acknowledge that men, too, are raped, but as with all the syndromes in this book, we concentrate on women because they are the gender predominantly subjected to this crime. American Medical Association estimates indicate that 95% of sexual assaults are perpetrated against females (2000, http://www.ama-assn.org). For analysis and discussion of how men are affected by rape, including suffering from Rape Trauma Syndrome, see the work of Rumney and Morgan-Taylor (1994, 1996, 1997a, b, c).

3 Throughout this chapter the terms 'victim' and 'complainant' are used to signify the woman/child who is raped. There are other terms that could also be used, such as 'survivor' or 'complainer' (a Scottish term referring to a victim of a crime), but we have chosen to adopt the terminology deployed in most of the literature.

4 It is interesting to note that, on the day following this judgement, female members of the Italian Parliament all wore jeans, as a form of protest against the ruling. When Italian women joined them in this action, it came to be known in the press as the 'Jeans Revolt'.

5 For readers unfamiliar with legal process, it may be useful to clarify that the decision to prosecute a person accused of rape (or any other criminal action) is taken by the State, in the public interest. It is not taken by the victim of the crime, although s/he is likely to testify as a witness.

6 The welcome success of this appeal illustrates the benefits of RTS testimony for individual women, as, without it, Ms Ejon's application for asylum would have failed. However, the wider issue remains: why should women's reluctance to disclose rape and sexual abuse be taken as evidence that their stories are inconsistent, embellished, or simply untrue? Why must a woman be formally characterised as mentally ill before her account will be believed? It is society's pervasive doubt in regard to women's abuse that generates this reaction. A more just strategy, on the part of law and politicians, would be to focus on dismantling this disbelief.

7 A summary and analysis of the US cases concerning admissibility of RTS evidence has been prepared by Dobbin and Gatowski (1997): *The Admissibility of Rape Trauma Syndrome: Summary of US State Caselaw*, unpublished, on file with the authors.

8 Note that Morgan was not accused of the rape of his wife. He could not be, for at the time of the case there was no prohibition on rape within marriage. Morgan was, however, convicted of aiding and abetting the rape.

9 Mark Pendergrast (1998), who has played a leading role in the debate about False Memory Syndrome (see Chapter 7), is among those who disagree with the abolition of the warning. He notes that '[u]ntil recently, judges were supposed to caution juries that such allegations were easy to make and difficult to defend, but this duty was abolished . . . [in] 1994, on the grounds that the warning was degrading to sex abuse victims. Such a ruling assumes guilt and should be reversed' (Pendergrast, 1998: 627). Abolition of the warning does not, of course, assume anything about the man's guilt; rather, abolition of the warning simply ceases the sanctioned practice of creating (false) doubts about women's tendency to tell the truth.

10 The outcome of this case was that the psychologist, who had been instructed by the defence, examined the victim prior to the trial and concluded, unexpectedly (from the point of view of the defence) that the victim *was* suffering from a severe case of PTSD. The defence decided, therefore, not to present the evidence. At a pre-trial appeal, the Supreme Court of New Mexico ruled that the prosecution could make use of the evidence. Although this is in some ways a positive outcome it does not alter the fact that the *victim* of a crime was forced to undergo an involuntary psychological examination.

6 Premenstrual Syndrome

1 'Xingu' (1911), reprinted in *Roman Fever* (1983), London: Virago Press, p. 37.

2 One of these groups was, in fact, the American Psychological Association. One might then ask why PMS should be included in this text. That is because, as we discuss in Chapter 2, once a diagnosis has entered the DSM, it goes on to influence psychologists' thinking, practice, and research, regardless of initial objections to it. The majority of criticism of the diagnosis within psychology has come from feminist psychologists (e.g. Choi and Salmon, 1995; Ussher, 1991; Walker, 1997), who occupy a marginal place within the discipline.

3 We thank Pamela Ferguson for making this observation.

4 In June 1997, women wishing to become professional boxers were denied a licence by the British Board of Boxing Control, on the 'medical' grounds that 'unfortunately many women suffer from PMT when they are more prone to accidents, they are more emotional and more labile (unstable), which makes them more prone to injury' (*The Scotsman*, 13 February 1998). This ruling was forcibly overturned by an industrial tribunal in August 1998, and the first-ever professional female boxing match took place in Britain in November 1998 (*The Scotsman*, 26 November 1998).

   Liza Picard (1998: 291) recounts having heard an Anglican cleric arguing against ordination of women because 'it would be self-evidently impossible . . . for a menstru- ating woman to administer communion', apparently based on a version of the old myth that maintains menstruating women turn wine sour and meat rancid.

   Valerie Hey (1985: 66) quotes the comments of Dr Rowland Berry, a therapist at a young offender's institution for women, which appeared in *The Guardian* (14 March 1983). When asked whether he thought that the all-male hierarchy might be detri- mental to the women's sense of self esteem, he replied, 'Good God, you couldn't have all women! The place would be rife with pre-menstrual tension and no sanity anywhere!'

5 In a Channel 4 television documentary entitled *Women's Bits*, aired in the UK in November 1999, Dr Dalton stated that she had testified in more than a dozen murder cases.

6 Laws (1990) conducts a more extended investigation of gynaecological texts.

7 In his medical text, published originally in 1957 and revised/reprinted nine times since then because of its status as a classic source, Jeffcoate offers opinions on a variety of gynaecological issues. Although not relevant to PMS *per se*, we cannot resist noting his comments on vaginal discharge and on the causes of frigidity, for they are among his most charming.

> On vaginal discharge: 'A woman sometimes complains of discharge when she really means *vulval odour*. . . . Providing a reasonable standard of cleanliness is maintained, vulval odour is never apparent to bystanders, and those women who complain of it have a disorder of the mind rather than the body. The idea usually arises from a misinterpretation of some innocent remark of an acquaintance, and thereafter becomes an obsession difficult to eradicate. The complainants adopt all possible means to ensure cleanliness yet still interpret every look or movement on the part of their fellow workers or social contacts as evidence that "they smell". Those women who have cause to complain of odour do not do so because they are as insensitive as they are dirty.' (Jeffcoate, 1987: 550, emphasis in original)

> On frigidity: 'Some women who are physically attractive, smartly dressed and spoiled by attention have too much love of self. The beautiful coquettish woman can make a singularly disappointing lover. There may be more obvious reasons for the loss of the sex urge – love for another man, disquiet over the husband's unfaith- fulness or other misdemeanours, and sexual perversion including homosexuality.' (Jeffcoate, 1987: 569)

8 There are a range of disposals available to UK judges, including requiring defendants to undergo out-patient treatment, which was a key condition of Sandie Smith's probation in both her 1981 and 1982 cases. Although the development of a similar mechanism in US jurisdictions might address Carney and Williams' concerns, it would not solve the problem of which treatments should be recommended for use with PMS sufferers, given that there is no agreement within the medical community about the effectiveness of particular treatments. Laws pointed out that this meant that 'British courts are *requiring* women to accept progesterone therapy' despite the fact that strong evidence supporting its effectiveness was 'in fact lacking' (Laws, 1983: 29, emphasis in original).

9 Indeed, Dalton's work has been one of the driving forces behind establishing a link between crime and PMS. Her findings are cited extensively as evidence of such a 'worrying' association. D'Emilio (1985), Reid and Yen (1981), and Wallach and Rubin (1971) are among those who draw heavily on her work in laying a foundation for their arguments. It is interesting to note that Reid and Yen (1981: 85) remark that they do consider it 'noteworthy' that women's crime rates are 'still lower than those seen in the noncycling male subject', but apparently do not think it noteworthy *enough* to allow it to influence their theoretical analysis.

10 D'Emilio (1985: 586–587) does propose ways in which the 'possible deleterious effects' of a PMS defence could be 'dispelled' and societal impacts minimised. For example, she suggests this could occur through limiting the availability of the defence to 'only those women most severely affected by the disorder' or by 'requiring a thorough and accurate diagnosis of the defendant as a chronic sufferer'. She specifically cites Dalton's method of charting cyclical symptoms and behaviours as an acceptable 'certification process'. However, these solutions are superficial, for all of the reasons we have been discussing in this chapter. On what basis are those women 'most severely affected' to be differentiated from others? Who is to have the power to decide? How is the law to deal with the fact that neither methods of diagnosis nor of treatment, including Dalton's, have reached any reasonable degree of general acceptance? D'Emilio's attempt to reconcile the individual/group conflict is inadequate, for it has not seriously engaged with any of the attendant issues.

7 False Memory Syndrome

1 *Tea and Leg-irons: New Feminist Readings from Scotland* (1992), London: Open Letters, p. 65.

2 The appeal was partially successful, in that one of the men had his conviction quashed, due to lack of evidence. The appeal was rejected for the other defendant.

3 While boys are victims of child sexual abuse, the majority of victims are female (Finkelhor, 1986), and the legal cases of alleged FMS have tended to involve female victims. Hence we concentrate on the position of women in this chapter.

4 Pamela Freyd is the mother of Jennifer Freyd, an academic psychologist who has made allegations of sexual abuse against her father. Pamela Freyd helped to set up the False Memory Syndrome Foundation in conjunction with her husband after asserting that her daughter's accusations were false. Jennifer Freyd steadfastly maintains her claims (Freyd, 1996: 197–199).

5 The 2000 update of the website omits some of the 1999 material quoted here. The 2000 references to the DSM are more muted, with the emphasis on the deficiencies of the DSM. These include decision-taking based on consensus rather than scientific evidence, and the inclusion of some diagnoses based more on current social interests rather than on scientifically derived principles. It may be that the obstacles facing the FMSF in gaining unequivocal validation of their position has led them to re-evaluate the benefits to their aims of DSM inclusion.

6 Just as there is a gendered aspect in regard to the victims of sexual abuse, so is there

one in regard to the perpetrators, most of whom are men – thus our use of this explicitly gendered term.

7 Depending on the facts and circumstances, the type of claim pursued might be for defamation or for negligence. There are, of course, sound financial reasons for targeting therapists, in that malpractice suits can be lucrative for a successful plaintiff. Affording abusers a right of redress against therapists not only represents a major doctrinal shift in tort liability law, it is also harmful to women. They are silenced as the focus of the dispute moves from their experience of abuse to the grievances of the alleged abuser. Women may also be denied the full benefits of therapy, as mental health professionals begin to practise defensive therapy and the cost of counselling rises as a result of increased costs for malpractice insurance.

8 Despite Meadowcroft's construction, FMS does not constitute a 'defence' as such but would be used as an 'explanation' of the allegations to undermine the credibility and reliability of the woman's testimony.

9 Mark Pendergrast is among those who decries this shift. 'Laws that extend the statute of limitations for "decades-delayed discovery" of sexual abuse should be repealed. (If the abuse was always remembered, but not reported because of fear, coercion, or other factors, the perpetrator should not be protected by the statute of limitations, as long as the abuse can be corroborated by external evidence. But that's different from bringing charges against an elderly parent based on dreams or hypnosis.)' (Pendergrast, 1998: 626). His proposed distinction between the two 'types' of situations is too simplistic, given the lack of corroborative external evidence that exists in almost all sexual abuse cases, especially those where the abuse occurred years ago. Pendergrast displays a suspicion toward women's and children's claims of which Wigmore (1940) and Williams (1978) would have been proud. He firmly places himself within their sceptical ranks when he later calls for a reinstitution of the mandatory corroboration warning in cases of sexual crimes, where judges were required to warn juries that 'such allegations are easy to make and difficult to defend' (p. 627). Pendergrast's use of Wigmore's own words, discussed in detail in Chapter 5, leaves little doubt about the angle from which he is approaching the issue of FMS.

10 On appeal, in 1999, the Supreme Court of Canada reversed the decision of the trial judge and held that the complainant's right to privacy for her medical records should not in this case give way to the accused's right to be able to make 'full answer and defence'. However, in a strong dissenting judgement, Justice Lamer argued that the rights of the accused were infringed by a failure to gain access to the complainant's records. His comments suggest that this issue is not comfortably settled.

11 It should be noted that not all clinicians would concede that the activities of the interview room were subjective and incapable of objective measurement.

12 The finding that most memories are recovered independently of therapy was an uncomfortable one for the British False Memory Society, whose Advisory Committee, in a letter to the editor of *The Psychologist*, criticised the questionnaire as unrepresentative and misleading (BFMS Advisory Committee, 1995: 507).

13 Pendergrast (1998) points out that Holmes does not state categorically that repressed memories cannot exist, for one cannot prove a negative (the classic null hypothesis).

14 The age at which a child/young woman was deemed capable of consent varied from state to state but was generally fixed by the state's Penal Code somewhere between the ages of 12 and 18 years.

15 For discussion of the alternative view that Multiple Personality Disorder has no genuine psychiatric foundation, see Brandon *et al.* (1998), Hacking (1995), Pendergrast (1998), and Webster (1996).

8 Moving beyond the implicit relation

1 *The Left Hand of Darkness* (1997), London: Orbit, p. 9. Originally published 1969 by Macdonald & Co.

2 There are a variety of other diagnoses that we have not discussed in this text, which advocates would like to see admitted into the DSM. Scientific methods and terminology are regularly invoked to support the arguments of the authors. Examples of such 'diagnoses' include Post-Abortion Syndrome (Lee, forthcoming; Lee and Gilchrist, 1997; Speckard and Rue, 1992), Divorce-Related Malicious Mother Syndrome (Turkat, 1999), and Munchausen's Syndrome by Proxy (Adshead and Brooke, 1999). We have little doubt that examination of these syndromes would provide further support for our arguments concerning the implicit relation.

3 Indeed, the term 'transformation' has come to be so associated with critical and postmodernist visions that Alan Sokal and Jean Bricmont (1996) used it in the title of their spoof article, 'Transgressing the Boundaries: Toward a Transformative Hermeneutics of Quantum Gravity', which was written to support and illustrate their position that postmodernist work in the sciences is vacuous and misleading. They discuss the reasons they undertook such a deceptive project in their 1998 book.

4 Hilary Rose (1994) has written explicitly on the links between science fiction, science, and feminism, examining the ways in which science fiction allows 'dreams of the future' (p. 209) and stressing that 'our imaginations are in charge of our futures' (p. 213).

5 This paper was originally published under the name Donald McCloskey, but since then the author has changed her name to Deirdre.

References

Adler, Zsusanna (1987) *Rape on Trial*, London: Routledge.

Adshead, Gwen and Brooke, Deborah (eds) (1999) *Munchausen's Syndrome by Proxy: Current Issues in Assessment, Treatment and Research*, World Scientific Publishing Company Inc.

Alcoff, Linda and Potter, Elizabeth (1993) (eds) *Feminist Epistemologies*, New York: Routledge.

Alexander, Lawrence A., Coleman, Jules L. and Schauer, Frederick (1995) 'Editorial', *Legal Theory* 1: 1–3.

Allen, Hilary (1987) *Justice Unbalanced: Gender, Psychiatry and Judicial Decisions*, Buckingham: Open University Press.

Allen, Hilary (1990) 'At the mercy of her hormones: premenstrual tension and the law', in P. Adams and E. Cowie (eds) *The Woman in Question*, London: Verso.

Allison, Julie A. and Wrightsman, Lawrence S. (1993) *Rape: The Misunderstood Crime*, Newbury Park, CA: Sage.

Allridge, Peter (1994) 'Forensic science and expert evidence', *Journal of Law and Society* 21: 136–150.

American Psychiatric Association (1980) *Diagnostic and Statistical Manual of Mental Disorders*, Third Edition [DSM-III], Washington, DC: American Psychiatric Association.

American Psychiatric Association (1987) *Diagnostic and Statistical Manual of Mental Disorders*, Third Edition Revised [DSM-III-R], Washington, DC: American Psychiatric Association.

American Psychiatric Association (1994) *Diagnostic and Statistical Manual of Mental Disorders*, Fourth Edition [DSM-IV], Washington, DC: American Psychiatric Association.

American Psychological Association (1994) *Working Group on the Investigation of Memories of Childhood Abuse: Interim Report*, Washington, DC: American Psychological Association.

Anastasi, Anne (1988) *Psychological Testing*, Sixth Edition, New York: Macmillan.

Andrews, Bernice, Morton, John, Bakerian, Debra A., Brewin, Chris R., Davies, Graham M. and Mollon, Phil (1995) 'The recovery of memories in clinical practice: experiences and beliefs of British Psychological Society practitioners', *The Psychologist* May: 209–214.

Armstrong, Louise (1978) *Kiss Daddy Goodnight: A Speak-Out on Incest*, New York: Hawthorn Books.

Armstrong, Louise (1996) *Rocking the Cradle of Sexual Politics: What Happened When Women Said Incest*, London: The Women's Press.

Aronowitz, Stanley (1988) *Science as Power: Discourse and Ideology in Modern Society*, Minneapolis: University of Minnesota Press.

Baars, Bernard J. (1984) 'View from a road not taken', *Contemporary Psychology* 29: 804–805.

Babbitt, Susan E. (1993) 'Feminism and objective interests: the role of transformation experiences in rational deliberation', in L. Alcoff and E. Potter (eds) *Feminist Epistemologies*, New York: Routledge.

Bachman, Ronet and Saltzman, Linda (1995) *Violence against Women: Estimates from the Redesigned Survey*, Washington, DC: Bureau of Justice Statistics.

Baddeley, Alan (1998) 'So where should we publish?', *The Psychologist* 11 (June): 312.

Baker-Ward, Lynne, Ornstein, Peter A., Gordon, Betty N., Follmer, Andrea and Clubb, Patricia A. (1995) 'How shall a thing be coded? Implications of the use of alternative procedures for scoring children's verbal reports', in M. Zaragoza *et al.* (eds) *Memory and Testimony in the Child Witness*, Thousand Oaks: Sage.

Bandalli, Sue (1995) 'Provocation: a cautionary note', *Journal of Law and Society* 22: 398–409.

Barnes, Barry (1977) *Interests and the Growth of Knowledge*, London: Routledge & Kegan Paul.

Bass, Ellen and Davis, Laura (1994) *The Courage to Heal: A Guide for Women Survivors of Child Sexual Abuse*, Third Edition, New York: Harper & Row.

Bayer, Ronald (1987) *Homosexuality and American Psychiatry: The Politics of Diagnosis*, Princeton, NJ: Princeton University Press.

Beasley, Chris (1999) *What Is Feminism? An Introduction to Feminist Theory*, London: Sage.

Behavioral Sciences and the Law (1995) Special Issue: 'Behavioral Science Evidence in the Wake of Daubert', 13(2).

Bell, Vikki (1993) *Interrogating Incest: Feminism, Foucault and the Law*, London: Routledge.

Benatar, May (1995) 'Running away from sexual abuse: denial revisited', *Families in Society* 76: 315–320.

Benedek, Elissa P. (1988) 'Premenstrual syndrome: a view from the bench', *Journal of Clinical Psychology* 49: 498–502.

Bennett, Mark (1999) 'Introduction', in M. Bennett (ed.) *Developmental Psychology: Achievements and Prospects*, London: Psychology Press.

Berkeley, Ellen P. and McQuaid, Matilda (eds) (1989) *Architecture: A Place for Women*, Washington, DC: Smithsonian Institution Press.

Berlin, Jesse A., Begg, Colin B. and Louis, Thomas A. (1989) 'An assessment of publication bias using a sample of published clinical trials', *Journal of the American Statistical Association* 84: 381–392.

Bernstein, David E. (1996) 'Junk science in the United States and the Commonwealth', *Yale Journal of International Law* 21: 123–182.

Bernstein, Richard J. (1983) *Beyond Objectivism and Relativism: Science, Hermeneutics and Praxis*, Philadelphia, PA: University of Pennsylvania Press.

Bienen, Leigh B. (1983a) 'A question of credibility: John Henry Wigmore's use of scientific authority in section 924a of the *Treatise on Evidence*', *California Western Law Review* 19: 235–268.

Bienen, Leigh B. (1983b) 'Rape reform legislation in the United States: a look at some practical effects', *Women's Rights Law Reporter* 6: 184–189.

Billig, Mick (1987) *Arguing and Thinking: A Rhetorical Approach to Social Psychology*, Cambridge: Cambridge University Press.

Birch, Diane J. (1998) 'Case and Comment: Commentary to R v B', *Criminal Law Review*, 406–408.

Blau, Theodore (1984) *The Psychologist as Expert Witness*, New York: Wiley.

Blackman, Derek E., Muller, Dave J. and Chapman, Antony J. (1984) 'Perspectives in psychology and law', in D.J. Muller, D.E. Blackman and A.J. Chapman (eds) *Psychology and Law*, Chichester: Wiley.

Bleier, Ruth (1984) *Science and Gender: A Critique of Biology and Its Theories on Women*, Oxford: Pergamon Press.

Bleier, Ruth (1988) 'A decade of feminist critiques in the natural sciences', *Signs* 14: 186–195.

Bloor, David (1977) *Knowledge and Social Imagery*, London: Routledge & Kegan Paul.

Bohan, Janis S. (1992) 'Reviewing psychology, re-placing women: an end searching for a means', in J. S. Bohan (ed.) *Seldom Seen, Rarely Heard: Women's Place in Psychology*, Boulder, CO: Westview Press.

Bordo, Susan (1990a) 'Feminism, postmodernism and gender-sceptism', in L. Nicholson (ed.) *Feminism/Postmodernism*, London: Routledge.

Bordo, Susan (1990b) 'Reading the body slender', in M. Jacobus, E. F. Keller and S. Shuttleworth (eds) *Body/Politics: Women and the Discourse of Science*, London: Routledge.

Borgida, Eugene and Brekke, Nancy (1985) 'Psycholegal research on rape trials', in A. W. Burgess (ed.) *Research Handbook on Rape and Sexual Assault*, New York: Garland.

Bowlby, John (1969) *Attachment and Loss*, New York: Basic Books.

Bowlby, John (1988) *A Secure Base: Parent–Child Attachment and Healthy Human Development*, New York: Basic Books.

Boyle, James (1991) 'Is subjectivity possible? The post-modern subject in legal theory', *University of Colorado Law Review* 62: 489.

Boyle, James (ed.) (1992) *Critical Legal Studies: Selected Readings*, New York: New York University Press.

Boyle, Mary (1997) *Re-thinking Abortion: Psychology, Gender, Power and the Law*, London: Routledge.

Bradley, Ben S. (1989) *Visions of Infancy: A Critical Introduction to Child Psychology*, Cambridge: Polity Press.

Brandon, Sidney, Boakes, Janet, Glaser, Danya and Green, Richard (1998) 'Recovered memories of childhood sexual abuse: implications for clinical practice', *British Journal of Psychiatry* 172: 296–307.

Bristow, Ann R. (1984) 'State v Marks: an analysis of expert testimony on rape trauma syndrome', *Victimology* 9: 273–281.

British False Memory Society Advisory Committee (1995) 'Further comment on recovered memories', *The Psychologist* November: 507–508.

British Psychological Society (1994) *Expert Testimony: Developing Witness Skills*, Video Training Package, Leicester.

British Psychological Society (1995) *The Report of the Working Party of the British Psychological Society on Recovered Memories*, London: British Psychological Society.

British Psychological Society (1998) *Psychologists as Expert Witnesses in Scotland*, Leicester: British Psychological Society.

Brown, Beverley (1990) 'Reassessing the critique of biologism', in L. Gelsthorpe and A. Morris (eds) *Feminist Perspectives in Criminology*, Milton Keynes: Open University Press.

Brown, Beverley, Burman, Michelle and Jamieson, Lynne (1993) *Sex Crimes on Trial*, Edinburgh: Edinburgh University Press.

Brown, Laura S. and Burman, Erica (1997) (eds) 'Feminist responses to the "false memory" debate', *Feminism and Psychology* 7: 7–16.

Brownmiller, Susan (1991) *Against Our Will: Men, Women and Rape*, London: Penguin. Originally published 1975.

Bruck, Maggie and Ceci, Stephen J. (1995) *Jeopardy in the Courtroom: A Scientific Analysis of Children's Testimony*, Washington DC: American Psychological Association

Budieri, D., Li Wan Po, A. and Dornan, J. (1994) 'Clinical trials of premenstrual syndrome: entry criteria and scales for measuring treatment outcomes', *British Journal of Obstetrics and Gynaecology* 101: 689–695.

Burgess, Ann W. and Holmstrom, Lynda L. (1974) 'Rape trauma syndrome', *American Journal of Psychiatry* 131: 981–999.

Burgess, Ann W. and Holmstrom, Lynda L. (1985) 'Rape trauma syndrome and post-traumatic stress response', in A. W. Burgess (ed.) *Research Handbook on Rape and Sexual Assault*, New York: Garland.

Burman, Erica (1994) *Deconstructing Developmental Psychology*, London: Routledge.

Burman, Michelle and Lloyd, Siobhan (1993) *Specialist Police Units for the Investigation of Violent Crime against Women and Children in Scotland*, Edinburgh: HMSO.

Busby, Karen (1997) 'Discriminatory use of personal records in sexual violence cases', *Canadian Journal of Women and the Law* 9: 148–177.

Busfield, Joan (1996) *Men, Women, and Madness: Understanding Gender and Mental Disorder*, London: Macmillan.

Byrd, Kevin R. (1994) 'The narrative reconstructions of incest survivors', *American Psychologist* 49: 439–440.

Cain, Patricia A. (1989) 'Feminist jurisprudence: grounding the theories', *Women's Law Journal*, 191–214.

Caplan, Paula (1995) *They Say You're Crazy: How the World's Most Powerful Psychiatrists Decide Who's Normal*, Reading, MA: Addison-Wesley.

Caringella-MacDonald, Susan M. (1988) 'Parallels and pitfalls: the aftermath of legal reform for sexual assault, marital rape, and domestic violence victims', *Journal of Interpersonal Violence* 3: 174–189.

Caringella-MacDonald, Susan M. (1991) 'An assessment of rape reform; victim and case treatment under Michigan's model', *International Review of Victimology* 1: 347–361.

Carney, Robert M. and Williams, Brian D. (1983) 'Premenstrual syndrome: a criminal defence', *Notre Dame Law Review* 59: 253–269.

Carson, David and Bull, Ray (1995) *The Handbook of Psychology in Legal Contexts*, Chichester: Wiley.

Casey, Juliette M. (1999) *Legal Defences for Battered Women Who Kill: Battered Woman Syndrome, Expert Testimony and Law Reform*, Unpublished doctoral dissertation, Edinburgh University.

Cattell, Raymond B. and Kline, P. (1977) *The Scientific Analysis of Personality*, London: Penguin.

Ceci, Stephen J. and Bruck, Maggie (1993) 'Suggestibility of the child witness: a historical review and analysis', *Psychological Bulletin* 113: 403–439.

Ceci, Stephen J. and Bruck, Maggie (1995) *Jeopardy in the Courtroom: A Scientific Analysis of Children's Testimony*, Washington, DC: American Psychological Association.

Ceci, Stephen J. and Loftus, Elizabeth (1994) '"Memory work": a royal road to false memories?', *Applied Cognitive Psychology* 8: 351–364.

Chait, Linda R. (1986) 'Premenstrual syndrome and our sisters in crime: a feminist dilemma', *Women's Rights Law Reporter* 9: 267–293.

Chalmers, Iain (1993) 'The Cochrane collection: preparing, maintaining, and disseminating systematic reviews of the effects of health care', *Annals of the New York Academy of Science* 703: 156–165.

Chambers, Gerry A. and Millar, Ann R. (1983) *Investigating Sexual Assault*, HMSO: Edinburgh.

Cheit, Ross (1994) Paper presented at the Mississippi Statewide Conference on Child Abuse and Neglect, Jackson, 29 April.

Chesler, Phyllis (1972) *Women and Madness*, New York: Doubleday.

Childs, Mary and Ellison, Louise (eds) (forthcoming) *Feminist Perspectives on Evidence*, London: Cavendish.

Choi, Precilla Y. L. and Salmon, Peter (1995) 'How do women cope with menstrual cycle changes?', *British Journal of Clinical Psychology* 34: 139–151.

Cohen, Lawrence H. (1979) 'Clinical psychologists' judgments of the scientific merit and clinical relevance of psychotherapy outcome research', *Journal of Consulting and Clinical Psychology* 47: 421–423.

Collier, Richard (1995) *Masculinity, Law and the Family*, London: Routledge.

Collins, Patricia Hill (1990) *Black Feminist Thought*, Boston, MA: Unwin Hyman.

Colman, Andrew M. (1991) 'Crowd psychology in South African murder trials', *American Psychologist* 46: 1071–1079.

Colman, Andrew M. and Mackay, R. D. (1993) 'Legal issues surrounding the admissibility of expert psychological and psychiatric testimony', *Issues in Criminological and Legal Psychology* 20: 46–50.

Comer, Ronald J. (1998) *Abnormal Psychology*, Third Edition, New York: W. H. Freeman.

Comment (1950) 'Psychiatric Evaluation of the Mentally Abnormal Witness', *Yale Law Journal* 59: 1324–1341.

Concise Oxford Dictionary of Current English (1995) H. W. Fowler and F. G. Fowler (original eds) Ninth Edition, D. Thompson (ed.) Oxford: Clarendon Press.

Conley, John M., O'Barr, William M. and Lind, E. Allan (1978) 'The power of language: presentational style in the courtroom', *Duke Law Journal*, 1375–1399.

Connelly, Clare (1996) 'Women who kill violent men', *Juridical Review*, 215–217.

Conway, Martin, A. (1990) 'Autobiographical memory and conceptual representation', *Journal of Experimental Psychology: Learning, Memory, and Cognition* 16: 799–812.

Conway, Martin, A. (1997) *Recovered Memories and False Memories*, Oxford: Oxford University Press.

Cornell, Drucilla (1991) *Beyond Accommodation*, New York: Routledge.

Cornell, Drucilla (1993) *Transformations*, New York: Routledge.

Cornell, Drucilla (1995) *The Imaginary Domain: Abortion, Pornography, and Sexual Harassment*, London: Routledge.

Cosmides, Leda (1989) 'The logic of social exchange: has natural selection shaped how humans reason? Studies with the Wason Selection Task', *Cognition* 31: 187–276.

Cosmides, Leda and Tooby, John (1992) 'Cognitive adaptations for social exchange', in J. K. Barkow, L. Cosmides and J. Tooby (eds) *The Adapted Mind: Evolutionary Psychology and the Generation of Culture*, New York: Oxford University Press.

Coursol, Allan and Wagner, Edwin E. (1986) 'Effect of positive findings on submission and acceptance rates: a note on meta-analysis bias', *Professional Psychology: Research and Practice* 17: 136–137.

Courtois, Christine A. (1997) 'Delayed memories of child sexual abuse: critique of the controversy and clinical guidelines', in M. A. Conway (ed.) *Recovered Memories and False Memories*, Oxford: Oxford University Press.

Crawford, Mary and Marecek, Jeanne (1989) 'Psychology reconstructs the female, 1968–1988', *Psychology of Women Quarterly* 13: 147–165; reprinted in J. S. Bohan (ed.) (1992) *Seldom Seen, Rarely Heard: Women's Place in Psychology*, Boulder, CO: Westview Press.

Cross, Rupert and Tapper, Colin (1995) *Evidence*, Eighth Edition, London, Butterworth.

Dalton, Katharina (1960a) 'Menstruation and accidents', *British Medical Journal* 2: 1425–1426.

Dalton, Katharina (1960b) 'Effect of menstruation on schoolgirls' weekly work', *British Medical Journal* 1: 326–328.

Dalton, Katharina (1961) 'Menstruation and crime', *British Medical Journal* 2: 1752–1753.

Dalton, Katharina (1964) 'The influence of menstruation on health and disease', *Proceedings of the Royal Society of Medicine* 57: 18.

Dalton, Katharina (1982) 'Legal implications of PMS', *World Medicine* 17 April: 93–94.

Dalton, Katharina (1994) *PMS: The Essential Guide to Treatment Options*, San Francisco: HarperCollins.

Damrosch, David (1995) *We Scholars: Changing the Culture of the University*, Cambridge, MA: Harvard University Press.

deLacoste-Utamsing, Christine and Holloway, Ralph L. (1982) 'Sexual diamorphism in the human corpus callosum', *Science* 216: 1431–1432.

D'Emilio, Joann (1985) 'Battered women's syndrome and premenstrual syndrome: a comparison of their possible use as defences to criminal liability', *St John's Law Review* 59: 558–587.

Dewey, John (1963) *Philosophy and Civilization*, New York: Little, Brown.

di Leonardo, Micaela (ed.) (1991) *Gender at the Crossroads of Knowledge: Feminist Anthropology in the Postmodern Era*, Berkeley, CA: University of California Press.

Dobash, Rebecca E. and Dobash, Russell P. (1979) *Violence against Wives*, New York: Free Press.

Dobash, Rebecca E. and Dobash, Russell P. (1992) *Women, Violence and Social Change*, London: Routledge.

Dobash, Rebecca E. and Dobash, Russell P. (eds) (1998) *Rethinking Violence against Women*, Thousand Oaks, CA: Sage.

Dobbin, Shirley A. and Gatowski, Sophia I. (1997) 'The admissibility of rape trauma syndrome: summary of US state case law', Paper presented at Law and Science Seminar, University College London, July 1997.

Doris, John (ed.) (1991) *The Suggestibility of Children's Recollections: Implications for Eye-Witness Testimony*, Washington, DC: American Psychological Association.

Downs, Donald A. (1996) *More than Victims: Battered Women, The Syndrome Society and the Law*, Chicago: University of Chicago Press.

DSM, see American Psychiatric Association.

Dutton, Mary Ann (1993) 'Understanding women's responses to domestic violence: a redefinition of battered woman's syndrome', *Hofstra Law Review* 21: 1191–1242.

Dutton, Mary Ann (1999) 'Multidimensional assessment of woman battering', *Psychology of Women Quarterly* 23: 195–198.

Easterbrook, Philippa J., Berlin, Jesse A., Gopalan, Ramana and Matthews, David R. (1991) 'Publication bias in clinical research', *Lancet* 337: 967–972.

Ebbinghaus, Hermann (1885) *Memory*, New York: Teacher's College, Columbia University, 1913. Reprinted in 1964, New York: Dover.

Edwards, Harry T. (1992) 'The growing disjunction between legal education and the legal profession', *Michigan Law Review* 91: 34–78.

Edwards, Susan S. M. (1989) *Policing Domestic Violence*, London: Sage.

Edwards, Susan S. M. (1992) 'Battered women syndrome', *New Law Journal* 142: 1350–1351.

Edwards, Susan S. M. (1996) *Sex and Gender in the Legal Process*, London: Blackstone Press.

Edwards, Susan S. M. and Halpern, Ann (1991) 'Protection for the victim of domestic violence: time for radical revision', *Journal of Social Welfare and Family Law*, 94–109.

Ehrenreich, Barbara and English, Deirdre (1979) *For Their Own Good: 150 Years of the Experts' Advice to Women*, London: Pluto.

Estrich, Susan (1986) 'Rape', *Yale Law Journal* 95: 1087–1184.

Estrich, Susan (1987) *Real Rape*, Cambridge MA: Harvard University Press.

Ewing, Charles P. (1987) *Battered Women Who Kill: Psychological Self-Defense as Legal Justification*, Lexington, MA: D. C. Heath.

Eysenck, Hans J. and Eysenck, S. B. G. (1969) *Personality Structure and Measurement*, London: Routledge & Kegan Paul.

Eysenck, Michael (1998) *Psychology: An Integrated Approach*, Harlow: Addison Wesley Longman.

Farrington, David P. (1993) 'Unacceptable evidence', *New Law Journal* 143: 806–808.

Farrington, David P. (1997) 'Foreword', in A. Kapardis *Psychology and Law: A Critical Introduction*, Cambridge: Cambridge University Press.

Federal Rules of Evidence (1975) St Paul, MN: West. Updated 1984.

Feild, Hubert S. and Bienen, Leigh B. (1980) *Jurors and Rape*, Lexington, MA: D. C. Heath.

Feldman, Martin L. (1995) 'May I have the next dance, Mrs Frye?', *Tulane Law Review* 69: 793–807.

Ferguson, Pamela R. (1993) 'Controversial aspects of the law of rape: an Anglo-Scottish comparison', in R. Hunter (ed.) *Justice and Crime: Essays in Honour of The Right Honourable The Lord Emslie*, Edinburgh: T. & T. Clark.

Figert, Anne E. (1996) *Women and the Ownership of PMS: The Structuring of a Psychiatric Disorder*, New York: Aldine de Gruyter.

Finkelhor, David (1984) *Child Sexual Abuse: New Theory and Research*, New York: The Free Press.

Finkelhor, David (1986) *A Sourcebook on Child Sexual Abuse*, Newbury Park, CA: Sage.

Fiske, Susan T., Bersoff, Donald N., Borgida, Eugene, Deaux, Kay and Heilman, Madeline (1991) 'Social science research on trial: use of sex stereotyping research in *Price Waterhouse* v *Hopkins*', *American Psychologist* 46: 1049–1070.

Fitzpatrick, Peter (1992) *The Mythology of Modern Law*, London: Routledge.

Fivush, Robyn and Shukat, Jennifer, R. (1995) 'Content, consistency and coherence of early autobiographical recall' in M. Zaragoza *et al.* (eds) *Memory and Testimony in the Child Witness*, Thousand Oaks, CA: Sage.

Fivush, Robyn, Pipe, Margaret-Ellen, Murachver, Tamar and Reese, Elaine (1997) 'Events spoken and unspoken: implications of language and memory development for the recovered memory debate', in M. A. Conway (ed.) *Recovered Memories and False Memories*, Oxford: Oxford University Press.

Flavell, John L., Miller, Patricia H. and Miller, Scott (1993) *Cognitive Development*, Third Edition, London: Prentice-Hall International.

FMSF Website (2000) www.fmsfonline.org Contact the False Memory Syndrome Foundation at 3401 Market Street, Philadelphia, PA 19104, USA, for further information.

Follini, Beth (1995) 'FMS: fraudulent, misogynist, and sinister', *Trouble and Strife* 31: 12–14.

Foucault, Michel (1979) *Discipline and Punish*, London: Penguin. Translated by A. M. Sheridan-Smith.

Foucault, Michel (1980) *Power/Knowledge*, London: Harvester Wheatsheaf.

Fox, Marie (1995) 'Legal responses to battered women who kill', in J. Bridgeman and S. Millns (eds) *Law and Body Politics*, Aldershot: Dartmouth.

Frank, Jerome (1949) *Law and the Modern Mind*, London: Stevens.

Frank, Robert (1931) 'Hormonal causes of premenstrual tension', *Archives of Neurology and Psychiatry* 26: 1053–1057.

Frazier, Patricia and Borgida, Eugene (1985) 'Rape trauma syndrome evidence in court', *American Psychologist* 40: 984–993.

Frazier, Patricia and Borgida, Eugene (1992) 'Rape trauma syndrome: a review of case law and psychological research', *Law and Human Behavior* 16: 293–311.

Freckleton, Ian (1994) 'When plight makes right: the forensic abuse syndrome', *Criminal Law Journal* 18: 29–49.

Fredman, Sandra (1997) *Women and the Law*, Oxford: Clarendon Press.

Freyd, Jennifer (1996) *Betrayal Trauma: The Logic of Forgetting Childhood Abuse*, Cambridge, CA: Harvard University Press.

Freyd, Jennifer (1997) 'Violations of power, adaptive blindness and betrayal trauma theory', *Feminism and Psychology* 7: 22–31.

Frug, Mary Joe (1985) 'Re-reading contracts: a feminist analysis of a contracts casebook', *American Universities Law Review* 34: 1065–1140.

Frug, Mary Joe (1992) *Postmodern Legal Feminism*, New York: Routledge.

Ganaway, George K. (1992) 'Some additional questions', *Psychology and Theology* 20: 201–205.

Gardner, Richard A. (1992) *True and False Accusations of Child Sex Abuse*, Cresskill, NJ: Creative Therapeutics.

Gellatly, Angus (1997) 'Cognitive processes and theory development: a reply to Spencer and Karmiloff-Smith', *Human Development* 40: 55–58.

Gelles, Richard, J. (1997) *Intimate Violence in Families*, Third Edition, Thousand Oaks, CA: Sage.

Gelles, Richard J. and Straus, Murray (1988) *Intimate Violence: The Causes and Consequences of Abuse in the American Family*, New York: Simon & Schuster.

Gerbasi, Kathleen C., Zuckerman, Miron and Reis, Harry T. (1977) 'Justice needs a new blindfold: a review of mock jury research', *Psychological Bulletin* 84: 323–345.

Gergen, Kenneth (1985) 'The social constructionist movement in modern psychology', *American Psychologist* 40: 266–275.

Getman, Julius (1992) *In the Company of Scholars: The Struggle for the Soul of Higher Education*, Austin, TX: University of Texas Press.

Ghate, Deborah and Spencer, Liz (1995) *The Prevalence of Child Sexual Abuse in Britain: A Feasibility Study for a Large-Scale National Survey of the General Population*, London: HMSO.

Giannelli, Paul C. (1980) 'The admissibility of novel scientific evidence: *Frye* v *United States*, a half-century later', *Columbia Law Review* 80: 1197–1250.

Gillespie, Cynthia K. (1989) *Justifiable Homicide*, Columbus, OH: Ohio State University Press.

Gilligan, Carol (1993) *In a Different Voice: Psychological Theory and Women's Development*, Cambridge, MA: Harvard University Press.

Ginsburg, Gerald and Richardson, James (1998) '"Brainwashing" evidence in the light of *Daubert*', in H. Reece (ed.) *Law and Science: Current Legal Issues, Volume 1*, Oxford: Oxford University Press.

Gleitman, Henry, Fridlund, Alan J. and Reisberg, Daniel (1999) *Psychology*, Fifth Edition, New York: W. W. Norton.

Gless, Alan G. (1995) 'Some post-Daubert trial tribulations of a simple country judge: behavioral science evidence in trial courts', *Behavioral Sciences and the Law* 13: 261–291.

Gold, Steven N., Hughes, Dawn and Hohnecker, Laura (1994) 'Degrees of repression of sexual abuse memories', *American Psychologist* 49: 441–442.

Goldstein, Eleanor with Farmer, Kevin (1992) *Confabulations: Creating False Memories, Destroying Families*, Boca Raton, FL: SIRS.

Gonda, Caroline (ed.) (1992a) *Tea and Leg-Irons: New Feminist Readings from Scotland*, London: Open Letters.

Gonda, Caroline (1992b) 'Exactly them words: histories of a murderous daughter', in C. Gonda (ed.), *Tea and Leg-Irons: New Feminist Readings from Scotland*, London: Open Letters.

Goodman-Delahunty, Jane and Foote, William E. (1995) 'Compensation for pain, suffering, and other psychological injuries: the impact of *Daubert* on employment discrimination claims', *Behavioral Sciences and the Law* 13: 183–206.

Gordon, Gerald H. (1978) *The Criminal Law of Scotland*, Second Edition, Edinburgh: W. Green.

Gordon, Gerald H. (1991) *Commentary to Thomas v Lowe*, SCCR 943.

Gotell, Lise (forthcoming) 'Colonization through disclosure: confidential records, sexual assault complainants and Canadian law', *Social and Legal Studies*.

Gove, Walter (1979) 'Sex differences in the epidemiology of mental illness: evidence and explanations', in E. Gomberg and V. Franks (eds) *Gender and Disordered Behavior*, New York: Bruner/Mazel.

Graycar, Regina and Morgan, Jenny (1990) *The Hidden Gender of Law*, Annandale, New South Wales: The Federation Press.

Greenawalt, Kent (1992) *Law and Objectivity*, Oxford: Oxford University Press.

Greene, Raymond and Dalton, Katharina (1953) 'The premenstrual syndrome', *British Medical Journal* 1: 1007–1014.

Greenwald, Anthony G. (1975) 'Consequences of prejudice against the null hypothesis', *Psychological Bulletin* 82: 1–20.

Groff, Suzanne E. (1994) 'Repressed memory or false memory: New Hampshire courts consider the dispute', *New Hampshire Bar Journal* 35: 57–58.

Gross, Richard (1996) *Psychology: The Science of Mind and Behaviour*, Third Edition, London: Hodder & Stoughton.

Grossman, Lisa R. and Pressley, Michael (1994) 'Introduction to the special issue on recovery of memories of childhood sexual abuse', *Applied Cognitive Psychology* 8: 277–280.

Gudjonsson, Gisli (1996) 'Results from the 1995 survey: psychological evidence in court', *The Psychologist* 9 (May): 213–217.

Guilliat, R. (1996) *Talk of the Devil: Repressed Memory and the Ritual Abuse Witch-Hunt*, Melbourne, Vic: Text Publishing Co.

Hacking, Ian (1995) *Rewriting the Soul: Multiple Personality and the Sciences of the Memory*, Princeton, NJ: Princeton University Press.

Hagen, Margaret, (1997) *Whores of the Court: The Fraud of Psychiatric Testimony and the Rape of American Justice*, New York: HarperCollins.

Hale, Sir Matthew (1678) *Pleas of the Crown: A Methodical Summary*, London: Professional Books. Reprinted in 1972.

Hall, Liz and Lloyd, Siobhan (1989) *Surviving Child Sexual Abuse: A Handbook for Helping Women Challenge Their Past*, Lewes: The Falmer Press.

Hall, Ruth E. (1985) *Ask Any Woman*, Bristol: Falling Wall Press.

Haney, Craig (1993) 'Psychology and legal change: the impact of a decade', *Law and Human Behavior* 17: 371–398.

Hanmer, Jalna, Radford, Jill and Stanko, Elisabeth (1989) *Women, Policing, and Male Violence*, London: Routledge.

Haraway, Donna (1986) 'Primathology is politics by other means', in R. Bleier (ed.) *Feminist Approaches to Science*, New York: Pergamon.

Haraway, Donna (1988) 'Situated knowledges: the science question in feminism and the privilege of partial perspective', *Feminist Studies* 14: 575–599.

Harding, Sandra (1986) *The Science Question in Feminism*, Ithaca, NY: Cornell University Press.

Harding, Sandra (1991) *Whose Science? Whose Knowledge? Thinking from Women's Lives*, Ithaca, NY: Cornell University Press.

Harding, Sandra (1993) 'Rethinking standpoint epistemology: "what is strong objectivity"?', in L. Alcoff and E. Potter (eds) *Feminist Epistemologies*, New York: Routledge.

Harlow, Harry (1959) 'Love in infant monkeys', *Scientific American* 200: 68–74.

Harris, Angela (1990) 'Race and essentialism in feminist legal theory', *Stanford Law Review* 42: 581–616.

Harrison, Kate (1991) 'No means no: that's final', *New Law Journal* 141: 1489–1490.

Hart, Herbert L. A. (1961) *The Concept of Law*, Oxford: Clarendon Press.

Hart, Herbert L. A. (1968) *Punishment and Responsibility: Essays in the Philosophy of Law*, Oxford: Clarendon Press.

Hayes, Monica L. (1994) 'The necessity of memory experts for the defense in prosecutions for child sexual abuse based upon repressed memories', *American Criminal Law Review* 32: 69–85.

Helfer, Ray E. and Kempe, C. Henry (1987) *The Battered Child*, Fourth Edition, London: University of Chicago Press.

Henderson, Sheila (1997) *Service Provision to Women Experiencing Domestic Violence in Scotland*, Edinburgh: The Scottish Office Central Research Unit.

Henwood, Karen and Nicolson, Paula (1995) 'Qualitative research', *The Psychologist*, March: 109–110.

Herman, Judith (1992) *Trauma and Recovery: The Aftermath of Violence: From Domestic Abuse to Political Terror*, New York: HarperCollins.

Hester, Marianne, Kelly, Liz and Radford, Jill (eds) (1996) *Women, Violence and Male Power*, Buckingham: Open University Press.

Hey, Valerie (1985) 'Getting away with murder: PMT and the press', in S. Laws, V. Hey and A. Eagan (eds) *Seeing Red: The Politics of Premenstrual Tension*, London: Hutchinson.

Hochman, John (1994) 'Recovered memory therapy and false memory syndrome', *Skeptic* 2: 58–61.

Hodgkinson, Tristram (1990) *Expert Evidence: Law and Practice*, London: Sweet & Maxwell.

Holmes, David S. (1990) 'The evidence for repression: an examination of 60 years of research', in J. Singer (ed.) *Repression and Dissociation: Implications for Personality, Theory, Psychopathology and Health*, Chicago: University of Chicago Press.

Holmes, David S. (1994) 'Is there evidence for repression? Doubtful', *Harvard Mental Health Letter*, 10 (June), 4–6.

Holmes, Oliver Wendell (1881) *The Common Law*, Boston, MA: Little, Brown.

Holtzman, Elizabeth (1986) 'Premenstrual symptoms: no legal defence', *St John's Law Review* 60: 712–715.

Home Office (1995) *Criminal Statistics: England and Wales*, Cm 3421, London.

Home Office Statistics (1985–1993) Home Office Statistics and Research Department, London.

Hopkins, Nick and Reicher, Steven D. (1996) 'The construction of social categories and processes of social change: arguing about national identities', in G. Breakwell and E. Lyons (eds) *Changing European Identities*, Oxford: Butterworth Heinemann.

Hopkins, Nick, Regan, Martin and Abell, Jackie (1997) 'On the context dependence of national stereotypes: some Scottish data', *British Journal of Social Psychology* 36: 553–563.

Howard, George S. (1985) 'The role of values in the science of psychology', *American Psychologist* 40: 255–265.

Hubbard, Raymond (1995) 'The earth is highly significantly round (p < .0001)', *American Psychologist* 50: 1098.

Hubbard, Ruth (1990) *The Politics of Women's Biology*, New Brunswick, NJ: Rutgers.

Hull, Michael, Joyce, David, Turner, Gillian and Wardle, Peter (1997) 'Premenstrual Syndrome', *Undergraduate Obstetrics and Gynaecology*, Oxford: Butterworth Heinemann.

Hunter, Rosemary (1996) 'Gender in evidence: masculine norms vs. feminist reforms', *Harvard Women's Law Journal* 19: 127–167.

Ibanez, Tomas (1991) 'Social psychology and the rhetoric of truth', *Theory and Psychology* 1: 187–201.

ICD, see World Health Organization.

Imwinkelried, Edward J. (1995) 'Expert testimony in the US: a different perspective', *New Law Journal Supplement* 145: 644–646.

Indiana Law Journal (1950) 'Psychiatric aid on evaluating credibility of rape complainants', *Indiana Law Journal* 26: 98.

Jackson, Stevie (1985) 'Introduction', in S. Laws, V. Hey and A. Eagan (eds) *Seeing Red: The Politics of Premenstrual Tension*, London: Hutchinson.

Jarvis, G. J. (1994) *Obstetrics and Gynaecology: A Critical Approach to the Clinical Problems*, Oxford: Oxford University Press.

Jasanoff, Sheila (1995) *Science at the Bar: Law, Science, and Technology in America*, Cambridge, MA: Harvard University Press.

Jeffcoate, Norman (1987) *Jeffcoate's Principles of Gynaecology*, Fifth Edition. Revised by V. R. Tindall, Originally published 1957, Butterworth.

Johnson, Holly (1996) *Dangerous Domains: Violence against Women in Canada*, Toronto: Nelson.

Johnson, Holly (1998) 'Rethinking survey research on violence against women', in R. E. Dobash and R. P. Dobash (eds) *Rethinking Violence against Women*, Thousand Oaks, CA: Sage.

Joint, Matthew (1995) *Road Rage*, Basingstoke, Hampshire: The Automobile Association.

Jonakait, Randolph N. (1994) 'Real science and forensic science', *Shepard's Expert & Scientific Evidence Quarterly* 1: 435–455.

Jones, Carol (1994) *Expert Witnesses*, Oxford: Clarendon Press.

Journal of Mental Science (1865) Volume 11: 427–431.

Juviler (1960) 'Psychiatric opinions as to credibility of witnesses: a suggested approach', *California Law Review* 48: 648–673.

Kapardis, Andreas (1997) *Psychology and Law: A Critical Introduction*, Cambridge: Cambridge University Press.

Kassin, Saul M. (1998) 'Clinical psychology in court: house of junk science', *Contemporary Psychology* 43: 321–324.

Kassin, Saul M., Ellsworth, Phoebe C. and Smith, Vicki L. (1989) 'The general acceptance of psychological research on eyewitness testimony: a survey of the experts', *American Psychologist* 44: 1089–1098.

Keller, Evelyn Fox (1983) *A Feeling for the Organism: The Life and Work of Barbara McClintock*, New York: W. H. Freeman.

Keller, Evelyn Fox (1985) *Reflections on Gender and Science*, New Haven, CT: Yale University Press.

Keller, Evelyn Fox (1987) 'Working scientists and feminist critiques of science', *Daedalus* 116: 77–91.

Keller, Evelyn Fox (1992) *Secrets of Life, Secrets of Death: Essays on Language, Gender and Science*, New York: Routledge.

Kelly, Katharine D. (1997) '"You must be crazy if you think you were raped": reflections on the use of complainants' personal and therapy records in sexual assault trials', *Canadian Journal of Women and the Law* 9: 178–195.

Kelly, Liz (1988) *Surviving Sexual Violence*, Cambridge: Polity Press.

Kennedy, Duncan (1983) *Legal Education and the Production of Hierarchy: A Polemic against the System*, Cambridge, MA: A Far Press.

Kennedy, Helena (1993) *Eve Was Framed: Women and British Justice*, London: Vintage Books.

Kenny, Anthony (1983) 'The expert in court', *Law Quarterly Review* 99: 197–216.

Kerr, Clark (1991) *The Great Transformation in Higher Education, 1960–1980*, Albany, NY: State University of New York Press.

Kessen, William (1979) 'The American child and other cultural inventions', *American Psychologist* 34: 815–820.

Kessen, William (1990) *The Rise and Fall of Development*, Worcester, MA: Clark Press.

Kessen, William (1996) 'The transcendental alarm', in C. F. Graumann and K. J. Gergen (eds) *Historical Dimensions of Psychological Discourse*, Cambridge: Cambridge University Press.

Kihlstrom, John F. (1997) 'Suffering from reminiscences: exhumed memory, implicit memory, and the return of the repressed', in M. A. Conway (ed.) *Recovered Memories and False Memories*, Oxford: Oxford University Press.

Kimble, Gregory A. (1989) 'Psychology from the standpoint of a generalist', *American Psychologist* 44: 491–499.

King, Michael (1986) *Psychology In and Out of Court*, Oxford: Pergamon Press.

Kingston, Beryl (1980) *Lifting the Curse: How to Relieve Painful Periods*, London: Ebury Press.

Kitzinger, Celia (1990) 'Resisting the discipline', in E. Burman (ed.) *Feminists and Psychological Practice*, London: Sage.

Kitzinger, Celia (1991) 'Feminism, psychology, and the paradox of power', *Feminism and*

Psychology 1: 111–129; reprinted in J. S. Bohan (ed.) (1992) *Seldom Seen, Rarely Heard: Women's Place in Psychology*, Boulder, CO: Westview Press.

Koch, Sigmund (1981) 'The nature and limits of psychological knowledge: lessons of a century qua "science"', *American Psychologist* 36: 257–269.

Koss, Mary P. (1993) 'Rape: scope, impact, intervention, and public policy response', *American Psychologist* 48: 1062–1069.

Koss, Mary P., Gidycz, Christine A. and Wisniewski, Nadine (1987) 'The scope of rape: incidence and prevalence of sexual aggression and victimization in a national sample of higher education students', *Journal of Consulting and Clinical Psychology* 55: 162–170.

Kramarae, Cheris and Spender, Dale (eds) (1993) *The Knowledge Explosion: Generations of Feminist Scholarship*, Hemel Hempstead: Harvester Wheatsheaf.

Kuhn, Thomas S. (1970) *The Structure of Scientific Revolutions*, Second Edition, Chicago: University of Chicago Press.

Kupenda, Angela Mae (1997) 'Making traditional courses more inclusive: confessions of an African American female professor who attempted to crash all the barriers at once', *University of San Francisco Law Review* 31: 975–992.

Kutchins, Herb and Kirk, Stuart (1988) 'The future of DSM: scientific and professional issues', *The Harvard Medical School Mental Health Letter*, 5: 4–6.

Lacey, Nicola (1993) 'Closure and critique in feminist jurisprudence', in A. Norrie (ed.) *Closure or Critique: New Directions in Legal Theory*, Edinburgh: Edinburgh University Press.

Lacey, Nicola (1996) 'Normative reconstruction in socio-legal theory', *Social and Legal Studies* 5: 131–157.

Lacey, Nicola (1998) *Unspeakable Subjects: Feminist Essays in Legal and Social Theory*, Oxford: Hart Publishing.

Lacey, Nicola and Wells, Celia (1998) *Reconstructing Criminal Law: Text and Materials*, London: Butterworth.

La Fontaine, Jean S. (1990) *Child Sexual Abuse*, Cambridge: Polity Press.

LaFree, Gary, Reskin, Barbara and Visher, Christy (1985) 'Jurors' responses to victims' behavior and legal issues in sexual assault trials', *Social Problems* 32: 389–407.

Laing, Ronald D. (1960) *The Divided Self: A Study of Sanity and Madness*, London: Tavistock.

Lancet (1981) 'Premenstrual syndrome', *Lancet*, 19 December, 1393–1394.

Landsman, Stephan (1995) 'Of witches, madmen, and products liability: an historical survey of the use of expert testimony', *Behavioral Sciences and the Law* 13: 131–157.

Largen, Mary Ann (1988) 'Rape-law reform: an analysis', in A. W. Burgess (ed.) *Rape and Sexual Assault*, Volume 2, New York: Garland.

Lauderdale, Helen J. (1984) 'The admissibility of expert testimony on rape trauma syndrome', *Journal of Criminal Law and Criminology* 75: 1366–1416.

Laws, Sophie (1983) 'The sexual politics of pre-menstrual tension', *Women's Studies International Forum* 6: 19–31.

Laws, Sophie (1985) 'Who needs PMT? A feminist approach to the politics of premenstrual tension', in S. Laws, V. Hey and A. Eagan (eds) *Seeing Red: The Politics of Premenstrual Tension*, London: Hutchinson.

Laws, Sophie (1990) *Issues of Blood: The Politics of Menstruation*, London: Macmillan.

Lee, Ellie (forthcoming) *Psychologising Abortion*, Unpublished Ph.D. Thesis, University of Kent.

Lee, Ellie and Gilchrist, Anne (1997) 'Abortion psychological sequelae: the debate and the research', in E. Lee and M. Lattimer (eds) *Issues in Pregnancy Counselling: What Do Women Need and Want?*, Canterbury: Pro-Choice Forum.

Lees, Sue (1996) *Carnal Knowledge: Rape on Trial*, London: Hamish Hamilton.

Lees, Sue (1997) *Ruling Passions: Sexual Violence, Reputation and the Law*, Buckingham: Open University Press.

Leippe, Michael R. and Romanczyk, A. (1987) 'Reactions to child (versus adult) eyewitnesses', *Law and Human Behaviour* 13: 101–131.

Leneman, Leah (1998) *Alienated Affections: The Scottish Experience of Divorce and Separation, 1684–1830*, Edinburgh: Edinburgh University Press.

Levine, Howard B. (1997) 'Psychic reality and historical truth', in C. Prozan (ed) *Construction and Reconstruction of Memory: Dilemmas of Childhood Sexual Abuse*, Northvale, New Jersey: Jason Aronson.

Levine, Murray (1999) 'Review essay: "the legal culture must assimilate the scientific culture" and vice versa?', *Law and Policy* 21.

Lewis, Penney and Mullis, Alastair (1999) 'Delayed criminal prosecutions for childhood sexual abuse: ensuring a fair trial', *Law Quarterly Review* 115: 265–295.

Lindsay, D. Stephen and Read, J. Don (1994) 'Psychotherapy and memories of child sexual abuse: a cognitive perspective', *Applied Cognitive Psychology* 8: 281–338.

Llewellyn, Carl (1960) *The Common Law Tradition: Deciding Appeals*, Boston: Little, Brown.

Llewellyn-Jones, Derek (1990) *Gynaecology, Volume II*, Fifth Edition, London: Faber & Faber.

Lloyd, Dennis (1994) *Introduction to Jurisprudence*, Sixth Edition, London: Sweet & Maxwell. Updated and edited by M. Freeman.

Lloyd, Genevieve (1984) *The Man of Reason: 'Male' and 'Female' in Western Philosophy*, London: Methuen.

Lloyd-Bostock, Sally M. (1981) 'Psychology and the law: a critical review of research and practice', *British Journal of Law and Society* 8: 1–28.

Loftus, Elizabeth F. (1983) 'Silence is not golden', *American Psychologist* 38: 564–572.

Loftus, Elizabeth F. (1991) 'Resolving legal questions with psychological data', *American Psychologist* 46: 1046–1048.

Loftus, Elizabeth F. (1993) 'The reality of repressed memories', *American Psychologist* 48: 518–537.

Loftus, Elizabeth F. (1994) 'The repressed memory controversy', *American Psychologist* 49: 443–445.

Loftus, Elizabeth F. and Ketcham, Katherine K. (1994) *The Myth of Repressed Memory: False Memories and Accusations of Sexual Abuse*, New York: St. Martin's Press.

Loftus, Elizabeth F. and Monahan, John (1980) 'Trial by data: psychological research as legal evidence', *American Psychologist* 35: 270–283.

London and Edinburgh Monthly Journal of Medical Science (1845) Volume 5, August: 632–636.

London Medical Gazette (1845) Volume 1: 166–171.

Lott, Bernice (1985) 'The devaluation of women's competence', *Journal of Social Issues* 41: 43–60; reprinted in J. S. Bohan (ed.) (1992) *Seldom Seen, Rarely Heard: Women's Place in Psychology*, Boulder, CO: Westview Press.

Luckhaus, Linda (1985) 'A plea for PMT in the criminal law', in S. Edwards (ed.) *Gender, Sex and the Law*, Oxford: Croom Helm.

Lunbeck, Elizabeth (1994) *The Psychiatric Persuasion: Knowledge, Gender, and Power in Modern America*, Princeton, NJ: Princeton University Press.

Luus, C. A. Elizabeth and Wells, Gary L. (1992) 'The perceived credibility of child eyewitnesses' in H. Dent and R. Flin (eds) *Children as Witnesses*, Chichester: Wiley.

McCloskey, Deirdre (1995) 'The discreet charm of the bourgeoise', *Feminist Economics* 1: 119–124.

McCloskey, Michael and Egeth, Howard E. (1983) 'Eyewitness identification: what can a psychologist tell a jury?', *American Psychologist* 38: 550–563.

McColgan, Aileen (1993) 'In defense of battered women who kill', *Oxford Journal of Legal Studies* 13: 508–529.

McGovern, Constance (1985) *Masters of Madness: Social Origins of the American Psychiatric Profession*, Hanover, NH: University Press of New England.

Mack, Kathy (1993) 'Continuing barriers to women's credibility: a feminist perspective on the proof process', *Criminal Law Forum* 4: 327–353.

Mack, Kathy (1994) '*B* v *R*: negative stereotypes and women's credibility', *Feminist Legal Studies* 2: 183–194.

Mackay, R. D. and Colman, Andrew M. (1996) 'Equivocal rulings on expert psychological and psychiatric evidence: Turning a muddle into a nonsense', *Criminal Law Review*, 88–95.

MacKinnon, Catharine A. (1982) 'Feminism, Marxism, and the state: an agenda for theory', *Signs* 7: 515–540.

MacKinnon, Catharine A. (1983) 'Feminism, Marxism, method and the state: towards a feminist jurisprudence', *Signs* 8: 635–663.

MacKinnon, Catharine A. (1987) *Feminism Unmodified: Discourses on Life and Law*, Cambridge, MA: Harvard University Press.

MacKinnon, Catharine A. (1989) *Toward a Feminist Theory of the State*, Cambridge, MA: Harvard University Press.

Mahoney, Michael J. (1977) 'Publication prejudices: an experimental study of confirmatory bias in the peer review system', *Cognitive Therapy and Research* 1: 161–175.

Marlowe, Douglas B. (1995) 'A hybrid decision framework for evaluating psychometric evidence', *Behavioral Sciences and the Law* 13: 207–228.

Marshall, Jane (1996) 'Heavy periods: the process of collusion and compromise in research', in E. Burman *et al.* (eds), *Challenging Women: Psychology's Exclusions, Feminist Possibilities*, Buckingham: Open University Press.

Martinson, Donna, MacCrimmon, Marilyn, Grant, Isabel and Boyle, Christine (1991) 'A forum on *Lavallee* v *R*: women and self-defence', *University of British Columbia Law Review* 25: 23–68.

Matoesian, Gregory M. (1993) *Reproducing Rape: Domination through Talk in the Courtroom*, Chicago: University of Chicago Press.

Matoesian, Gregory M. (1995) 'Language, law, and society: policy implications of the Kennedy Smith rape trial', *Law and Society Review* 29: 669–701.

Mayhew, Patricia, Maung, Natalie A. and Mirrlees-Black, Catriona (1993) *The 1992 British Crime Survey*, London: HMSO.

Melton, Gary B. and Limber, Susan (1989) 'Psychologists' involvement in cases of child maltreatment: limits of role and expertise', *American Psychologist* 44: 1225–1233.

Melton, Gary B. and Wilcox, Brian L. (1989) 'Changes in family law and family life: challenges for psychology', *American Psychologist* 44: 1213–1216.

Memon, Amina and Young, Mark (1997) 'Desperately seeking evidence: the recovered memory debate', *Legal and Criminological Psychology* 2: 131–154.

Memon, Amina, Vrij, Aldert and Bull, Ray (1998) *Psychology and Law: Truthfulness, Accuracy and Credibility*, London: McGraw-Hill.

Merton, Robert K. (1973) *The Sociology of Science*, Chicago: University of Chicago Press.

Miles, Rosalind (1993) *The Women's History of the World*, London: HarperCollins.

Miller, George A. (1966) *Psychology: The Science of Mental Life*, London: Penguin.

Minda, Gary (1995) *Postmodern Legal Movements: Law and Jurisprudence at Century's End*, New York: New York University Press.

Minow, Martha (1986) 'Law turning outward', *Telos* 73: 79–100.

Minow, Martha (1990) 'Words and the door to the land of change: law, language, and family violence', *Vanderbilt Law Review* 43: 1665–1699.

Monahan, John and Walker, Laurens (1988) 'Social science research in law: a new paradigm', *American Psychologist* 43: 465–472.

Monahan, John and Walker, Laurens (1994) *Social Science Research in Law: Cases and Materials*, Third Edition, Westbury, NY: Foundation Press.

Montoya, Margaret E. (1994) 'Mascaras, trenzas, y grenas: un/masking the self while un/braiding Latina stories and legal discourse', *Chicano–Latino Law Review* 15: 1–37.

Morawski, Jill G. (1994) *Practicing Feminism, Reconstructing Psychology: Notes on a Liminal Science*, Ann Arbor: University of Michigan Press.

Morgan, Elaine (1972) *The Descent of Woman*, New York: Stein and Day.

Morgan, Michael (1996) 'Qualitative research: a package deal?', *The Psychologist* 9 (January): 31–32.

Morgan, Michael (1998) 'Qualitative research: science or pseudo-science?', *The Psychologist* 11 October: 481–483.

Morowski, Jill G. (1985) 'The measurement of masculinity and femininity: engendering categorical realities', *Journal of Personality* 53: 196–223.

Mossman, Mary Jane (1986) 'Feminism and legal method: the difference it makes', *Australian Journal of Law and Society* 3: 30.

Muehlenhard, Charlene L., Powch, Irene G., Phelps, Joi L. and Guisti, Laura M. (1992) 'Definitions of rape: scientific and political implications', *Journal of Social Issues* 48: 23–44.

Muensterberg, Hugo (1908) *On the Witness Stand: Essays on Psychological Crime*, New York: Clark Boardman.

Mulligan, Nora (1983) 'Premenstrual syndrome', *Harvard Women's Law Journal* 5: 219–227.

Mullis, Alastair C. (1997) 'Compounding the abuse? The House of Lords, child sexual abuse and limitation periods', *Medical Law Review* 5: 22–62.

Murphy, Susan (1992) 'Assisting the jury in understanding victimization: expert psychological testimony on battered women syndrome and rape trauma syndrome', *Columbia Journal of Law and Social Problems* 25: 277–312.

Naffine, Ngaire (1990) *Law and the Sexes: Explorations in Feminist Jurisprudence*, Sydney: Allen & Unwin.

National Institute of Mental Health (1999) http://www.nimh.gov/publicat/numbers.

National Judicial College (1999) http://www.judges.org/educate.

Naylor, C. David (1997) 'Meta-analysis and the meta-epidemiology of clinical research', *British Medical Journal*, 315: 617–619.

Neuliep, James W. and Crandall, Rick (1993) 'Reviewer bias against replication research', *Journal of Social Behavior and Personality* 8: 22–29.

New Mexico Female Intimate Partner Violence Death Review Team (1998) *Getting Away with Murder*, Albuquerque, NM: Center for Injury Prevention Research and Education, University of New Mexico.

Nicolson, Donald (1995) 'Telling tales: gender discrimination, gender construction, and battered women who kill', *Feminist Legal Studies* 3: 185–206.

Nicolson, Donald and Sanghvi, Rohit (1993) 'Battered women and provocation: the implications of *R* v *Ahluwalia*', *Criminal Law Review* 728–738.

Nicolson, Paula (1991) 'Explanations of postnatal depression: structuring knowledge of female psychology', *Research on Language and Social Interaction* 25: 75–96.

Nicolson, Paula (1995) 'Feminism and psychology', in J. A. Smith, R. Harré and L. van Langenhove (eds) *Rethinking Psychology*, Thousand Oaks, CA: Sage.

Norrie, Alan (1993a) *Crime, Reason and History*, London: Weidenfield & Nicolson.

Norrie, Alan (ed.) (1993b) *Closure and Critique: New Directions in Legal Theory*, Edinburgh: Edinburgh University Press

Oakley, Anne (1979) *Becoming a Mother*, Oxford: Martin Robertson.

O'Barr, William M. (1982) *Linguistic Evidence: Language, Power and Strategy in the Courtroom*, New York: Academic Press.

O'Connor, Pat (1992) *Friendships between Women: A Critical Review*, Hemel Hempstead: Harvester Wheatsheaf.

O'Donovan, Katherine (1985) *Sexual Divisions in Law*, London: Weidenfeld & Nicolson.

O'Donovan, Katherine (1991) 'Defences for battered women who kill', *Journal of Law and Society* 18: 219–240.

O'Donovan, Katherine (1993) 'Law's knowledge: the judge, the expert, the battered woman, and her syndrome', *Journal of Law and Society* 20: 427–437.

O'Donovan, Katherine (1997) 'With sense, consent or just a con?' in N. Naffine and R. Owens (eds) *Sexing the Subject of Law*, Sydney: Law Book Company.

O'Donovan, Katherine (1998) 'Fabled explanations of bias', in C. McGlynn (ed.) *Legal Feminisms: Theory and Practice*, Aldershot: Ashgate.

Ofshe, Richard and Watters, Ethan (1994) *Making Monsters: False Memories, Psychotherapy, and Sexual Hysteria*, New York: Scribner's.

Olsen, Frances (1990) 'Feminism and critical legal theory: an American perspective', *International Journal of Society and Law* 18: 199–215.

Pahl, Jan (ed.) (1985) *Private Violence and Public Policy*, London: Routledge.

Parker, Ian (1992) *Discourse Dynamics: Critical Analysis for Social and Individual Psychology*, London: Routledge.

Parlee, Mary B. (1973) 'The premenstrual syndrome', *Psychological Bulletin* 80: 454–465.

Pattullo, Polly (1983) *Judging Women: A Study of Attitudes that Rule our Legal System*, London: National Council for Civil Liberties.

Payne, David G., Elie, Claude J., Blackwell, Jason M. and Neuschatz, Jeffrey S. (1996) 'Memory illusions: recalling, recognizing, and recollecting events that never occurred', *Journal of Memory and Language* 35: 261–285.

Pendergrast, Mark (1998) *Victims of Memory: Incest Accusations and Shattered Lives*, London: HarperCollins.

Penrod, Steven D., Fulero, Solomon M. and Cutler, Brian L. (1995) 'Expert psychological testimony on eyewitness reliability before and after Daubert: the state of the law and the science', *Behavioral Sciences and the Law* 13: 229–259.

Peters, Douglas P. and Ceci, Stephen J. (1982) 'Peer review practices of psychological journals: the fate of published articles, submitted again', *Behavioral and Brain Sciences* 5: 187–195.

Pezdek, Kathy and Banks, William P. (1996) *The Recovered Memory/False Memory Debate*, San Diego: Academic Press.

Picard, Liza (1998) *Restoration London*, London: Phoenix.

Pizzi, William T. (1995) 'Expert testimony in the US', *New Law Journal* 145: 82–83.

Polkinghorne, Donald (1983) *Methodology for the Human Sciences: Systems of Inquiry*, Albany: State University of New York Press.

Poole, Debra A. and White, Lawrence T. (1995) 'Tell me again: stability and change in the repeated testimonies of children and adults', in M. Zaragoza *et al.* (eds) *Memory and Testimony in the Child Witness*, Thousand Oaks, CA: Sage.

Poole, Debra A., Lindsay, D. Stephen, Memon, Amina and Bull, Ray (1995) 'Psychotherapy and the recovery of memories of childhood sexual abuse: US and British practitioners' opinions, practices, and experiences', *Journal of Consulting and Clinical Psychology* 63: 426–437.

Potter, Jonathan and Wetherell, Margaret (1987) *Discourse and Social Psychology*, London: Sage.

Prilleltensky, Isaac (1989) 'Psychology and the status quo', *American Psychologist* 44: 795–802.

Prozan, Charlotte K. (1997) *Construction and Reconstruction of Memory: Dilemmas of Childhood Sexual Abuse*, Northvale, New Jersey: Jason Aronson.

Psychology of Women Section Review, The (1999) Volume 1.

Quilligan, Edward J. and Zuspan, Frederick P. (1990) *Current Therapy in Obstetrics and Gynecology*, London: W. B. Saunders Co.

Raitt, Fiona E. (1998) 'A new criterion for the admissibility of scientific evidence? The metamorphosis of helpfulness', in H. Reece (ed.) *Law and Science: Current Legal Issues 1998, Volume 1*, Oxford: Oxford University Press.

Raitt, Fiona E. (forthcoming) 'Gender and the rules of evidence', in M. Childs and L. Ellison (eds) *Feminist Perspectives on Evidence*, London: Cavendish.

Redmayne, Mike (1997) 'Presenting probabilities in court: the DNA experience', *International Journal of Evidence and Proof* 1: 187–214.

Reid, Robert L. and Yen, S. S. C. (1981) 'Current developments: premenstrual syndrome', *American Journal of Obstetrics and Gynecology* 139: 85–104.

Renvoize, Jean (1982) *Incest: A Family Pattern*, London: Routledge.

Rhode, Deborah (1989) *Justice and Gender: Sex Discrimination and the Law*, Cambridge, MA: Harvard University Press.

Rich, Adrienne (1980) *On Lies, Secrets and Silence*, London: Virago.

Richardson, James T. and Ginsburg, Gerald P. (1998) '"Brainwashing" evidence in light of *Daubert*: science and unpopular religions', in H. Reece (ed.) *Law and Science: Current Legal Issues 1998, Volume 1*, Oxford: Oxford University Press.

Rittenhouse, C. Amanda (1991) 'The emergence of premenstrual syndrome as a social problem', *Social Problems* 38: 412–425.

Robbins, Susan P. (1995) 'Wading through the muddy waters of recovered memory', *Families in Society* 76: 478–489.

Roberts, Helen (1985) *The Patient Patients: Women and Their Doctors*, London: Pandora.

Roberts, Paul (1998) 'Expert evidence in Canadian criminal proceedings: more lessons from North America', in H. Reece (ed.) *Law and Science: Current Legal Issues, Current Legal Issues 1998, Volume 1*, Oxford: Oxford University Press.

Roediger, Henry L. and McDermott, Kathleen B. (1995) 'Creating false memories: remembering words not presented in lists', *Journal of Experimental Psychology: Learning, Memory, and Cognition* 21: 803–814.

Rorty, Richard (1980) *Philosophy and the Mirror of Nature*, Oxford: Billing & Sons.

Rose, Gillian (1993) *Feminism and Geography*, Cambridge: Polity Press.

Rose, Hilary (1994) *Love, Power and Knowledge: Towards a Feminist Transformation of the Sciences*, Oxford: Polity Press.

Rosenthal, Robert (1979) 'The "file drawer problem" and tolerance for null results', *Psychological Bulletin* 86: 638–641.

Rosenzweig, Mark R. (1991) 'The scientific status of psychology', *International Journal of Psychology* 26: 514–542.

Rosewater, Lynne B. (1985) 'Schizophrenic, borderline or battered?', in L. Rosewater and L. Walker (eds) *Handbook of Feminist Therapy: Women's Issues in Psychotherapy*, New York: Springer.

Rosewater, Lynne B. (1988) 'Battered or schizrophenic? Psychological tests can't tell', in K.Yllo and M. Bograd (eds) *Feminist Perspectives on Wife Abuse*, Newbury Park, CA: Sage.

Ross, David, Dunning, David, Toglia, Michael and Ceci, Stephen (1991) 'The child in the eyes of the jury: assessing mock jurors' perceptions of the child witness', *Law and Human Behavior* 14: 5–23.

Rosser, Sue V. (1994) *Women's Health: Missing From US Medicine*, Bloomington: Indiana University Press.

Royal College of Psychiatry (1997) *Working Group on Reported Recovered Memories of Child Sexual Abuse*, London: Royal College of Psychiatry.

Rubinow, David R. and Roy-Byrne, P. (1984) 'Premenstrual syndromes: overview from a methodologic perspective', *American Journal of Psychiatry* 141: 163–172.

Rumney, Philip and Morgan-Taylor, Martin (1994) 'A male perspective on rape', *New Law Journal* 144: 1490–1493.

Rumney, Philip and Morgan-Taylor, Martin (1996) 'Sentencing for male rape', *New Law Journal* 146: 262.

Rumney, Philip and Morgan-Taylor, Martin (1997a) 'Recognizing the male victim: gender neutrality and the law of rape, Part One', *Anglo-American Law Review* 26: 198–234.

Rumney, Philip and Morgan-Taylor, Martin (1997b) 'Recognizing the male victim: gender neutrality and the law of rape, Part Two', *Anglo-American Law Review* 26: 330–356.

Rumney, Philip and Morgan-Taylor, Martin (1997c) 'Male rape trauma syndrome in the US courts: *People* v *Yates*', *International Journal of Evidence and Proof* 1: 232–242.

Russell, Diane E. H. (1984) *Sexual Exploitation: Rape, Child Sexual Abuse, and Workplace Harassment*, Newbury Park, CA: Sage.

Russell, Diane E. H. (1986) *The Secret Trauma: Incest in the Lives of Girls and Women*, New York: Basic Books.

Saks, Michael J. (1989) 'Legal policy analysis and evaluation', *American Psychologist* 44: 1110–1117.

Sales, Bruce D., Shuman, Daniel W. and O'Connor, Maureen (1994) 'In a dim light: admissibility of child sexual abuse memories', *Applied Cognitive Psychology* 8: 399–406.

Sampson, Edward E. (1981) 'Cognitive psychology as ideology', *American Psychologist* 36: 730–743.

Sandland, Ralph (1995) 'Between "truth" and "difference": poststructuralism, law and the power of feminism', *Feminist Legal Studies* 3: 3–47.

Santrock, John W. (1996) *Psychology, Alternative and Enhancement Chapters*, Fifth Edition, New York: McGraw-Hill.

Sarason, Samuel B. (1981) 'An asocial psychology and a misdirected clinical psychology', *American Psychologist* 36: 827–836.

Sattar, Ghazala and Bull, Ray (1996) 'Child witnesses in court: psycho-legal issues', *Solicitors Journal* April: 401–403.

Saward, Jill with Green, Wendy (1990) *Rape: My Story*, London: Bloomsbury.

Scales, Ann C. (1986) 'The emergence of feminist jurisprudence: an essay', *Yale Law Journal* 95: 1373–1403.

Schacter, Daniel L. (1996) *Searching for Memory: The Brain, the Mind, and the Past*, New York: Basic Books.

Schacter, Daniel L. and Curran, Tim (1995) 'The cognitive neuroscience of false memories', *Psychiatric Annals* 25: 726–730.

Schacter, Daniel L., Norman, Kenneth A. and Koutstaal, Wilma (1997) 'The recovered memories debate: a cognitive neuroscience perspective', in M. A. Conway (ed.) *Recovered Memories and False Memories*, Oxford: Oxford University Press.

Schneider, Elizabeth M. (1980) 'Equal rights to trial for women: sex bias in the law of self-defence', *Harvard Civil Rights–Civil Liberties Law Reports* 15: 623–647.

Schneider, Elizabeth, M. (1986) 'Describing and changing: women's self-defence work and the problem of expert testimony on battering', *Women's Rights Law Report* 9: 195–197.

Schneider, Susan M. (1992) 'Can this marriage be saved?', *American Psychologist* 46: 1055–1057.

Schooler, Jonathan W., Bendiksen, Miriam and Ambadar, Zara (1997) 'Taking the middle line: can we accommodate both fabricated and recovered memories of sexual abuse?', in M. A. Conway (ed.) *Recovered Memories and False Memories*, Oxford: Oxford University Press.

Schuller, Regina A. and Hastings, Patricia A. (1996) 'Trials of battered women who kill: the impact of alternative forms of expert evidence', *Law and Human Behavior* 20: 167–187.

Schuller, Regina A. and Vidmar, Neil (1992) 'Battered women syndrome evidence in the courtroom: a review of the literature', *Law and Human Behavior* 16: 273–291.

Schuman, Joan and Galvez, Mara (1996) 'A meta/multi-discursive reading of "False Memory Syndrome"', *Feminism and Psychology* 6: 7–29.

Scott, Wilbur J. (1990) 'PTSD in DSM-III: A case in the politics of diagnosis and disease', *Social Problems* 37: 294–310.

Scottish Office, The (1995) *Statistical Bulletin: Criminal Justice Series*, Edinburgh.

Scottish Office, The (1996) *Statistical Bulletin: Criminal Justice Series*, Edinburgh.

Scottish Office, The (1997) *Statistical Bulletin: Criminal Justice Series*, Edinburgh.

Scottish Partnership on Domestic Violence (1998) *Draft Workplan for Partnership*, Edinburgh: Scottish Office Home Department.

Scully, Diane (1986) *Unrelenting Sexual Violence: A Study of Convicted Rapists*, London: HarperCollins Academic.

Sedley, Sir Stephen (1997) 'Law and public life', in Lord Nolan and S. Sedley (eds) *The Making and Remaking of the British Constitution*, London: Blackstone Press.

Seligman, Martin E. P. (1975) *Helplessness: On Depression, Development and Death*, San Francisco: Freeman.

Sheldon, David H. (1992) 'The admissibility of psychiatric and psychological evidence', *Scots Law Times*, 301–305.

Sheldon, David H. and MacLeod, Malcolm D. (1991) 'From normative to positive data: expert psychological evidence re-examined', *Criminal Law Review*, 811–820.

Sheldon, Sally (1997) *Beyond Control: Medical Power and Abortion Law*, London: Pluto Press.

Sherif, Carolyn Wood (1979) 'Bias in psychology', in J. Sherman and E. T. Beck (eds) *The Prism of Sex: Essays in the Sociology of Knowledge*, Madison: University of Wisconsin Press. Reprinted in J. S. Bohan (ed.) (1992) *Seldom Seen, Rarely Heard: Women's Place in Psychology*, Boulder, CO: Westview Press.

Shields, Stephanie A. (1975) 'Functionalism, Darwinism, and the psychology of women: a study in social myth', *American Psychologist* 30: 739–754. Reprinted in J. S. Bohan (ed.) (1992) *Seldom Seen, Rarely Heard: Women's Place in Psychology*, Boulder, CO: Westview Press.

Shotter, John and Gergen, Kenneth J. (eds) (1989) *Texts of Identity*, London: Sage.

Showalter, Elaine (1987) *The Female Malady: Women, Madness, and English Culture, 1830–1980*, London: Virago Press.

Showalter, Elaine (1997) *Hystories: Hysterical Epidemics and Modern Media*, New York: Columbia University Press.

Shuttleworth, Sally (1990) 'Female circulation: medical discourse and popular advertising in the mid-Victorian era', in M. Jacobus, E. Fox Keller and S. Shuttleworth (eds) *Body/Politics: Women and Discourses of Science*, London: Routledge.

Simes, R. John (1986) 'Publication bias: the case for an international registry of clinical trials', *Journal of Clinical Oncology* 4: 1529–1541.

Smart, Carol (1984) *The Ties That Bind: Law, Marriage and the Reproduction of Patriarchal Relations*, London: Routledge & Kegan Paul.

Smart, Carol (1989) *Feminism and the Power of Law*, London: Routledge.

Smart, Carol (1990) 'Law's power, the sexed body and feminist discourse', *Journal of Law and Society* 17: 194–210.

Smart, Carol (1992) 'The woman of legal discourse', *Social and Legal Issues: An International Journal* 1: 29–44.

Smart, Carol (1995) *Law, Crime, and Sexuality: Essays in Feminism*, London: Sage.

Smith, John and Hogan, Brian (1999) *Criminal Law*, Ninth Edition, London: Butterworth.

Smith, Jonathan A. (1995) 'Qualitative methods, identity and transition to motherhood', *The Psychologist* March: 122–125.

Smith, Jonathan A. (1999) 'Identity development during the transition to motherhood: an interpretative phenomenological analysis', *Journal of Reproductive and Infant Psychology* 17: 267–280.

Smith, Jonathan A., Harré, Rom and van Langenhove, Luk (eds) (1995) *Rethinking Psychology*, London: Sage.

Smith, Paige H., Smith, Jason B. and Earp, Jo Anne (1999) 'Beyond the measurement trap: a reconstructed conceptualization and measurement of woman battering', *Psychology of Women Quarterly* 23: 177–193.

Smith, Richard and Roberts, Ian (1997) 'An amnesty for unpublished trials', *British Medical Journal* 314: 686–687.

Smith, Roger (1981) *Trial by Medicine: Insanity and Responsibility in Victorian Trials*, Edinburgh: Edinburgh University Press.

Sokal, Alan and Bricmont, Jean (1996) 'Transgressing the boundaries: toward a transformative hermeneutics of quantum gravity', *Social Text* 46/47: 217–252.

Sokal, Alan and Bricmont, Jean (1998) *Intellectual Impostures*, London: Profile Books.

Sommer, Barbara (1984) 'PMS in the courts: are all women on trial?', *Psychology Today* August: 36–38.

Sommer, Barbara (1987) 'The file drawer effect and publication rates in menstrual cycle research', *Psychology of Women Quarterly* 11: 233–242.

Sommers, Christina Hoff (1994) *Who Stole Feminism? How Women Have Betrayed Women*, New York: Simon & Schuster.

Soothill, Keith and Soothill, Debbie (1993) 'Prosecuting the victim?: a study of the reporting of barristers' comments in rape cases', *Howard Journal* 32: 12–22.

Soothill, Keith, Walby, Sylvia and Bagguley, Paul (1990) 'Judges, the media, and rape', *Journal of Law and Society* 17: 211–233.

Spanier, Bonnie B. (1995) *Im/partial Science: Gender Ideology in Molecular Biology*, Bloomington: Indiana University Press.

Speckard, Anne C. and Rue, Vincent M. (1992) 'Postabortion syndrome: an emerging public health concern', *Journal of Social Issues* 48: 95–119.

Spencer, Janine and Karmiloff-Smith, Annette (1997) 'Are we misconstruing children or scientists?', *Human Development* 40: 51–54.

Spender, Dale (1985) *Man Made Language*, London: Routledge.

Sprince, Alan (1998) 'Negligently inflicted psychiatric damage: a medical diagnosis and prognosis', *Legal Studies* 18: 59–77.

Staats, Arthur W. (1991) 'Unified positivism and unification psychology: fad or new field?', *American Psychologist* 46: 899–912.

Stanko, Elizabeth (1985) *Intimate Intrusions: Women's Experience of Male Violence*, London: Routledge.

Stanko, Elizabeth (1988) 'Hidden violence against women', in M. Maguire and J. Pointing (eds) *Victims of Crime: A New Deal?*, Buckingham: Open University Press.

Stern, Jerome M. and Simes, R. John (1997) 'Publication bias: evidence of delayed publication in a cohort study of clinical research projects', *British Medical Journal* 315: 640–645.

Stone, Lawrence (1990) *Road to Divorce: England 1530–1987*, Oxford: Oxford University Press.

Straus, Murray (1980) 'Measuring intra-family conflict and violence: the Conflict Tactics Scale', *Journal of Marriage and the Family* 41: 75–88.

Straus, Murray (1990) 'Measuring intra-family conflict and violence: the Conflict Tactics Scales', in M. Straus and R. Gelles (eds) *Physical Violence in American Families: Risk Factors and Adaptions to Violence in 8,145 Families*, New Brunswick, NJ: Transaction.

Sullins, Carolyn D. (1998) 'Suspected repressed childhood sexual abuse: gender effects on diagnosis and treatment', *Psychology of Women Quarterly* 22: 403–418.

Szasz, Thomas (1972) *The Myth of Mental Illness*, St Albans: Paladin.

Szasz, Thomas (1973) *The Manufacture of Madness*, St Albans: Paladin.

Tabachnick, Barbara G. and Pope, Kenneth S. (1997) 'Therapist responses to recovered and never-forgotten memories of child sex abuse: a national survey of licensed psychologists', *Violence against Women* 3: 348–360.

Tarlock, A. Dan (1996) 'The futile search for environment laws based on "good science"', *International Journal of Biosciences and the Law*, 1: 9–19.

Tavris, Carol (1992) *The Mismeasure of Woman*, New York: Simon & Schuster.

Temkin, Jennifer (1987) *Rape and the Legal Process*, London: Sweet & Maxwell.

Temkin, Jennifer (1993) 'Sexual history evidence: the ravishment of section 2', *Criminal Law Review*, 3–20.

Tetreault, Patricia A. (1989) 'Rape myth acceptance: a case for providing educational expert testimony in rape jury trials', *Behavioral Sciences and the Law* 7: 243–257.

Thomson, Michael (1998) 'Rewriting the doctor: medical law, literature and feminist strategy', in S. Sheldon and M. Thomson (eds) *Feminist Perspectives on Health Care Law*, London: Cavendish.

Thornton, Margaret (1986) 'Feminist jurisprudence: illusion or reality?', *Australian Journal of Law and Society* 3: 5.

Thornton, Peter (1995) 'A new look at eye witness testimony', *New Law Journal* 145: 94–98.

Tremper, Charles R. (1987) 'Sanguinity and disillusionment where law meets social science', *Law and Human Behavior* 11: 267–276.

Tuana, Nancy (1993) *The Less Noble Sex: Scientific, Religious, and Philosophical Conceptions of Woman's Nature*, Bloomington: Indiana University Press.

Turkat, Ira Daniel (1999) http//www.deltabravo.net/custody/malice/htm.

Turner, John C., Oakes, Penelope J., Haslam, S. Alexander and McGarty, Craig (1994) 'Self and collective: cognition and social context', *Personality and Social Psychology Bulletin* 20: 454–463.

Tushnet, Mark (1991) 'Critical legal studies: a political history', *Yale Law Journal* 100: 1515–1544.

Twining, William (1973) 'The bad man revisited', *Cornell Law Review* 58: 275–293.

Twining, William (1985) *Theories of Evidence: Bentham and Wigmore*, London: Weidenfeld & Nicolson.

Uglow, Steve (1997) *Evidence: Text and Materials*, London: Sweet & Maxwell.

Underwager, Ralph and Wakefield, Hollida (1990) *The Real World of Child Interrogations*, Springfield, IL: Charles C. Thomas.

Underwager, Ralph and Wakefield, Hollida (1994) *The Return of the Furies: Analysis of Recovered Memory Therapy*, Chicago: Open Court.

US Attorney-General (1984) *Task Force on Family Violence*, Washington, DC: Attorney-General.

Ussher, Jane M. (1990) 'Choosing psychology or not throwing the baby out with the bathwater', in E. Burman (ed.) *Feminists and Psychological Practice*, London: Sage

Ussher, Jane M. (1991) *Women's Madness: Misogyny or Mental Illness?*, Hemel Hempstead: Harvester Wheatsheaf.

Ussher, Jane M. (1997) *Fantasies of Femininity: Reframing the Boundaries of Sex*, London: Penguin.

van Langenhove, Luk (1995) 'The theoretical foundations of experimental psychology and its alternatives', in J. A. Smith, R. Harré and L. van Langenhove (eds) *Rethinking Psychology*, Thousand Oaks, CA: Sage.

Victim Support (1992) *Domestic Violence: Report of a National Inter-Agency Working Party*, London: Victim Support.

Victim Support (1996) *Women, Rape, and the Criminal Justice System*, London: Victim Support.

Walker, Anne E. (1997) *The Menstrual Cycle*, London: Routledge.

Walker, Laurens and Monahan, John (1987) 'Social frameworks: a new use of social science in law', *Virginia Law Review* 73: 559–598.

Walker, Lenore E. (1979) *The Battered Woman*, New York: Harper & Row.

Walker, Lenore E. (1984) *The Battered Woman Syndrome*, New York: Springer.

Walker, Lenore E. (1990) *Terrifying Love: Why Battered Women Kill and How Society Responds*, New York: Harper Perennial.

Walkerdine, Valerie (1988) *The Mastery of Reason*, London: Routledge.

Wallach, Aleta and Rubin, Larry (1971) 'The premenstrual syndrome and criminal responsibility', *UCLA Law Review* 19: 209–312.

Ward, Colleen A. (1995) *Attitudes toward Rape: Feminist and Social Perspectives*, London: Sage.

Waring, Marilyn (1989) *If Women Counted*, San Francisco: Harper & Row.

Warshaw, Robin (1988) *I Never Called It Rape*, New York: Harper & Row.

Webster, Richard (1996) *Why Freud Was Wrong: Sin, Science and Psychoanalysis*, London: Fontana Press.

Weisstein, Naomi (1971) 'Psychology constructs the female, or the fantasy life of the male psychologist', *Journal of Social Education* 35: 362–373; reprinted in J. S. Bohan (ed.) (1992) *Seldom Seen, Rarely Heard: Women's Place in Psychology*, Boulder, CO: Westview Press.

Wells, Celia (1994) 'Battered woman syndrome and defences to homicide: where now?', *Legal Studies* 14: 266–276.

Wenneras, Christine and Wold, Agnes (1997) 'Nepotism and sexism in peer-review', *Nature* 387: 341–343.

Wertheim, Margaret (1997) *Pythagoras' Trousers: God, Physics, and the Gender Wars*, London: Fourth Estate.

Wetherell, Margaret and Edley, Nigel (1999) 'Negotiating hegemonic masculinity: imaginary positions and psycho-discursive practices', *Feminism and Psychology* 9: 335–356.

Whitehead, R. E. (1934) 'Notes from the Department of Commerce: women pilots', *Journal of Aviation Medicine* 5: 47–49.

Wigmore, John H. (1937) *Wigmore on Evidence, Volume IIIA*, Boston: Little, Brown. Reprinted and edited by Chadbourne in 1970, Boston: Little, Brown.

Wigmore, John H. (1940) *Wigmore on Evidence, Volume I*, Third Edition, Boston: Little, Brown.

Wilkinson, Sue (1997) 'Still seeking transformation: feminist challenges to psychology', in L. Stanley (ed.) *Knowing Feminisms: On Academic Borders, Territories, and Tribes*, Thousand Oaks, CA: Sage.

Williams, Glanville (1978) *Textbook of Criminal Law*, First Edition, London: Stevens and Sons.

Williams, Glanville (1983) *Textbook of Criminal Law*, Second Edition, London: Stevens and Sons.

Williams, Glanville (1987) 'Child witnesses', in P. Smith (ed.) *Criminal Law Essays in Honour of J. C. Smith*, London: Butterworth.

Williams, Glanville (1992) 'Rape is rape', *New Law Journal* 142: 11–13.

Williams, Linda Meyer (1994) 'Recall of childhood trauma: a prospective study of women's memories of child sexual abuse', *Journal of Consulting and Clinical Psychology* 62: 1167–1176.

Williams, Linda Meyer (1995) 'Recovered memories of abuse in women with documented child sexual victimization histories', *Journal of Traumatic Stress* 8: 649–674.

Williams, Patricia (1991) *The Alchemy of Race and Rights*, Cambridge, MA: Harvard University Press.

Wilson, Elizabeth A. (1998) *Neural Geographies: Feminism and the Microstructure of Cognition*, London: Routledge.

Winbolt, Barry (1996) 'False memory syndrome: an issue clouded by emotion', *Medicine, Science and the Law* 36: 100–109.

Wolpert, Lewis (1998) 'What lawyers need to know about science', in H. Reece (ed.) *Law and Science: Current Legal Issues 1998, Volume 1*, Oxford: Oxford University Press.

Wood, Linda A. and Rennie, Heather (1994) 'Formulating rape: the discursive construction of victims and villians', *Discourse and Society* 5: 125–148.

Worell, Judith and Johnson, Norrie (eds) (1997) *Feminist Visions: New Directions in Education and Practice*, Washington, DC: American Psychological Association.

World Health Organization (1994) *International Classification of Diseases and Related Health Problems*, Tenth Edition [ICD-10], Geneva: WHO.

Yale Law Journal (1950) 'Psychiatric evaluation of the mentally abnormal witness', *Yale Law Journal* 59: 1324–1338.

Yapko, Michael (1997) 'The troublesome unknowns about trauma and recovered memories', in M. A. Conway (ed.) *Recovered Memories and False Memories*, Oxford: Oxford University Press.

Yllo, Kersti and Bograd, Michele (1988) *Feminist Perspectives on Wife Abuse*, Newbury Park, CA: Sage.

Young, Allan (1995) *The Harmony of Illusions: Inventing Post-Traumatic Stress Disorder*, Princeton, NJ: Princeton University Press.

Yuille, John C. (1989) 'Expert evidence by psychologists: sometimes problematic and often premature', *Behavioral Sciences and the Law*, 7: 181–196.

Yuille, John C. and Wells, Gary L. (1991) 'Concerns about the application of research findings: the issue of ecological validity', in J. Doris (ed) *The Suggestibility of Children's Recollections*, Washington, DC: American Psychological Association.

Zaragoza, Maria S., Graham, John R., Hall, Gordon C., Hirschman, Richard and Ben-Porath, Yossef S. (eds) (1995) *Memory and Testimony in the Child Witness*, Thousand Oaks, CA: Sage.

Zeedyk, M. Suzanne and Raitt, Fiona E. (1997) 'Psychological theory in law: legitimating the male norm', *Feminism and Psychology* 7: 539–546.

Zeedyk, M. Suzanne and Raitt, Fiona E. (1998) 'Psychological evidence in the courtroom: critical reflections on the general acceptance standard', *Journal of Community and Applied Social Psychology* 8: 23–39.

Zimbardo, Philip G. (1992) *Psychology and Life*, Thirteenth Edition, New York: HarperCollins.

Zonana, Howard (1994) '*Daubert* v *Merrell Dow Pharmaceuticals*: a new standard for scientific evidence in the courts?', *Bulletin of the American Academy of Psychiatry and Law* 22: 309–325.

Name Index

Subject Index